A Dynamic Approach to Seco

Language Learning & Language Teaching (LL&LT)

The LL&LT monograph series publishes monographs, edited volumes and text books on applied and methodological issues in the field of language pedagogy. The focus of the series is on subjects such as classroom discourse and interaction; language diversity in educational settings; bilingual education; language testing and language assessment; teaching methods and teaching performance; learning trajectories in second language acquisition; and written language learning in educational settings.

Editors

Nina Spada
Ontario Institute for Studies in Education,
University of Toronto

Nelleke Van Deusen-Scholl
Center for Language Study
Yale University

Volume 29

A Dynamic Approach to Second Language Development.
Methods and techniques
Edited by Marjolijn H. Verspoor, Kees de Bot and Wander Lowie

A Dynamic Approach to Second Language Development

Methods and techniques

Edited by

Marjolijn H. Verspoor

Kees de Bot

Wander Lowie

University of Groningen

John Benjamins Publishing Company

Amsterdam / Philadelphia

The paper used in this publication meets the minimum requirements of American National Standard for Information Sciences – Permanence of Paper for Printed Library Materials, ANSI z39.48-1984.

Library of Congress Cataloging-in-Publication Data

A dynamic approach to second language development methods and techniques / edited by
    Marjolijn H. Verspoor, Kees de Bot, Wander Lowie.
p.   cm. (Language Learning & Language Teaching, ISSN 1569-9471 ; v. 29)
Includes bibliographical references and index.
1.   Second language acquisition. 2.   Language and languages--Study and teaching.   I.
    Verspoor, Marjolyn. II. De Bot, Kees. III. Lowie, Wander, 1959- IV. Title. V. Series.
P118.2D96   2011
418.0071--dc22   2010044921
ISBN 978 90 272 1998 5   (Hb ; alk. paper)
ISBN 978 90 272 1999 2   (Pb ; alk. paper)
ISBN 978 90 272 8735 9   (Eb)

Table of contents

List of *How to* sections

Acknowledgements

We hereby would like to thank four generations of students at the MA Applied Linguistics program at the University of Groningen who have had to struggle and suffer through our first feeble attempts to explain DST methodology and techniques. We are also grateful to two anonymous reviewers and the series editors, Nina Spada and Nelleke Van Deusen-Scholl, who have given invaluable suggestions for improvement. Last but not least, we have appreciated the help of two of our former students: Nienke Van Der Hoeven-Houtzagers for her help in copy-editing and Esther De Meijer for making sure the *how to* sections were clear.

Introduction

Kees de Bot, Wander Lowie & Marjolijn Verspoor

It has now been 13 years since Diane Larsen-Freeman published her seminal article on complex systems and second language acquisition (Larsen-Freeman 1997). As she has noticed herself in various publications, it took the applied linguistic world a few years to realize that a paradigm shift was about to take place. Several publications and meetings on both sides of the Atlantic have taken place since that time and this repetitive mentioning – iterations in dynamic parlance – of relevant aspects of complexity and dynamic systems theories has now led to a solid position of this perspective on language learning and teaching.

In several publications, the short history of the complexity/dynamic approach to second language development SLD has been spelled out and there is no need to do so here. However, it may be useful to look at the most recent and important set of articles on this issue: the special 60th anniversary issue of Language Learning on language as a complex adaptive system (December 2009, issue 59, supplement). In their opening position paper, Clay Beckner, Richard Blythe, Joan Bybee, Morten H. Christiansen, William Croft, Nick C. Ellis, John Holland, Jinyun Ke, Diane Larsen-Freeman, Tom Schoenemann, or the 'Five Graces group', as they call themselves, lay out the most important aspects of language as a complex adaptive system (CAS). In this article – compulsory reading for all students of applied linguistics (AL) interested in this new approach – the authors show that a multitude of factors play a role in the emergence of first and second languages, but their conclusions on how to do research on language as a complex system are disappointing:

> In the various aspects of language considered here, it is always the case that form, user and use are inextricably linked. However, such complex interactions are difficult to investigate *in vivo*. Detailed, dense longitudinal studies of language use and acquisition are rare enough for single individuals over a time course of months. (….) However there are other ways to investigate how language might emerge and evolve as a CAS. A valuable tool featuring strongly in our methodology is mathematical or computational modeling. (Beckner et al. 2009, 12)

Although the authors are careful to mention the limitations of modeling as empirical research, they see modeling as the only viable approach, probably a reflection of several of the authors' scientific histories and preferences. In our opinion, however, the current paucity should not lead to an "either or" choice: Modeling can not replace empirical data but should simulate empirical data to test theoretical insights.

First of all, language development itself, with its many distinct constructions at different levels (sounds, morphemes, words, phrases and clauses) that can easily be observed and counted, lends itself par excellence to contribute to our knowledge of complex systems. Secondly, there are already several longitudinal data bases that provide detailed and dense data of language development over longer stretches of time (see van Dijk & van Geert 2007, or Steinkrauss 2009 on L1). Of course, simulations are valid and may be the way to move forward, but only in interaction with real data, especially when they simulate real data, can test hypotheses, or consider possible alternative developmental tracks when factors interact in specific ways.

The ultimate test of a theory, following Jordan's (2004) insightful discussion of theories on second language development, lies in its ability to generate powerful and testable hypotheses. Whether CAS, complexity theory (CT) or dynamic systems theory (DST) meets this requirement remains to be seen because prediction is not what the dynamic approach is after. It predicts that systems and variables will influence each other's change over time, but the outcome of these interactions is by definition unpredictable at lower levels of the system. One of the most important outcomes of this perspective is that the focus is once more on the learner, but this time not as a generalized hypothetical representative of a larger sample, but as a developing system on its own.

The main thrust of this book is to show different ways of looking at the development of individual learners. One aspect of the focus on the individual learner is the renewed interest of intraindividual and interindividual variation over time. Inspired by the groundbreaking work by Paul van Geert and his colleagues, we are now more than before aware of the relevance of information on variation and its sources. This is one of the perspectives that is elaborated in more detail in various contributions in this volume. Variation can be studied as the outcome of interactions between variables, and only through carefully looking at such variables and their interaction in longitudinal data can we slowly expand the range of variables we know to play a role in the developmental processes we are interested in.

The aim of this volume is to show how different types of data can be gathered and analyzed to inform us about the process of language development from a dynamic perspective. In contrast to Beckner et al., the contributors to this volume do not see mathematical modeling and simulations as the only approach. There are different types of data that we can study using the tools of DST and CT. Data on variation, dense data gathering and analysis, but also simulation data related to longitudinal data on development are seen as important sources of information. Applied linguists are not cognitive scientists, and though they should inform themselves about the contributions of modeling and simulations, they should not rely on them without carefully analyzing linguistic data first.

This book is meant for researchers and students who would like to apply dynamic systems methods and techniques such as variability analyses and modeling to longitudinal language data. The chapters explain the general principles with many actual examples from previously published and new data. In addition, starting from chapter three and continuing to chapter six, readers are directed to the 'How to' sections in Chapter 8 at the end of the book, which provide detailed information about the actual techniques and tools we used to code, analyze, present and model the data. Finally, on our website SLD_Methods (DOI:10.1075/lllt.29.website), readers can find the original files that we worked with and practice doing the analyses or examine the exact formulae we used.

The first two chapters present the theoretical framework for a DST approach.

Chapter 1, "Researching SLD from a DST perspective" by Kees de Bot and Diane Larsen-Freeman, reviews the basics of DST and shows the relation between traditional research and a DST approach to applied linguistics. One of the main questions is what the major contribution of a DST approach to language development is.

Chapter 2, "DST and a usage-based approach to SLD" by Marjolijn Verspoor and Heike Behrens, examines to what extent different usage-based approaches to language development are in line with DST thinking and address the research questions that a DST perspective to SLD could focus on.

Chapters 3 to 6 discuss actual case studies, each focusing on a different linguistic subsystem, to present different aspects of DST inspired research questions, techniques and methodologies. All four chapters use the data of real learners and show that even though they all keep developing, there is a great deal of variability as they discover and try out new words and constructions at all levels.

Chapter 3, "Coding and extracting the data" by Monika S. Schmid, Brian MacWhinney, and Marjolijn Verspoor, discusses the type of variables at different levels (e.g. lexical, syntactic, morphological, and so on) that may interact over time. It discusses an advanced Dutch learner of English in terms of how her sentence complexity and lexical sophistication develop over a three-year period. The main objective of this chapter is to show which variables may be interesting to look at and how to operationalize them. The *How to* sections at the end of the book show efficient techniques to code and extract data using existing software (CHAT), how extra tiers may be added to code for variables not automatically coded in CHAT, how to automatize processes using macros, and how the data may be extracted in CLAN, and then become available for analyses by importing the data in Excel pivot tables. CHAT/CLAN is widely used in the AL community (and includes an enormous shared corpus). The *How to* sections will explain the general principles and refer to the existing CHAT/CLAN handbooks where necessary. They also explain which data can be extracted automatically and which data can then be further analyzed using Excel pivot tables.

Chapter 4, "Variability analyses in language development" by Marijn van Dijk, Marjolijn Verspoor and Wander Lowie, points out the differences between traditional analyses that usually ignore variability and DST. The chapter discusses how eight Spanish learners of English acquire the grammatical negative formation subsystem. The main objective of this chapter is to show what variability can tell us about development and how to test whether the patterns found are meaningful or not. From a DST perspective, variability can actually be analyzed as data because the different patterns may give insight into the developmental process. Different techniques are shown to make the variability and general patterns visible within a spreadsheet program. Then techniques such as "detrending" and "Monte Carlo Analyses" are introduced to see if the patterns found are meaningful or not. The *How to* sections at the end of the book explain in detail how to make variability graphs in a spreadsheet program, make min-max graphs, make a moving window of correlations, detrend the data and run a Monte Carlo with software that can be downloaded for free.

Chapter 5, "Visualizing interactions between variables" by Marjolijn Verspoor and Marijn Van Dijk, is a preparation for the chapter on modeling. It first discusses the different relations variables may have to each other: They may support or compete with each other, and one may be conditional for another. The chapter then revisits the advanced learner from Chapter 3 to show various techniques to make the interactions such as support, competition or condition among different variables more visible so that they can be tested through simulation. The *How to* section at the end of the book shows how to do a moving window of correlations.

Finally, Chapter 6, "Modeling development and change" by Wander Lowie, Tal Caspi, Henderien Steenbeek, and Paul van Geert, shows how patterns that have been found in variability analyses as presented in Chapters 4 and 5 can be generalized in computer simulations. The chapter first explains what the differences are between deterministic and dynamic models and the main principles dynamic models are based on. Then by means of a case study on the development of the lexical subsystem of an advanced learner of English, it shows how theoretical assumptions about relationships between variables can be tested using growth models that simulate iterations. By comparing the outcomes of the growth models to empirical data, we can test whether our theoretical assumptions were justified. The *How to* sections at the end of the book gives details on how to use the program Van Geert (2003) has developed in Excel-VBA code and model data.

In our book we have limited ourselves to second language development as that has been our own expertise, but we hope that other researchers may find ways to apply these techniques to other areas of applied linguistic research as well.

Researching Second Language Development from a Dynamic Systems Theory perspective

Kees de Bot & Diane Larsen-Freeman

1. Introduction

The objective of this book is to present recently developed research methods and techniques in second language development (SLD) from a dynamic systems theory (DST) perspective. The objective of this chapter is to introduce DST briefly. It begins with a brief discussion of theory construction and goes on to introduce characteristics of dynamic systems. It concludes by suggesting some ways that research from a DST perspective can be conducted.

2. Theories in applied linguistics

The aim of scientific research is to develop theories that can describe and explain phenomena. In the history of science some of the greatest minds have developed thoughts about what constitutes a good theory, what phenomena should be described and what explanation actually is. It is of course beyond the scope of the present chapter to give a full treatment of the thinking about theorizing in science, but it may be useful to touch upon some of the issues because many of them are still debated today as fiercely as they have been in the past. In a way, applied linguistics (AL) is a young branch of science, and therefore some of the discussions that have more or less settled in "older" sciences still go on in this field. On the other hand, some would argue that it is also a sign of maturity that a research community reflects on what its main theories and paradigms are. That is certainly the case in AL. We are fortunate to have several books on theories of SLA (Mitchell & Myles (1998[2004]), Larsen-Freeman & Long (1991), Gass & Selinker (2001), Nortega (2009)) and an excellent overview of general issues in theory building in science as they apply to AL in Jordan's "Theory Construction in Second Language Acquisition" (2004).

   The focus of this chapter is on one domain of AL, namely second language development (SLD). It is traditional in AL to refer to this domain as second language acquisition (SLA); however, we prefer "development" for the reasons we give below. Long gives the following much quoted definition of an SLA theory:

> SLA theory encompasses the simultaneous and sequential acquisition and loss of second, third, fourth, etc. languages and dialects by children and adults learning naturalistically or with the aid of instruction, as individuals or in groups, in second or foreign language settings.   (Long 1993: 225)

While this is already a fairly broad definition, we would like to broaden it even further by moving from acquisition to development and from development to use. This leads us to the following definition:

> A theory of SLD describes and ultimately explains the development and use of more than one language in individuals.

By including the notion of "use", we want to make it clear that in our view several issues of multilingual processing, such as L1 interference and code-switching, are explicitly part of what we consider to be SLD. This allows for the inclusion of research on psycholinguistic aspects of multilingualism that in our view is crucial for our understanding of SLD. By using "development" rather than "acquisition", we want to make it clear that linguistic skills can grow and decline, and that accordingly, language acquisition and language attrition are equally relevant outcomes of developmental processes. Also implicit in the use of the term "development" is our belief that there is no one point at which it can be said that a language is completely acquired. Its development is ongoing. Our own perspective on development is based on notions in dynamic systems theory in which there is basically no distinction between development and use (we will come back to this later in this chapter), but we acknowledge that in most research and theories the two notions are treated separately.

It follows from our definition of a theory of SLD that theories can be descriptive and explanatory. Most theories are descriptive, and such descriptions are essential for our understanding of many phenomena, but very few theories are actually explanatory. The difference between descriptive and explanatory theories can be easily illustrated with the theory that the earth moves around the sun. This is a theory that describes the earth's path, but it does not explain why the earth moves around the sun. Even though most SLD theories aim to be explanatory, few theories actually are, partly because for many phenomena there are no comprehensive accounts for all outcomes and partly because making absolute claims about human phenomena is problematic. Nonetheless, for many researchers, explanation is the highest goal and they frown upon "mere" description.

There are two ways that theories form: through induction and through deduction. These two approaches can be summarized as "research then theory" and "theory then research" respectively. Jordan (2004) discusses this inductive/deductive distinction in detail and gives it a historical perspective, but we will limit ourselves to the discussion of some examples to show how these two approaches are used in SLD research.

In the *inductive* approach the researcher begins with gathering data on the phenomena to be studied. There is no preconceived theory that is used to gather the data. However, we must be aware that there is no description without a theory: There will always be some basic assumptions concerning the nature of acceptable data, such as "language phenomena are not completely random" or "words are relevant units of analysis". An example could be a study on prosody in L2 learning. First, the researcher has to define what she will be looking for: pitch contours, stress patterns, variation in volume or other phenomena. Then she will try to categorize phenomena to find out whether there is any systematicity in the data. Following that categorization process, she will then try to arrive at some general statements that aim at explaining the relations between the phenomena. This is then the core of a theory. The researcher doesn't start with a theory and try to find data to support or falsify it, but takes the data as a starting point and attempts to distill some underlying principles. As a next step, these principles can be used as a starting point in order to find further support and eventually arrive at a more generalisable theory.

In the *deductive* approach, the theory is the starting point. On the basis of the theory, a number of testable hypotheses are set up and data are gathered that provide evidence to support or falsify the hypothesis. The hypothesis has to be narrow enough to get relevant information on the phenomena studied. An example could be the role in second language development of watching subtitled TV, in which the subtitles are in a known language. The theory predicts that comprehensible input leads to acquisition, so watching more subtitled TV will lead to more acquisition, "all other things being equal". The normal procedure will then be to set up an experiment in which two groups are compared: one group who watches a large amount of TV and the other group who watches a smaller amount and performs some other task in the L2 for the time equivalent to the first group's television-watching. The gain scores in proficiency over time are used as the dependent variable. If the first group outscores the second group, the hypothesis is confirmed, and the theory supported. Of course, this example is a simplification, and we will come back to it to show that this kind of experimentation needs to be much more complex.

In the evaluation of theories, the notion of what constitutes proof is essential: A theory makes certain assumptions, and empirical data are gathered to test whether these assumptions hold or not. An assumption could be that there is a relation between the storage capacity in working memory and SLD: More capacity leads to development; less capacity may lead to stagnation or even decline of language skills. What would be proof for such an assumption? If we can establish that one group of learners has a small working memory capacity and another group has a large working memory capacity, the prediction is that the first group will show less development than the second group. But even if our expectations are confirmed, can we be sure that we have proof for our assumption? There may also be other aspects in which the two groups differ; for example, the group with the larger working memory may also have a higher aptitude for language learning, so we cannot be sure that the differences found in language proficiency are caused by the larger working memory. Another possibility is that people who practice learning an L2 a lot will have a larger working memory, so the larger memory capacity is a result and not a cause of language learning.

It seems, then, that proving a theory is not as simple as it may seem. It is in the end the community of researchers that defines whether a theory is adequate or not. However, within the SLD community, there is not much explicit discussion on whether a particular theory is valid, probably because many theories in AL have come from different fields where their worth has already been proven.

2.1   DST as a theory of SLD

This is not a chapter on the details of dynamic systems, also known as complex systems, and complex adaptive systems. While the history of the application of complex dynamic systems in the field of applied linguistics is fairly brief, a range of publications have been published in recent years (de Bot 2008; de Bot, Lowie & Verspoor 2005; de Bot, Verspoor & Lowie 2007; Jessner 2008; Larsen-Freeman 1997, 2002, 2006, in press; Larsen-Freeman & Cameron 2008a, 2008b; van Geert 1998, 2008; Verspoor, de Bot & Lowie 2004; Verspoor, Lowie & van Dijk 2008). More detailed information on various aspects can be found in these publications. In this chapter we will focus on issues that are relevant for the methodology of researching SLD from a DST perspective.

3.   The basic characteristics of dynamic systems

"Systems" are groups of entities or parts that work together as a whole. We talk about the economic system, the social system, the system of a computer, and so on. At the human level we use terms such as the circulatory system, the articulatory system, and the cognitive system. Systems consist of subsystems and are themselves part of a larger system. Systems are embedded in other systems. The term "dynamic" also has a fairly straightforward meaning. Dynamic refers to the changes that a system undergoes due to internal forces and to energy from outside itself.

The theoretical framework we will present in this chapter is based on DST, and in its most basic form, it is exactly that: systems that change through forces. Sometimes the system changes continuously, sometimes discontinuously, even chaotically.

Despite its relative newness, DST has attracted much interest, and this interest has resulted in whole institutes devoted to the study of DST and more books and articles on this topic than anyone can ever read. In areas germane to our interests there are several articles and books on language and language learning as dynamic systems (Larsen-Freeman 1997, 2002; Van Geert 1994b; Herdina & Jessner 2002; de Bot, Lowie & Verspoor 2005; de Bot & Makoni 2005; Larsen-Freeman & Cameron 2007, 2008b; Verspoor, de Bot & Lowie 2008) and on DST approaches to the human cognitive system (Thelen & Smith 1994; Port & van Gelder 1995; Beer 2000; Spivey 2007).[1]

DST started as a branch of theoretical mathematics, and its initial aim was to model the development of complex systems. Later on, the mathematical tools that had been developed proved to be useful for the analysis of problems such as the movement of the moon under the influence of the sun, the earth and other planets. Because there are systems on every level in the physical world, DST has found applications in a wide range of fields, ranging from epidemiology to economics to meteorology, and it has been used to solve practical problems ranging from heartbeat control to drilling holes for oil. What all these fields and applications have in common is that the phenomena they want to study or to change do not seem to follow predictable patterns of development.

In order to understand dynamic systems better, in this section we discuss their basic characteristics. These include:

a. Sensitive dependence on initial conditions
b. Complete interconnectedness
c. Nonlinearity in development
d. Change through internal reorganization and interaction with the environment
e. Dependence on internal and external resources
f. Constant change, with chaotic variation sometimes, in which the systems only temporarily settle into "attractor states"
g. Iteration, which means that the present level of development depends critically on the previous level of development
h. Change caused by interaction with the environment and internal reorganization
i. Emergent properties

We will discuss each of these characteristics here with some indications as to how they may play a role in SLD.

---

1. There are numerous web sites on DST. A very informative one is: http://www.calresco.org/sos/sosfaq.htm#2.11 Checked August 12, 2009

3.1   Sensitive dependence on initial conditions

Sensitive dependence on initial conditions has become famous as "the butterfly effect", which refers to the well-known example of the meteorologist Edward Lorenz, who showed that minimal differences in beginning conditions of systems can have massive effects later on. This has potentially a far-reaching impact on processes of change. For language learning it may mean that minimal differences between learners may, even when they go through similar learning experiences, lead to very different learning outcomes. In other words, similar teaching approaches do not necessarily lead to similar learning. For our research this means that we need to have detailed information on the initial conditions if we want to be able to explain differences and similarities in learning outcomes.

However, here we have already encountered one of the really complicated aspects of DST: In order to predict how development will take place, we need an extraordinary amount of information about those initial conditions. And, as we will see later on, at the start we don't know what the complete list of relevant conditions looks like: Does your grandmother's level of proficiency in French when she was young play a role in your learning of Swahili? Probably not, but it is possible – her aptitude or enthusiasm for French may have been passed on to you. Paulson (2005: 345) maintains that "the impossible amount of information needed for exact predictions is typical of chaotic systems".

It is not only our limitation in identifying all of the relevant variables and initial conditions. Our predictions are still limited by the next two characteristics of dynamic systems: their interconnectedness and their nonlinearity.

3.2   Complete interconnectedness

In a dynamic system all parts are connected to all other parts. Looking at language as a dynamic system means that subsystems such as the lexical system, the phonological system and the syntactical system are interconnected, which in turn means that changes in one system will have an impact on all other systems. This is not to say that all connections between systems are equally strong: Some systems will be only loosely connected, while for other systems the connections are very strong and the mutual impact of changes will be equally effective. In Figure 1 this complex interaction between variables is represented. It concerns the relationship between changes in proficiency at three moments in time and the relation with language contact, attitude/motivation and the use of strategies. A change in proficiency from Time 1 to Time 2 will be affected by proficiency in other languages, attitudes and motivation, language contact and language awareness at Time 1. But the change in proficiency will in turn have an impact on these factors: Enhanced skills may lead to a change in attitude and contact with the language and use of strategies. These changes will then impact on the ongoing process of language development from Time 2 to Time 3. This is in turn influenced by changes in proficiency in the other languages and so on. The picture clearly shows how complex interactions become, even when there are only three variables.

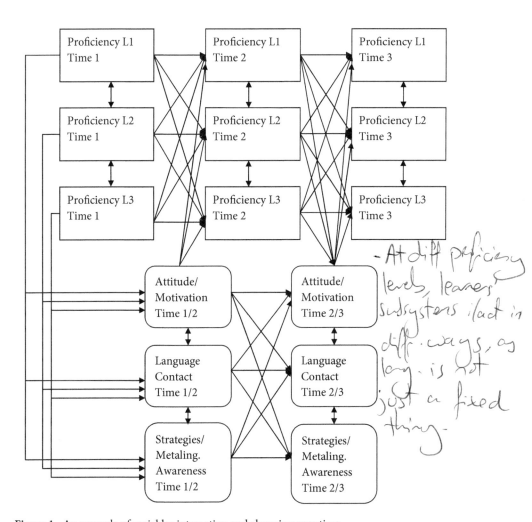

Figure 1. An example of variables interacting and changing over time

This raises the second major problem in doing research from a DST perspective: How can you study a system and its subsystems when everything is interconnected? How valid is it to study developmental changes in the phonological system without taking into account the changes that may occur at the syntactical and lexical level? There is no clear solution for this problem. On the basis of existing research, it may be possible to estimate what may be more or less relevant variables to include, and common sense may help as well. At the same time, some rather unexpected variables may in the end explain findings better than the more obvious ones. An example is the finding from a study by van der Slik, Driessen and de Bot (2006), who studied school performance of pupils with a Dutch and an immigrant background in the Netherlands. A large array of variables was included in the design, and in the end the variable explaining most was not ethnic background, level of education of parents or characteristics of the school, but whether the father had a paid job or not. In this study several thousands of pupils were tested, which allowed for testing the impact of a large set of variables. In most studies on SLD, the sample size (number of participants) is fairly small, and therefore only a small number of variables can be analyzed statistically, as we will see in Chapter 4.

3.3   Nonlinearity in development

We tend to think in terms of linear development. We imagine linear relations between cause and effect: When you have to learn vocabulary in a foreign language, you expect to learn twice as many words when you invest twice as much time in learning them. However, for dynamic systems the relation between cause and effect is often nonlinear, that is, there is no proportionate effect for a given cause.

In an interesting study, Meara (2004) showed that attrition of lexical skills can be simulated by setting up a simple computer model – a network of interconnected words, and then studying the effect of switching off one word after another. Because each word is connected to other words, switching off one word will have an effect on many other words in the network. Meara's model shows that switching off one word after another does not lead to a similarly linear decline of words in the lexicon. There is enormous variation in how the network reacts: In some cases the system remains largely intact until very many words are switched off, while in other cases there is dramatic decline right after the first few words are switched off. Of course, a simple simulation of a lexical network is not how the brain really works, but such simulations do give us some idea of how nonlinear development operates.

The nonlinearity is closely related to the interconnectedness of the system. The more components interact, the more problematic it becomes to predict how the system will change. If you are interested in learning tones in Mandarin, many variables will play a role in predicting how learning takes place. The amount of time spent listening to tones, listening skills, attention, motivation, knowledge of other tone languages, musicality, environmental noise levels, all of these factors may play a role. The impact of each single variable may be linear in the sense that twice as much noise may make perception and therefore learning twice as problematic, but the complexity is not additive. It is magnified because all of these variables interact. Learning L2 tones may be influenced directly by musicality, but more likely the musicality will be affected by, and will affect, motivation to learn, and motivation may interact with time invested and noise levels, and so on. So, in addition to the direct effect of the variables, there is interaction between the variables, and this interaction is dynamic in the sense that it changes due to the impact the factors have on each other. So the motivation to learn tones may change due to the success in learning, which may then affect the amount of time invested. In other words, some variables may be more or less stable, such as earlier experience in learning tone languages, and musicality, while others are more dynamic, such as time invested, motivation, attention and listening skills. And even the stable variables may not be really static; learning a new tone language adds to the experience with tone languages, and musicality may also change with experience. Still, the stable/dynamic variables distinction may be useful to keep in mind when setting up research, since the impact of stable variables is more likely to be continuous and therefore doesn't need to be assessed repeatedly, while the impact of dynamic variables is probably discontinuous and therefore needs to be assessed at regular intervals.

3.4   Change through internal reorganization and interaction with the environment *So, how do subsystems change when you go better? pp. percieve

As we have indicated earlier on, we use the term "development" rather than acquisition or attrition. From a DTS perspective there is no goal or direction in development; there is only change. Two forces are at work constantly: interaction with the environment and internal self-organization. A simple example may help to clarify this. Suppose you have built a sandcastle on the beach. At first, when the sand is still wet and clinging, the castle will keep its shape. From the outside and from a distance, it looks like a stable and inert system. But you know that internally all sorts of processes are taking place. Due to changes in humidity, the adhesive powers of the grains of sand decline, making the links between the parts of the system weaker and weaker. There are also external forces: First the wind and the sand hit the castle and then there is the shaking of the ground due to people passing by. If you look carefully, you will see little changes all along. But the castle may stand for quite some time, and then for some reason, a part starts to crumble. We will never know why that part crumbled first or what made it crumble. We cannot look inside the sandcastle because that would interfere with the internal reorganizational processes going on. The castle will not disappear steadily once the first signs of decline present themselves; one part will crumble, while another will stand unexpectedly long.

3.5   Dependence on internal and external resources

Every developing system is constrained by limited resources. For a frictionless pendulum, the energy that went into setting it in motion continues to keep it moving. Most natural systems need a constant flow of additional resources: Economic systems need labor and production to keep them going, and the brain needs oxygen and nutrients to function. Language learning and language use are equally dependent on resources. Van Geert and colleagues (van Geert 2008; van Geert, Savelsbergh & van der Maas 1997) distinguish between resources for learning that are internal to the system and resources that are external:

Internal resources, resources within the learning individual: the capacity to learn, time to learn, memory capacity, problem solving skills, internal informational resources such as conceptual knowledge and motivational resources. The list can be extended endlessly: Vision and audition, general health, mobility and so on, they may all play a role.

External resources, resources outside the learning individual: spatial environments to explore, time invested by the environment to support learning, external informational resources such as the language used by the environment, motivational resources such as reinforcement by the environment and material resources (books, TV sets).

By definition, internal and external resources interact: Time to learn is related to time invested by the environment, audition is related to the effectiveness of auditory resources and many other connections can be made. Also note that systems and resources are interconnected: Memory capacity is a resource for language proficiency, but language proficiency may also be a resource for memory capacity. Higher levels of proficiency allow for larger holistic units to be stored in memory.

3.6   Constant change, in which the systems only temporarily settle into "attractor states"

As we have indicated above, systems are constantly in interaction with their environment and reorganize themselves as a result of internal changes. We also mentioned the nonlinearity of development. To make this clear, we can go back to the sandcastle example: Internal and external forces are constantly working, and the seemingly stable system is actually dynamically changing all the time. When it goes beyond a critical stage, it will change (we see the crumbling of the castle as "decline", but of course for the system this is just another state). The castle crumbles, but is not reduced to an amorphous pile of sand in one continuous process. One tower of the castle collapses, but then the flow of sand stops: The system settles into a new form. This is called an "attractor state", defined as the state the systems prefers to be in over other states at a particular point in time. Attractor states are not defined by an external force; they result from the developments in the system. Why a given state is an attractor state and why the system will never settle in the opposite, or so called "repellor state" is unclear and such stages cannot be predicted. Minor differences in initial conditions may also lead to different attractor states.

For SLD, the phenomenon of fossilization could be described as the result of attractor states the system settles into. Fossilization refers to the stagnation in development of L2 learners who acquire a part of the language system and do not seem to develop it further. Though the notion of fossilization and the empirical evidence for it are far from clear (see Larsen-Freeman 2005), the idea of a developing language system settling into a specific state helps to clarify what an attractor state is. It takes a considerable amount of energy to make the system break away from the attractor state and move on. The metaphor used to explain attractor states is that of a surface such as that of the moon, partly smooth, partly with holes and mountains. A ball rolling over that surface will be "attracted" to the holes and be "repelled" by the mountains. Once the ball is in a hole, it takes much more energy to make it move again than to keep it rolling over the smooth surface. Related to this is the notion of "basins of attraction". To continue the surface metaphor: This indicates that there are not only holes, but also slightly depressed plains forming shallow bowls. The distance to the attractor state itself can be fairly long and it may take quite some time to reach it, but once the system is in the basin of attraction it will continue to move in that direction. Basins of attraction can take many forms, from depressed plains to river-like meandering forms.

This is all very theoretical and reflects the mathematical thinking behind DST. Still, the idea of preferred stages and directions a system is attracted to is relevant for our understanding of SLD. Some of the problems with what fossilization is and how you can prove it may actually be solved by taking this perspective: Attempts to explain why some people's L2s fossilize at some point and manifest certain deviant forms have not been very successful. Maybe fossilization cannot be predicted because it is the result of the complex interactions that are typical of dynamic systems. It may also explain why there is such variation in what is seen as fossilization: different factors, different initial stages, and different interactions.

3.7   Chaotic variation over time (sometimes)

Due to the interaction of variables over time, the path that a dynamic system takes may be difficult to anticipate. Language learners may go through phases of fluency and disfluency for no obvious or discernible reason. Chaotic variation, variation that is impossible to predict, results. It may be caused by a range of factors, such as physical fatigue, memory overload or temporary disfunctioning of a part of the brain.

3.8   Iteration

The development of a system has been compared with a dance. The dance as a system is not the simple repeated steps, but the complex interaction between the two dancers, the steps they take, and the environment. The dance emerges from the repetition of the same basic steps in an ever-changing setting, the room to move for the dancers, the rhythm of the music, the intentions of the dancers and so on. Iterations are the repeated applications of the same procedure over and over again. But with every step, the dance changes, the next step is different from the previous one and the one that follows. Thus iterations are "analogous to beginning at a certain step and doing a dance step: then starting from a new location each time, doing the dance step over and over again" (Hayles 1990: 153 in Paulson 2005). For development this means that the present level depends critically on the previous level (van Geert 1994b). In other words, in the present state of the system, its complete history is represented.

This line of thinking leads to some pretty far-reaching implications. One that Larsen-Freeman (1997, 2010) refers to is that there is basically no difference between using the language and language change: Every time an element of a language is used, its status in the system is changed and therefore the whole system transformed, even if only to increase the probability of the element's being selected the next time. Other times, a form takes on new meaning. For example, when reading a certain text, some words may be unknown, but on the basis of a context the meaning can be inferred. Each time the word is seen, the previous presentation of that word, with all its semantic, conceptual and syntactic information, will be refreshed and changed slightly due to the context it appeared in.

To give an example, if English learners do not know the word "cougar" and read:

1. "Cougars like open spaces"
2. "Cougars have sharp teeth"
3. "Cougar hunt rabbits"

they may have an image of an animal that is probably similar to that of a fox. After reading:

4. "Cougars are the largest animals of the cat family in America"
5. "Cougars are known to have devoured young babies in urban areas"

the picture of a fox-like animal has changed into that of a cat-like animal such as a lion and a much more threatening one. In the meaning of what a cougar is, the old information from sentences 1–3 is still there, but the current representation of that animal is influenced heavily by the information in 4–5.

3.9   Change caused by interaction with the environment and internal reorganization

Systems will change due to interaction with their environment and due to internal reorganization. A simple dynamic system such as a pile of sand will change due to external forces such as the wind or changes in temperature. Such changes will lead to a reorganization of the system till it settles in a new attractor state. For language learning we can illustrate such changes by looking at the acquisition of new words. When a learner has one word for a certain way of moving, "walk", all types of walking will be referred to using this word. When at some point the word "stroll" is acquired, the lexical system will reorganize itself by differentiating various ways of walking.

3.10   Emergent properties

Emergent properties of a system are features not previously observed as functional characteristics of the system. Generally, higher level properties are regarded as emergent – ones that arise from the interaction of low-level components. An automobile is an emergent property of its interconnected parts. That property disappears if the parts are disassembled and just placed in a heap. So an automobile is more than the sum of its parts, but it is dependent on all those parts to function. Then, too, the properties emerge at different levels of scale, so it is possible for a traffic jam to emerge from the interaction of many automobiles. The most often cited example of emergent properties that are the result of a change is that water turns into ice when the temperature is lowered below zero. The potential to become ice is not an inherent characteristic of water, but an emergent property that comes out in specific conditions.

In research and theories on language development, emergentism, that is the potential of complexity arising out of the interaction between simple processing procedures and a rich environment, is now one of the leading theories (Ellis & Larsen-Freeman 2006; Ellis 2008). The idea of emergentism is often presented as an alternative to theories based on innateness of language, and in particular Chomsky's universal grammar, although some do not see their incompatibility (Plaza Pust 2008).

4.   DST and language learning: Bringing the social and the psychological together

There are three more characteristics that are important to consider when reflecting on theory in SLD from a DST perspective. First, cognition is not a separate module located in specific parts of our brains. It is distributed over different parts of the brain and the rest of the body. It could be argued that there is a lot of cognition in a sculptor's hands or a football player's feet. There is no clear boundary between the cognitive system and the rest of the human system. This means that the cognitive system is what is called *"embodied"*. Second, the cognitive system is also not bounded within the individual. Cognition is a *shared* property, and it can be shared with a computer: The hard drive can be seen as an extension of its user's cognitive system, and it can be shared with other people. Finally, cognition is *situated*. This means that the setting in which cognitive functions have been carried out are part of the cognition itself.

A well-known example is what Paul Meara calls the "Boulogne Ferry effect": the idea that after crossing the Channel between Britain and France, on entering the harbor of Boulogne, the situation evokes memories of being in a French-speaking environment at some time in the past and subsequently makes French vocabulary more accessible than it would ordinarily be.

The fact that cognitive activities are embodied, shared, and situated means that a traditional distinction in AL research between sociolinguistic and psycholinguistic approaches no longer holds. The social situation of language use and development and the psycholinguistic processing that takes place can only be artificially separated. Instead of studying the social and the psychological independently, or arguing about their relative importance, 'We should be looking for how to connect cognitive acquisition and social use…. Forcing us away from reductionism and towards holism' (Larsen-Freeman 2002: 40–41; see also Larsen-Freeman 2007).

5. Conducting research from a dynamic systems perspective

It may have occurred to readers that many of the characteristics of dynamic systems just discussed represent significant challenges to traditional ways of researching SLD. For instance, if everything is interconnected, how is it possible to study anything apart from everything else? If the process is nonlinear, how is it possible to make any predictions that are likely to hold up? And, if so much of SLD is dependent on initial conditions, and the initial conditions are many and variable, how is it possible to take all relevant factors into account? We admit that these and other questions are not easy to answer. However, researchers have a responsibility to seek support for their theories. As such, in this section of the chapter, we will outline some of the implications for research methods from a dynamic systems perspective, as we see them.

We start with the challenge that the interconnectedness of subsystems presents. As we have already indicated, dynamic systems emerge from the interconnectedness of their subsystems or parts. Thus, it is not possible to arrive at a satisfactory componential explanation (Clark 1997: 104). In other words, it is not possible to explain behavior by examining the component parts one by one and adding up our observations. Having said this, we think it both necessary and acceptable from a DST perspective to investigate a focal part of a system, as long as we are open to explanations from outside of the focus and that we can justify the focus we have chosen. For instance, it does not make sense to study situated and embodied cognition apart from the context in which it operates.

This is because the context of a language-learning activity includes both the intrinsic dynamics of the learner, that is, what individuals bring to the activity, and the external resources, which are outside the individual. It should not, therefore, be difficult to see why in DST the study of learners cannot be undertaken apart from the context. As van Geert and Steenbeek have written:

> Although it is statistically possible to separate context- and person-aspects, such separation requires the assumption of independence of persons and contexts. This assumption is untenable under a dynamic interpretation of performance. On a short time scale, context affordances and person abilities result from the real-time interaction between the two and are, therefore, inherently dependent on one another. On a longer time scale, persons tend to actively select and manipulate the contexts in which they function, whereas contexts on their turn help shape the person's characteristics and abilities.   (van Geert & Steenbeek 2008: 83)

Also, we can only make claims about the focal area – not the whole system. As we have just seen with the psychological and social dimensions of SLD, we should look at what connects the parts, not what each contributes independently. In other words, we adopt a system-level point of view to investigate change in behavior.

Of course, it is a common quest in science to seek the broadest possible generalization for observed behavior. Perhaps, though, when it comes to dynamic systems, we should think in terms of "particular generalizations" (Gaddis 2002: 62) rather than universal ones. In other words, we can point to tendencies and patterns we have found, but resist implying that they are applicable beyond our own research site and data.

Moreover, as we have illustrated earlier with our example of your grandmother's proficiency in French having an effect on your learning of Swahili, it is impossible to anticipate all the factors that are at play in a given situation. Even if it were possible to anticipate all the factors, they do not make a uniform contribution, that is, their influence ebbs and flows. In addition, we have also pointed to the butterfly effect, the sensitivity of the system to its initial conditions. All this, combined with the fact of the nonlinearity of the system, makes the prospect of predicting the behavior of dynamic systems a risky business indeed.

In conventional science, explanation produces predictions in the form of testable hypotheses. This is not a procedure that can be readily applied to dynamic systems. Just stop and think about a classic experiment. In an experiment to test the efficacy of a particular instructional treatment, a pretest is administered, an experimental group receives the treatment and a control group some other type of instruction. A posttest is then administered to both groups. If there is a significant difference between the pretest and posttest results, then the inference is made that the instructional procedure(s) were effective. However, with a nonlinear system it is possible for no effect to follow a treatment, or conversely, for an effect to show up that was not caused by the experimental treatment, but rather was due to some earlier experience or contextual factor. In other words, predicting simple, proximate, linear causality, in which some variables are said to play a determining role, is not part of the research enterprise governing dynamic systems. In its place, we propose retrodiction, or "explaining after by before" (van Geert & Steenbeek 2005). After a change has taken place, we can look back and describe what happened. We can observe the trajectory or the "trace" (Byrne 2002) of the system, explaining the next state by the preceding one. Of course, we may have expectations of how a process will unfold, or even of its outcomes, based on prior experience, but essentially, adopting a dynamic systems perspective brings about a separation of explanation and prediction. In actual fact, this may not be a unique limitation on research from a DST perspective. After all, geologists can explain earthquakes due to plate tectonics, and biologists accept the theory of evolution as an explanation for speciation. However, geologists have yet to be able to predict when an earthquake will strike, and no biologist can predict next year's flu strain.

If a classic experiment of the type that we have just outlined is not appropriate for researching dynamic systems, perhaps "formative experiments" are. In formative experiments, the focus is on the implementation of the treatment, rather than only on the endpoint. Furthermore, in classic experiments, there is an attempt to control all the factors, so as to warrant the claim that one factor was key. In contrast, in formative experiments, researchers are interested in the adaptations in a variety of factors that are made along the way to keep the instructional treatment on track.

> In a formative experiment, the researcher sets a pedagogical goal and finds out what it takes in terms of materials, organisation, or changes in the intervention in order to reach the goal.   (Newman 1990 in Reinking & Watkins 2000: 388).

There is another implication for research methods from a DST perspective – and this has to do with the matter of causality. As we have seen, dynamic systems resist explanations of simple linear causality. To say that X causes Y, as in motivation causes language learning success, does not work in DST. For one thing, there are many contributing factors to language learning success. To single out one, even one conceivably as powerful as motivation, may give a spurious result. This is because motivation itself is influenced by other factors, such as the attitudes of the learners and speakers of the target language. And its influence is reciprocal, with attitudes being affected by motivation. Moreover, no factor remains static. It is not the case that a learner is motivated or not motivated. Motivation waxes and wanes, sometimes from moment to moment. It is never a steady state (Dörnyei 2009).

At the very least, then, we need to look for the causal interconnections, the reciprocity that occurs when one factor changes and influences another. Another AL example of reciprocal causality that can be perceived in dynamic systems is the co-adaptation that takes place between interlocutors. To cite a well-known example in our field, when a native speaker and a nonnative speaker of a given language interact, the native speaker may adjust his or her language to make it easier to process.

Coadaptation is mutual, however. Presumably, the nonnative speaker is also adapting his or her language, fitting it to the situation at hand. The language resources of both interlocutors, then, are dynamically altered as each adapts to the other. Thus, in DST-inspired research, instead of investigating single variables, we study patterns that emerge from interactions. Extant research methodologies that enable inspection of changing iterative patterns are discourse analyses of native and nonnative speech, conversation analysis and corpus analysis. Then, too, in many ways, qualitative research methods, such as ethnographies, are well-suited for such investigations in that they "attempt to honor the profound wholeness and situatedness of social scenes and individuals-in-the-world" (Atkinson 2002: 539), by studying real people in their human contexts and interactions, rather than aggregating and averaging across individuals as happens in experimental and quantitative studies.

Gaddis (2002: 64) observes that in the real world, "everything is connected in some way to everything else". The independence of any individual variable then becomes questionable, as does the idea of a single cause giving rise to a complex event. Rather, it is likely that there are multiple and interconnected causes underlying any shift or outcome. "We may rank their relative significance, but we'd think it irresponsible to seek to isolate – or 'tease out' – single causes for complex events" (Gaddis 2002: 65). Of course because the future is unknowable, it does not follow that there is no continuity from the past. "Some continuities will be sufficiently robust that contingencies will not deflect them" (Gaddis 2002: 56).

Describing the dynamics of a dynamic system requires further comment. Even when a dynamic system is in its attractor state, it is still constantly changing, as a result of changes in and interaction in its parts. Recall the example of the sandcastle on the beach. No visible change is taking place, but evaporation of the moisture that is responsible for the sand's taking shape is occurring. This, as well as other forces, will lead eventually to a nonlinear change in which the castle, or more likely a portion of it, will fall. In other words, even when a system is stable, it is not static.

Furthermore, a dynamic system will show degrees of variability around attractor states and these degrees offer useful information about changes that the system is about to undergo. Thus, variation in the behavior of the system is not noise to be averaged away, or measurement error, but rather data to be mined (van Geert & van Dijk 2002). For example, changes in variability can be indicators of development. If we smooth away variability, by averaging, we lose the very information that may shed light on emergence (Larsen-Freeman 2006). If, instead, we pay attention to the nature of changes in stability and variability, we may find new ways of understanding SLD. Van Dijk and van Geert (2002) present several new methods that are especially useful for visualizing and describing intra-individual variability in observational data of individual children that were followed closely over a fairly short period of time. Such "dense" data are rare for SLD, but are badly needed to get a better insight into development over time. There are a number of methods to study variability that deviate from traditional approaches. These will be discussed in Chapter 4.

Another way that dynamism has been studied in dynamic systems is through computer modeling and simulations, such as discussed in reference to the Meara study earlier on in this chapter. Simulations can be very helpful because they force you to make your assumptions about the behavior of a particular dynamic system explicit. Furthermore, you can run the simulation on a computer again and again, altering the factors slightly and looking for the changes that result. The evolution of a system can happen in a matter of seconds, rather than years. Thus, in simulations we can manipulate developmental processes in a way we can never do in the real world, and doing so may provide us with interesting insights into how systems may develop. However, although computer simulations try to mimic real life as much as possible, they are by definition reductions of reality. If we cannot test them with real data, simulations remain a shaky ground to build theories on. A warning by Cowan (2003) is appropriate here: "Modelers become quite invested in their models and usually can account for most new data, if not through the central assumptions of the model then through tangential assumptions that have been conveniently added" (442).

Another dimension to researching dynamic systems pertains to the fact that, as we have said, systems are embedded within other systems. As we saw earlier, just as an automobile is an assemblage of parts, so too a traffic jam results from the gridlock of automobiles. In other words, dynamic systems operate at various levels of scale. In order to honor this, researchers must also think about investigating systems on different levels of scale. To give one example here – we can and should look for change in language processing over time through such methods as microdevelopment. The work by Behrens (2009) is a good example (though it also shows what an incredible amount of time goes into the development of such data bases). She gathered day by day information on language development of one child and also included the caretaker's speech. This allows not only for a detailed study of change over time, but also for a comparison between input and development.

To be true to SLD, however, we would also want to investigate the changes that take place at another level of scale. For instance, very recently a number of studies have been published in which eye movements have been used as an indication of online processing (Paulson 2005; Spivey 2007). These studies are able to capture change over time during task completion: By analyzing the eye movements in experiments in which the task changed during the experiment, the researchers were able to track the changes in attention that were caused by the change in experimental conditions. Such online techniques may help us to see change happening in the moment.

As may be clear from this chapter, a DST approach to SLD research may be different in a number of aspects from research that does not take a dynamic perspective. It is not our goal to promote the former approach here and declare the end to research based on the latter approach. For the moment we want to point out what needs to be kept in mind when a DST perspective is taken.

6.   Conclusion

In summary, a DST perspective, by rejecting the very notion of linear causality, undoes the conventional expectation that a good theory is one that describes, explains, and predicts. Description and explanation are possible, and these may be good enough. Instead of generalizable predictions, then, we are content to point to tendencies, patterns, and contingencies. Instead of single causal variables, we have interconnecting parts and subsystems that co-adapt and that may display sudden emergence of new modes of behavior. A good application of DST describes the system, its constituents, their contingencies, and also their interactions. Teasing out the relationships and describing their dynamics for systems at different levels of scale are key tasks of the researcher working from a DST perspective.

Dynamic Systems Theory and a usage-based approach to Second Language Development

Marjolijn Verspoor & Heike Behrens

1. Introduction

In Chapter 1, we discussed a DST approach to second language development research. DST is a general theory that explains how any complex system, which consists of a set of interrelated variables that continually mutually affect each other, may change over time. The goal of this chapter is to focus on the specific variables that may play a role within second language development. To do so, however, we first need to establish that language itself is a complex, dynamic system. Therefore, before focusing on the variables, we will first discuss some language theories that have explicitly or implicitly treated language or language development as a complex, dynamic system.

For many decades, a dominant view to language theory and language acquisition has been that language is modular, with separate and independent subsystems for sound, meaning and structure. These subsystems would interact with one another through interfaces. The main focus within this paradigm has been on the syntactic structure, which is regular and predictable: There is a universal grammar (UG) (all languages share basic principles) and humans are endowed with an innate language acquisition device, which enables humans to decode the language specific structural settings. The main arguments for this approach have been that language users are creative because they can produce sentences that they have never heard or used before, and that there are "constraints" because there are limits to the structures and shapes sentences may have. The main focus within this paradigm has been to find universals: What do humans have in common while developing their L1 or L2?

Even though this view of language has by no means been accepted by all applied linguists and has often been implicitly rejected or ignored, it is only recently that a more coherent picture has emerged of a completely different theoretical point of view of language and language acquisition, that requires neither a specialized language faculty nor a universal grammar to account for creativity and constraints. There is not one single theory that deals with all aspects of what language is, how it is organized, how it is processed, how it is used, how it changes, how it is acquired and how it is learned as a second language, but there is a group of compatible theories that together could fall under the umbrella of "usage-based" or "emergentist" theories and are compatible with a dynamic systems theory (DST) approach: cognitive linguistics, emergentism, connectionist theories, grammaticalization theory, activation theory, and usage-based L1 acquisition. All of these theories highlight certain aspects of language, language change, language acquisition, or the developmental process, but none of these theories by themselves gives a coherent picture of all these aspects at the same time. However, as Nick Ellis (1998) and a recent publication by Robinson and Ellis (2008) have attempted to show, these theories complement each other and can be applied to second language development theory. What follows is a brief description of these theories and a summary of the implications such a dynamic, usage-based approach may have for second language development (SLD) and the data that we will discuss later in this chapter.

2.   Language as a complex system

Cognitive linguistic (CL) theory (Langacker 2008) addresses what language is and how it relates to human cognition and conceptualization. The assumption is that language is primarily about making meaning. CL strongly rejects the modular view of language that is independent of all other human cognition and conceptualization. It argues that language is directly influenced by human cognition and processing abilities and reflects therefore human categorization, conceptualization, imagination, and schematization. It further argues that a continuum of constructions at all levels (morpheme, word, collocation, phrase, formulaic sequence, clause, sentence) reflects the conceptualization and structural organization underlying human languages and their processing (Langacker 2008; Goldberg 2003). CL is very much in line with a DST perspective because of the complete interconnectedness of the subsystems both in the mind and in the linguistic system, and because of the assumed dependency on both internal and external resources, such as perception, cognition, conceptualization, and human interaction.

But how has such a completely interconnected linguistic system developed to begin with? Hopper (1998) argues that the regular patterns that we find in any language at all levels do not occur because of some preprogrammed language faculty, but because they have simply emerged. In emergent grammar there is no such thing as an abstract grammar in the mind, but a network of expressions and constructions as a result of an iterative process: "different kinds of repetition, some of which concern what would more conventionally be called lexical, some idiomatic, and some morphological or grammatical" (Hopper 1998: 158). The regular patterns found in language are therefore the result of language use and are actually nothing but conventions established through time (cf. Evans & Levinson 2009: 444f.).

> The notion of Emergent Grammar is meant to suggest that structure, or regularity, comes out of discourse and is shaped by discourse in an ongoing process. Grammar is, in this view, simply the name for certain categories of observed repetitions in discourse.   (Hopper 1998: 156)

Hopper's line of thinking is in line with DST in that it considers language and language change a result of interaction with the environment and internal reorganization. Implicit in this view is that the present level of change depends critically on the previous level of change. Grammaticalization studies (e.g. Bybee 2008) have shown how established patterns in languages may change through use, overuse and abuse, often starting with a small change in one part of the system, which then eventually will affect other parts of the system. This view is in line with DST thinking in that systems are constantly changing, that small changes in one place may have an effect on other parts of the system, and that these changes are not linear.

The idea that language is creative and that new constructions and complexities occur is also compatible with connectionist models (e.g. Elman 1995) that have shown that through simple iterations complex patterns may emerge. In other words, complex patterns do not have to be innate because they can also emerge through small iterations. Also the UG argument that language must be innate because there are "constraints", i.e. there are natural limits to what is possible in a language can be countered with a DST perspective. Even though there are many approaches to complexity, chaos and dynamic systems, they share the common assumption that eventually all complex systems begin to self-organize, show regularities and will settle in so-called attractor states temporarily.

The idea that language learning is an iterative process is also in line with activation theory (Rumelhart & McClelland 1987): The more frequently one hears something, the more easily it is activated, the more frequently it is used and the faster it is learned. Within activation theory, most work has been done at the lexical level, but MacWhinney also developed a computational model with self-organizing maps (SOMs) at different linguistic levels (morphology, syllable structure, lexicon, syntax and so on). In line with other usage-based theories, MacWhinney's unified model (UM) (2008) takes input as the source for learning. It learns by comparing the input, searching for similarities and differences. However, MacWhinney's model emphasizes that in addition to pure frequency, the role of cue availability, validity and reliability helps determine the course of acquisition, which relates to the opacity of patterns. *Cue availability* refers to how often a cue is present in the input, and *cue reliability* refers to whether a cue is always used consistently. *Cue validity* is the product of cue availability and reliability. A fully valid cue is a cue that is always there when it needs to be for communication purposes (in other words, it is fully available) and that is used consistently (it is fully reliable). A good example of a valid cue would be the verb *is* after *he* or *she*. An example of cues that are not valid at all is in the English article system. We can be sure that *a* and *the* are probably the most frequent words in the language (cue availability), but their use is notoriously difficult to acquire for learners whose L1 does not have a similar system. The reason is that both *a* and *the* have many different uses and functions, so the cue reliability and therefore the cue validity are very low. In other words, in line with DST thinking, MacWhinney points out that there cannot be just one causal factor in acquisition, but a combination of factors that interact.

To summarize, even though cognitive linguistics focuses on the meaningful inter-relationships within the language system in general, it recognizes that this system is complex and dynamic, that it is has emerged through social interaction, and that it will keep on changing. Emergentist and connectionist approaches focus especially on how it is possible that complexities can emerge in language through simple iterations, and grammaticalization theory concentrates on the detailed processes that may occur in language change. Activation theory and MacWhinney's unified model focus especially on the factors, such as frequency of occurrence, that play a role in language acquisition and use. In line with DST, all these usage-based theories implicitly or explicitly agree that the patterns that may occur at the general system level (a language in general) will also occur at the more specific, individual level.

Now that the learning theories related to DST have been briefly presented, we will discuss the specific variables that play a role in L2 development and how these may interact dynamically.

3.   The role of frequency

A longitudinal study in L1 acquisition with 44 American children from different socioeconomic backgrounds showed that not only the quality of interaction matters (e.g. the amount of positive or negative feedback in communication) but most criti-cally the quantity (Hart & Risley 1995). A child that hears 50 utterances per hour on average has been exposed to 250,000 utterances by age 4, but a child that hears an aver-age of 800 utterances per hour has an experience of 4 million utterances. The intensity of communication thus has exponential effects, and Hart and Risley found quantity of interaction to be the most relevant predictor for later success in school.

Frequency is an important factor in usage-based theories of language develop-ment and processing. But what exactly do we count, and how do we store this infor-mation? Critically, a distinction between type and token frequency has to be made. Token frequency measures the number of occurrences of a particular type: E.g. the word *dog* may appear 10 times in a particular conversation. Token frequency leads to entrenchment, i.e. each encounter leaves a memory trace, so that the more often we experience or do something, the more stable its representation becomes. However, token frequency does not lead to generalization or abstraction. For this we need type frequency or variation. Consider hearing the word *dog* ten times as opposed to having two tokens of *dog*, three tokens of *poodle* and five tokens of *dachshund*. In the latter case we see variation, and with enough experience in context we will work out that *poodle* and *dachshund* are subsets of the more general category *dog*. And if we compare their use in language with other words, we may notice that they all share grammatical properties with other elements we call "nouns" (e.g. being preceded by determiners and adjectives, showing agreement with the finite verb), although they may have nothing in common semantically. In other words, abstract part-of-speech categories derive from linguistic units being used in similar environments (MacWhinney 2008; Redington, Chater & Finch 1998).

The complexity of language processing becomes clearer if we consider a simple utterance such as *Tom likes his new dachshund Seppl*. It instantiates a transitive construction at the sentence level and is constructed from several other constructions, such as a pronoun-NP, a complex NP composed out of a possessive, an adjective and a proper noun, and a 3rd person singular verb. We could break this count down even further to the morphological level and the different phonemes. And at the same time the utterance instantiates the concrete words *Tom*, *likes*, *his* and so forth. But do we keep a count of all these different types all the time? Research from adult processing seems to suggest that we do, as frequency effects on all levels of representation are among the strongest effects we find in psycholinguistics (meaning that all things being equal, more frequent elements are processed more quickly and accurately than their equally complex but less frequent counterparts). Thus frequency leads to automatization, which makes processing faster and less error prone. Even newborns react differently to words they have heard in the womb, although they have no cues to what these words mean or that language means anything at all. But memorizing linguistic material will help them to break into the speech stream later on (Clark 2009).

While frequency effects in language processing provide evidence that we do rely on our previous linguistic experience, it is not fully understood to date what exactly we store and how this differs from learner to learner. Exemplar-based models of language assume that we store all exemplars and that the stored exemplars form "clouds" of similar exemplars, from which we build categories (Pierrehumbert 2003). In language development, the course of first language acquisition tells us that the child's memory and perceptual abilities filter the input. Researchers have argued that young children's limited working memory span may be beneficial to language learning, as they tend to focus on adjacent elements, where most of the grammatical information is encoded (e.g. congruence between determiners and nouns, agreement between the subject and the following verb). Likewise, content words tend to be stressed, so that it follows quite naturally that they are identified before the more frequent function words. This entails that some of the material that is there is not processed initially, or processed differently. Our ability to process the entire signal available increases with our experience with language, so it seems likely that the exemplars we store change over time (cf. Verspoor, de Bot & Lowie 2008). Also, storage may be influenced by the attention we pay to the event, so that some utterances may "count more" than others. These issues are largely unexplored empirically, but from a DST perspective they can be explained by the fact that what we pay attention to will change as we progress developmentally, and that what we pay attention to may also be situation-specific. It is therefore likely that what we count or what we store changes with development.

4.   The role of L1 in L2 acquisition

A usage-based view also implies that the L1 may play an important role in the acquisition of an L2 because the learner brings knowledge of language(s) to the acquisition task. This not only implies that L2 learners have knowledge of a linguistic system (its structure and its underlying categorization and conceptualization), which can give them a head start because unlike babies they need not work out what language and communication is about, but also that their processing system has been highly attuned to the properties of their first language.

> As Usage-Based Theory views linguistic knowledge as a set of automatized patterns which are schematic to varying degrees, the first language must be viewed as both a help and a hindrance to Second Language Acquisition. To the extent that the constructions in the second language are similar to those of the first language, the L1 constructions can serve as the basis for L2 constructions, with only the particular lexical or morphological material changed. However, since even similar constructions across languages are likely to differ in detail, the acquisition of the L2 pattern in all its detail is hindered by the L1 pattern.
> (Bybee 2008: 232)

Bybee's view is very much in line with what Ringbom (1987) concluded after extensive research on Finnish and Swedish speakers in the mid 1970s: Similarities served as facilitators. The idea that the L1 may play an important role in L2 acquisition is in line with the DST notion of sensitive dependence on initial conditions. It is much easier for learners to learn languages that are similar than languages that are different. It also implies that learners with different L1s have different problems in learning the same L2. MacWhinney (2008: 347–349) summarizes results on the developing mental lexicon of second language learners and argues that L2 is parasitic on L1 because learners will transfer when they can. The beginning learner links the new words to the existing ones in the L1. When the two languages are very similar and conceptually close, this positive transfer will not lead to problems or obvious mistakes, especially since learners tend to transfer general terms rather than specific ones. As the L2 becomes stronger, the learner will establish more and more conceptual links to the L2 and to the

L2 lexicon. Ultimately the associations between words in the L2 may become stronger than to the words of the L1. Associations of words within one language also explain why bilinguals do not mix languages excessively, since they are used to hearing, for example, English words in English contexts and Spanish ones in Spanish contexts (Hernandez, Li & MacWhinney 2005).

5. Dynamic language development

So far we have just talked about the dynamic complex language system as if it were a system on its own, but little has been said about children or people actually using the system. Why would a human want to spend so much effort to master a system anyway? Within a usage-based approach to first language acquisition, Lieven and Tomasello (2008) argue that children do not primarily want to learn to speak and "acquire language", but rather they want to belong to the social group, participate in their communication and express their intentions. In other words, learning to use a language (and other socially accepted behavior) is a means to an end: social interaction. This also entails that the modern, process-oriented view of the child is that of an active agent, not just a brain that waits for an innate grammar to be activated or that is passively formed by the input it receives:

> The task of the developing child is to become an active, knowledgeable participant of a language community. To do so, she uses whatever predispositions and knowledge she has to increase her understanding even as she engages in it. It is in this sense that she bootstraps her way to adult competence as an active, social child. (Shatz 2009: 8)

Children learn language from actual "usage events", which are particular utterances in particular contexts, and starting with isolated items or small chunks, they eventually recognize the repeated patterns and build up increasingly complex and abstract linguistics representations. In other words, children's early language is not the result of a top-down effect based on innate highly abstract structures and constructions allowing generalizations, but a bottom-up process based on an inventory of highly specific, item-based schemas that develop from pivot-like structures in piecemeal fashion over the early childhood years (Tomasello 2003). Such a line of thinking is also supported by Ellis (2002), who argues that one of the main factors to drive the (L2) acquisition process is input frequency. He gives examples in the processing of phonology, phonotactics, reading, spelling, lexis, morphosyntax, formulaic language, language comprehension, grammaticality, sentence production, and syntax.

If children learn language from language use, i.e. the language they hear, they need not only to remember what they have heard, but also to process it in such a way that they not only reproduce, but also reconstruct the system. Only if they perform a productive analysis of the input can they construct utterances they have not heard before, one of the key properties of the human language faculty. Research over the past decades has shown that even babies have remarkable skills in speech recognition and memory for speech sounds. Newborns can distinguish their mother's voice from other voices, and they recognize words they have heard before in the womb. They can distinguish their mother tongue from other languages a few days after birth (cf. Clark 2009, Chapter 3 for a summary).

Apart from being able to memorize and recognize linguistic units, children must identify their internal make-up and the patterns they occur in. In order to segment words out of the continuous speech stream, they initially rely on prosodic and perceptual properties. Regardless of their absolute frequency, words that appear in stressed or salient utterance in final- or initial position are easier to process than elements that are not salient (Peters 2009). In order to segment words out of continuous speech, they can make use of statistical information. It has been demonstrated that children are sensitive to statistical information, in particular transitional probabilities. Units that tend to co-occur together are likely to form a unit. Consider the sequence *prettybaby*: There is a high likelihood that in Child Directed Speech, *pre-* is followed by *-ty*, but a very low likelihood that *ty-* is followed by *ba*. Thus, *pretty* is a probable word while *tyba* is not (Saffran 2003). The processing abilities are not specific to language processing, but they do help children identify relevant linguistic units. Unlike adults, to come to the task of learning a language with a highly developed conceptual system, children have to learn the possible meaning of words as well. Here, social cognitive skills such as intention reading are essential (see Tomasello 2003 for a summary).

By the time children produce their first meaningful word, around their first birthday, they can draw on a massive amount of experience with language. But it still takes them several months before they start producing word combinations. Both corpus-based and experimental studies show that children initially rely strongly on the kind of patterns they hear in the input language and vary them only gradually (Tomasello 2000, 2003; Lieven, Behrens, Speares & Tomasello 2003). Even the acquisition of common sentence structures such as the transitive can take several years, as the generality of the structure is found only at a rather abstract level. A transitive sentence in English is defined by its Subject-Verb-Object structure, but in concrete utterances, subjects, verbs and objects come in many different shapes and sizes (Tomasello 2000). For example, *I love you, John hits Bill, the doctor sees the problem* are all transitive sentences, but they do not share lexical material and are semantically different in the degree of agency.

It is therefore not surprising that children initially rely on the patterns they hear and generalize only gradually. With an example from German morphology, we would like to illustrate that the nature of the generalization changes over time and that the system is never fully settled. As an example, we will summarize findings from the acquisition of the German plural by a monolingual German-speaking boy, Leo (Behrens 2002). Leo was followed with a dense sampling technique. Between ages 2 and 3, his parents made a one-hour recording five days a week. In addition, they kept a diary on his most advanced utterances of each day. This dataset allows us to track his development from day to day.

The German plural is formed in eight different ways: zero marking or marking by the affixes -n, e, or er, some of which can occur with vowel raising (umlaut) (cf. Table 1).

Table 1. The eight German plural classes

affix	-s	-(e)n	-e	-er	Zero
- Umlaut	Auto-s	Bahn-en, Fahne-n	Fisch-e	Kind-er	Lehrer-0
+ Umlaut	–	–	Bänk-e	Räd-er	Kästen-0

The plural marker that a given noun takes depends on the gender of the noun and its phonotactic properties (syllable structure and final sounds). The system is complex to describe, as some plural markers are clearly predictable (almost all feminine nouns and all nouns ending on schwa take the n-plural, nouns with the pseudosuffixes -el, -er, and -en are zero-marked unless they are feminine, when they get the -n marker.) The plural of other types of neuter and masculine nouns is harder to predict, a given noun root would be suitable to various markers, and in some cases this variability is indeed attested in language change or dialectal variation. But what are the cues language learners can rely on? They can draw on the gender and phonotactics of the noun root. Critically, for a full mastery of the system they need to process both, as the phonotactics of the root are not enough (cf. masculine der Zahn → die Zähne "tooth – teeth" with feminine die Bahn → die Bahnen). Another cue is the resulting plural noun forms (product oriented schemas, Köpcke 1998). Most noun plurals are bisyllabic and thus follow the iconicity principle that plural forms have more "substance", in that they are longer than the singular.

In the dense database we find that Leo has produced plurals of all types within only three weeks after producing his first plural form. And he starts to generalize very quickly. Within six weeks after producing the first plural noun, he has overgeneralized all plural markers including the umlaut. Overgeneralization errors are an indicator of productivity because they show that the learners go beyond the input: They will not have heard the form from others. The quick emergence of such errors suggests that the distinction between singular and plural is a very salient one and that Leo identifies the different plural allomorphs quickly since he does not settle on just a singular marker for overgeneralization. A closer look at his error patterns reveals that his errors are not haphazard and that they change over time. First of all, it is remarkable that some plural classes are almost always correctly inflected. For example, he always adds the -*n* plural to nouns on schwa and we may conclude he observed the fully predictable pattern for this noun type. This is not just an effect of the high frequency of these patterns, as we also find very low error rates on the low frequency -*s* and -*er* classes. Other classes, however, show error rates of up to 40%: Figure 1 depicts the error rates on the four most error-prone plural classes over the first five months of development. Data are analyzed in biweekly intervals, and we only included data points where at least 10 plural forms were attested. Errors mainly affect the classes with an umlaut as well as the zero marked class.

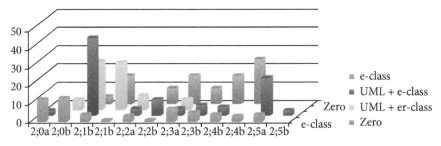

Figure 1. Leo's errors on plural classes in percent (age 2; 0–2; 5; biweekly intervals). Source: Behrens 2002)

While the Umlaut is no longer productive (i.e. new loan nouns in German do not take an Umlaut as the plural) so that the existing members may have to be learned lexically, the zero-marked class is (new nouns in German may have the zero plural, as in *Manager* "managers"). But the zero marked class represents a gap in the system because the child may start out with the assumption that plurals should be marked and therefore adds an ending to the stem. Figure 1 shows that the type of errors changes over time, as the child's generalizations may become more and more specific. We thus find not only variation over time, but also variation at a given point in time: Within the same month, Leo produces *Voge-n, Vogel-n,* and *Vögel-n* as the plural for *Vogel* "bird" (target: *Vögel*), and *Huhn-e, Hühn-e, Huhn-er* for *Huhn* "chicken" (target: *Hühn-er*) (for details cf. Behrens 2002).

Leo's error rate gets lower as his command of the language grows, and our default assumption in first language acquisition seems to be that the system settles once it has reached a "correct" representation. But if we look at the boy's later development, we realize that certain errors may occur again, even when the correct form has been produced several times. For example, Leo was obsessed with trains, but even after many correct plurals *Bahnen* he produced *Bahne* at a later point in development. Common theories of language acquisition within a UG or usage-based paradigm would not predict such errors. However, dynamic systems theory would assume that a system is never fully settled but that every attractor state can be overcome. This may in fact be a very useful property of the human mind, as speakers have to deal with ongoing language change in several respects. One could move to a different region where there are different orthographic norms or subtle variation in pronunciation or inflection. Therefore variability and a system that is not settled can be advantageous because the system that has to be processed may change. If our mind did not allow for any variation after a certain number of exposures or productions, we would not be able to adapt to new situations. When the second author moved from Germany to Switzerland a few years ago, she quickly adapted to the regional differences in plural formation and verb inflection and started to use *Pärke* as the plural to *Park*, thus overruling the entrenched Standard German form *Parks*. Or, to be more precise, she now has two plurals for the same nouns, one used in German and one in Swiss contexts. Without such flexibility we could not adopt to the manifold varieties within one language or to language change, which may happen quite quickly, when, for example, an expression becomes fashionable or politically incorrect.

Free variability also occurs in the L2 acquisition process. R. Ellis (1994) cites the study by Cancino, Rosansky and Schumann (1978) and concludes that "free variation occurs during an early stage of development and then disappears as learners develop better organized L2 systems" (Ellis 1994: 137). Such observations are in line with observations by Thelen and Smith (1994: 342), who suggest that variability is a metric of stability and a harbinger of changes. Variability is needed at the individual level for a learner to explore and select. For example, only when learners have access to a variety of forms are they able to select those that help them develop, so the more different forms they can select from, the more likely development is to take place. Within a similar vein, Bertenthal (1999), in a study on crawling patterns in infants, suggests that variability offers flexibility, driving development following Darwinian principles. Principles of variation and selection lead to storing and repeating behaviors that were successful more frequently than behaviors that were less successful.

Siegler (2007) suggests two other possible hypotheses for variability, which may not necessarily be mutually exclusive. Variability may reflect simultaneous activation of conflicting representations, which would facilitate the extension of the more advanced representation (Goldin-Meadow & Alibali 2002). Another view is that new strategies are often constructed from subroutines of existing approaches, and that assembling subroutines from different strategies is easier if the relevant strategies have been used recently and thus are relatively active (Shrager & Siegler 1998).

From a DST point of view, both free and systematic variability will be relatively high when the system is reorganizing and low in a more stable system. As van Dijk (2003) in L1, Larsen-Freeman (2005), Verspoor et al. (2008) and Spoelman and Verspoor (2010) in L2 studies report, the degree and pattern of variability at the individual level can tell us more about the developmental process, not only when we look at errors, but also when different types of constructions appear in the language. By tracing the different constructions and lexical measures over time, we may discover if the development of these measures is quick or slow, complex or simple or stagnating. We also discover the interactions between variables and the stages they go through. If the variability is low, we may assume that the system has stabilized for a particular period and for a particular aspect, whereas if the variability is high this means that the system is changing and moving towards another state or stage in the development until the system has settled again. This is reflected with bigger jumps when the data are analyzed and projected, and it is indicative that something is happening in the system and that the system is going through a period of transition before it settles again at a different level or attractor state. In other words, variability within a system is a precursor of change and of subsequent development.

6.   Individual patterns in language development

Many usage-based studies in L1 acquisition (Lieven & Tomasello 2008) and some in L2 acquisition (e.g. Diane Larsen-Freeman as early as 1976) have investigated the relation between frequency effects and development and have indeed found positive correlations at group levels. Much of this type of research has focused on the commonalities of groups of learners with averages for different learners taken as representing the "average" learner. Implicit in such investigations has been the assumption that learners develop along similar lines, a view that might hold to explain change and development at a macro level, but at the same time a view that ignores the messy, every day variability within learners and between learners that may drive the acquisition process, the varied strategies they may use and choose from to make meaning. If, as a usage-based approach holds, all learners have to find their own individual ways to detect and discover the repeated patterns for themselves, we might also expect differences among individuals.

A convincing case for the great amount of variability normally found among individuals in L1 development is given by Fenson, Bates, Goodman, Reznick and Thal (2000) in their article "Measuring Variability in Early Child Language: Don't Shoot the Messenger". They respond to Feldman et al. (2000), who had criticized the MacArthur Communicative Development Inventories, which is a standardized vocabulary acquisition test, as having too much variability, too little stability, and insufficient ability to predict early language delay. In this article, Fenson et al. argue that variability should not be seen as measurement deficiencies but as an authentic reflection of individual differences in early language development. They present data obtained in three different conditions, in a longitudinal study (Jahn-Samilo,

Goodman, Bates, Appelbaum & Sweet 2000), in parent-report data for 36 object names, and in child performance for the same 36 words in an elicited word production task administered monthly in the laboratory from 12 to 30 months, and find great variability between children from 16 to 30 months of age. Thus, they conclude, the vast variability does not reflect any psychometric deficiency, but a fact about early language growth that any valid measure must faithfully record.

The critique by Feldman et al. (2000) represents the traditional view that variability should be seen as noise in the data that should be eliminated or ignored, rather than as data that could give insight into the developmental process.

Longitudinal studies show the variability that may occur at the individual level, and how strategies may change over time, but does this mean that all studies at the group level are meaningless? Siegler (2006) points out that in a study that combined a micro-genetic and cross-sectional component (Siegler & Svetina 2002), the patterning of changes and non-changes proved to be quite comparable. The longitudinal and cross-sectional groups matched on 10 of the 11 indices of change that were examined. In contrast to the cross-sectional study, though, the longitudinal microgenetic study had yielded data that could show *how* the changes had taken place: Learners will reject and generate new strategies in two separate processes. Children would shift away from their predominant error on about a dozen trials before they discovered how to solve the problems correctly. Meanwhile, they generated a variety of incorrect approaches. In other words, cross-sectional data may give us information about the general stages learners will go through, but will not show the exact mechanisms of the changes.

7. Conclusion

As far as language learning is concerned from a usage-based, emergentist perspective, there is much more to learn in an L2 than its morphology and syntax. In fact, there is no real division between morphology, lexicon, collocations, formulaic phrases, and constructions. They are all constructions at different levels, but there is no clear division between them. Therefore, if we want to learn about language development, we should try to examine as many (overlapping) subsystems as possible, to see not only how each one of these emerges and develops over time, but also how the different subsystems may interact. For example, if we want to examine how learners develop more complex sentence structures over time, it might be interesting to see whether all types of dependent clauses emerge simultaneously or if some occur before others or even if some types of clauses go at the expense of others.

In trying to communicate, learners will take advantage of all the resources they have to get their message across; in speaking they will use gestures and facial expressions to indicate what they want to say. They will at first most likely focus on meaning and not be concerned too much with form. Similarly, in writing, they will think of strategies to get their meaning across. One often used strategy is to use the L1 to guess at a possible L2 word: for example, by writing an L1 word with an English spelling.

If language learning is a bottom-up process, where language is nothing more than a set of conventions, learners have to find their own strategies to express their intentions. They will pick up those conventions that they have heard most frequently, but in trying to express them, they may also try a set of varying strategies, from more simple ones to more complex ones, correct or incorrect, and often in juxtaposition. Eventually, however, they discard the least effective ones and use a combination of the more effective ones. This would mean that especially at the beginning stages, learners will show the greatest amount of interindividual variability. It also means it is useful to follow individuals along their developmental paths to see how and when new forms and constructions appear or disappear, change, or settle.

In our explorative studies presented in the next chapters, we will assume that learners basically move from the simplest, most frequent items that are most similar to their L1, to the items that are more complex, less frequent and less similar at all levels. At the earliest stages, learners will have to rely most on their strongest resource, their L1, and will transfer both positively and negatively. As they have more input and interaction in the L2, they will make more and more use of L2 words and constructions, but learning is not linear. Before learners are able to use the more complex structures, they have to make do with what they already have, so they may overextend the simpler constructions to express more complex ideas (use a simple present tense to express a past situation or juxtapose two simple sentences to suggest a more complex relation between the two sentences), so we may see peaks of overuse in some constructions. When more complex structures emerge, they may start to emerge around the same time, but the learner will start with a few fixed exemplars and then extend the use to other constructions. The most proficient learner is able to balance the different types of structures best.

Because each learner will have to discover the patterns of the target language on his or her own, we expect individual differences, for example related to initial conditions such as L1, age, aptitude, motivation, and so on, but as most learners will move from the simples constructions to the more complex ones, there are also general patterns common to most learners.

Coding and extracting data

Monika S. Schmid, Marjolijn Verspoor & Brian MacWhinney

1. Introduction

When investigating SLD, a usage-based and dynamic systems point of view proceeds from assumptions which are different from those of traditional approaches. DST researchers are not interested in monitoring whether L2 learners converge towards the native norm in the data they produce but rather in how the language system develops over time. In particular, the notion that a complex dynamic system consists of subsystems which are never entirely stable and may exhibit a great deal of variability, particularly during stages where the whole system is undergoing intensive development, is relevant here. This entails that DST approaches to SLD cannot confine themselves to data gathered on the development of one linguistic structure or rule but must take a broader perspective on the full range of the linguistic repertoire of a learner.

Such a perspective cannot be gained on the basis of many of the traditional experimental methods of research in applied linguistics. While specific tasks that are often used to gauge the state of an individual learner or a group of learners may provide additional insight into what is going on with respect to the acquisition of some specific feature(s), the full range of the linguistic repertoire can only truly be investigated on the basis of (spoken or written) data produced under relatively natural conditions – that is, data where all aspects of the linguistic production process (the selection of the vocabulary, the sentence frame, grammatical aspects such as tense, mood and voice, orthography or phonology and so on) are, as far as possible, fully under the control of the learner.

The reason for this approach is that, while the process of SLD usually implies an overall increase in linguistic knowledge, accuracy across all linguistic levels and complexity of vocabulary and style, there may be trade-offs between the individual components of language, in particular in situations where there is intensive development of one of these components. For example, a student who has previously shown an exceptionally broad vocabulary may, at some point in time, appear to regress with respect to lexical sophistication. This "dip" in her development may appear puzzling if the other aspects of her linguistic repertoire are not taken into account. However, when a full analysis is carried out, it may appear that at the same time, there is a marked increase in the length and complexity of the sentences she produces. In other words, at this point in time the student is diverting a large part of the limited cognitive resources she has available for the production and finalization of messages in her second language to the syntactic component of her linguistic knowledge, and therefore does not use the full range of vocabulary skills which she obviously has had at her disposal, as an analysis of her previous (and subsequent) performance can show. This trade-off would not have been apparent in a test tapping only into her vocabulary knowledge. Below, we will present an analysis of an individual case of SLD based on a sequence of written texts produced over a longer learning span, and show points at which such trade-offs emerge from the data.

Before that, however, we will address the issue of how to analyze spontaneously produced data. It has to be acknowledged that this is a highly costly and effortful process. One reason why researchers often prefer to rely on experimental data elicited by means of a specific test is that these can be gathered from a group of second language learners at the same time (exam-style), coded quickly and dichotomously (in terms of correct or incorrect responses), and quantified in terms of percentages of accurate responses which are easy to analyze statistically.

Spontaneously produced data, on the other hand, present a number of obstacles. Firstly, in particular where the researcher wants to rely on spoken data, they have to be elicited from each learner separately, either by means of a free interview or (if it is the aim to keep the topic constant across the data) by a task, for example, involving the description or retelling of a stimulus such as a picture or a film. This already means that the process of collecting the data may be far more time-intensive than where controlled experimental tasks are involved. Secondly, the transcription of such data is also invariably an extremely time-consuming process.

Both these obstacles can be circumvented to some degree by setting learners a specific topic and asking them to write a certain amount of text on this matter. This, of course, is a solution which may not be applicable in all cases, as written and spoken data are by no means equivalent expressions of a learner's linguistic knowledge and development. In either case, however, any kind of investigation which attempts to deal with naturalistic data, be they spoken or written, will have to expend a great deal of thought, time and care on the process of coding. This is particularly true for investigations such as the ones that are carried out from a DST perspective, which attempt to paint a full picture of the development of an individual's proficiency across all components of their linguistic repertoire.

In order to capture this process, the coding of linguistic data cannot be confined to the simple counting of errors. Nor may it even be enough to calculate accuracy as a function of the proportion of obligatory contexts, since an increase in proficiency – particularly at higher levels – often involves options which are stylistically determined, for example the use of the passive voice. This means that a large number of features may have to be coded not only across all obligatory, but across all possible contexts.

A good understanding of the available computer resources can help us make onerous processes of transcription, coding and analysis far more efficient. In the following, we will take you through a case study. First we will look at the raw textual material and discuss what measures we decided to look at.

> In the *How to* sections at the end of the book, (Chapter 8, Sections 2.1–2.5), we will give step-by step examples of how we coded and extracted the data. In the chapter itself we will emphasize how the data can be visualized and interpreted.

2.   The case study: Measures to be analyzed

The corpus investigated here consists of 22 text files collected a three-year period from an advanced student of English who majored in English at a university in the Netherlands. Her first language, Dutch, is typologically similar to English, and after six years of English instruction at high school she was quite an advanced user of English even when she entered university. She attended classes in academic writing, literature and linguistics and for each of these classes had to hand in written assignments. The texts were on different topics, such as literature, culture and society, or linguistics, but they were all written under similar circumstances (at home without time pressure) in an academic register. We took a random sample of about 200 words from each text (containing only full sentences) and ordered these excerpts chronologically. These data were previously investigated by Verspoor, Lowie and van Dijk (2008). The analyses presented here, however, differ from the original ones in that they were recoded using automatized functions, and concern different variables. Below are parts of three samples, the first assignment, one from the mid-range (13th), and the final one (22nd).

> *1. Practising an exam question for 20th century English fiction*
>
> The story is about the relationship between a father and his two daughters and about the way he influenced them. After their father's death, the two grown-up sisters, Constantia and Josephine weren't controlled by their father anymore and also they couldn't rely on him anymore. They were forced to make more decisions on their own now, in which they didn't succeed. They couldn't even decide on trivial matters like whether they would like their fish to be boiled or to be fried. Even at the end of the story, they couldn't make up their minds about ordinary matters. The story ends with a dialogue between the two women about the question whether they should keep Kate as a maid or fire her. The father had always prevented them to make decisions on their own.
>
> *13. The master and his slave*
>
> As the relationship between Prospero and Ariel is not equal, it is not perfect either. In the first part of the scene, it becomes clear that Ariel wants to fool Prospero by letting him know in an ironic way what he thinks of Prospero's demand. The absurdity of all the things he says to be willing to do for his master in a dramatic way give his statement ironic overtones. The strongest evidence that Ariel

and all his quality are not to Prospero's bidding task comes from the end of the play where Ariel asks in a way of indignation. The term of toil already tells us that the does not like working for Prospero at all, since it stands for hard, unpleasant work. Without knowing what it is that Prospero wants he does not like the idea of helping him again because he does not like to endure another hardship. In other words, he does not really want to dive into the fire for Prospero.

22. Task-based language learning and teaching

Focused tasks are tasks that elicit use of specific linguistic features, either by design or by the use of methodological procedures that focus attention on form in the implementation of a task. One of the major purposes of these tasks for learners is to induce their incidental attention to some specific linguistic forms when processing either input or output. Focused communicative tasks involving both reception and production (the main focus of this chapter) also serve clear goals for both researchers and teachers. For researchers, they provide a means of measuring whether learners have acquired a specific feature. They are often preferred to tests because they provide evidence of what learners do when they are not consciously focused on using a form correctly and thus can be considered to elicit implicit knowledge rather than explicit knowledge. Many SLA researchers would consider that only when learners demonstrate they are able to use a feature spontaneously in communicative activity can they be said to have acquired it. Focused tasks are of value to teachers because they provide a means of teaching specific linguistic features communicatively – under "real operating conditions".

Even a cursory glance at the samples reveals that at the end the writer uses more complex language. At the beginning the sentences are shorter (from an average sentence of about 18 words at first to 23 and 26, respectively). The early sample also contains many dependent clauses with finite verbs, often with a pronoun (*he* and *they*) whereas at the end other types of complex constructions appear: The noun phrases are longer (e.g. the noun phrase *tasks that elicit use of specific linguistic features, either by design or by the use of methodological procedures that focus attention on form in the implementation of a task* contains 29 words). Furthermore, there are many non-finite constructions, such as *to induce their incidental attention to some specific linguistic forms when processing either input or output*. The vocabulary also appears to have become more advanced. For example, in the first text the writer uses rather everyday, familiar words, such as *influence, force* and *control*, but in the last text there are less frequent words which are more typical of the academic register, such as *elicit, induce,* and *acquire*. To what degree the familiarity and frequency of lexical items differs can, for example, be established using the British National Corpus (BNC) online (http://www.natcorp.ox.ac.uk/): Here, the three verbs cited from the first text all score between 10,000 and 30,000 hits, while the three verbs from the last one range between 250 and 2000, and so are used far less frequently overall. We will discuss ways of measuring such factors below.

Our main research question from a DST perspective is how this development took place. Do all the variables that indicate increased complexity develop simultaneously, or do they compete? For example, how and when do the finite dependent clauses decrease and how and when does the student start using longer noun phrases and more non-finite structures? Do these variables develop slowly and smoothly or do they show peaks and troughs? Another question is to what degree a more sophisticated lexicon and sentence complexity are related. Does the appearance of a more academic vocabulary consisting of overall less frequent items precede more complex syntactic structures, or do they go hand in hand?

To answer these questions we have to examine the relevant variables. In order to do this, we first have to decide which variables may be relevant and how we can "operationalize" them, i.e. make it possible to count and quantitatively evaluate them. However, until we have looked at the different variables we may not know which ones are most relevant. Our coding procedure should therefore cast the net as widely as possible, to allow us to determine which variables are useful for our analysis. (Note that it is safer to code too many than too few things.)

We know from previous studies (e.g. Wolfe-Quintero, Inagaki, & Kim 1998) that sentence length is usually a good indicator of complexity (the longer the sentence, the more complex it will typically be); the average number of words per sentence/utterance may therefore be a useful variable. However, sentence length alone tells us nothing about the way the sentence has become more complex. We know that beginners use more simple sentences and advanced students more complex ones. In addition to sentence length, we therefore should code sentence type: simple, compound, complex and compound-complex. Previous studies (cf. Wolfe-Quintero et al. 1998) have also indicated that more advanced language learners use more dependent clauses, so these should be coded as well. However, as we are specifically interested in the developmental process (which types of clauses occur first, which later), we will code different types of such finite clauses: adverbial, relative and nominal clauses (the latter are clauses used as subject or object or after a preposition). The text samples analyzed here also showed an increase of non-finite structures towards the end of the developmental period we observed, so these are coded separately.

In addition to these measures of sentence complexity, we also want to establish development in the lexicon/vocabulary. There are various approaches to this. A very simple way of measuring lexical diversity is to calculate the so-called type-token ratio (TTR). This is simply the number of *different* words (types) contained in a certain stretch of text, divided by the *total* number of words (tokens). For a stretch of text in which each word occurs only once, the TTR would therefore be 1. However, straightforward type-token ratios can be problematic due to the presence of *function words* (e.g. determiners, prepositions, adverbs) which are highly frequent. This means that, as texts become longer, the type-token ratio invariably goes down. A number of different ways to compensate for this have been devised and are described in Vermeer (2000). We shall confine the discussion here to one such measure, the so-called D, which is based on the probability of new words appearing in longer and longer stretches of text. The precise calculation of D is rather complicated (for a full discussion see McKee, Malvern & Richards 2000); fortunately, there are programs which can perform the analysis for you automatically. One such tool, the CLAN program, which was developed in the CHILDES project (http://childes.psy.cmu.edu/), will be discussed in detail below.

In addition to purely quantitative measures that consider some kind of relationship between total words and total different words, there are a number of other indications of lexical diversity. Consider the following two stretches of text (from Jarvis 2006):

Text 1:
There was a girl who was alone and hungry. She stole some bread from a bakery and tried to run away, but she ran into a man, and they both fell down. That gave the police enough time to find her and catch her.

Text 2:
A destitute and lonely young female stole a loaf of bread from a bakery. She attempted to flee, but she collided with a man who was walking toward her, and both of them fell down. In the meantime, a policeman arrived and detained them.

As Jarvis points out, both utterances contain exactly the same number of tokens (44) as well as types (35), so that the TTR of both texts is identical. However, it is obvious that the second text uses lexical items which are less frequent to describe the same set of circumstances (e.g. "tried to run away" vs. "attempted to flee") in a manner that is similar to the lexical development pointed out for our learner above. In line with suggestions by other researchers, (e.g. Laufer & Nation 1995), Jarvis therefore suggests that, in addition to "blind" measures of lexical diversity, such as TTRs and D, other factors, such as the rarity of the items used, should be considered. From previous studies (cf. Grant & Ginther 2000) we know that, as proficiency increases, L2 writers compose longer essays with more unique words, and, on the average, longer words. More proficient writers also use different types of words (relatively more adjectives, adverbs and prepositions). We will look at all of these to help us chart the path of development of our advanced writer.

Another measure that may tell us something about more sophisticated vocabulary is word length, as more proficient writers tend to use longer words at least in English (Grant & Ginther 2000). One of the reasons for this is that less frequent, more academic words tend to be longer. For example, in Text 1, the average word length is 3.7 characters and in Text 2 it is 4.4 characters. Such an analysis, however, also has to take into account issues of word class. In Text 1 there are more function words such as pronouns, prepositions, anxillary verbs like *to be*, and so on, which tend to be shorter than content words such as nouns, verbs, adjectives and adverbs. Text 1 has 16 content words and 28 function words, whereas Text 2 has 20 content words and 24 function words. If average word length is calculated on the basis of content words only, the difference between the two texts is even clearer: Text 1 has an average word length of 4.62 and Text 2 of 6.35 characters. It may therefore be interesting to distinguish between content and function words in analyses of word frequency and word length, since a higher rate of function words can confound the issue.

Finally, Laufer and Nation (1995, 1999) propose that the "Lexical Frequency Profile" (LFP) of a learner should be based on analyses which measure how many of the words used belong to the 1000 most frequent words in the language, how many to the next 1000, and so on, taken in conjunction with counts of "rare" or "advanced" words, and words which belong to specific registers, such as academic writing. Such analyses can indeed provide insight into vocabulary knowledge, but they require that word frequency lists are available for the language under investigation, and they are also very time-consuming to conduct.

We therefore propose that investigations of relatively large learner corpora may adopt a less costly approach by using their own corpus as the basis for a frequency count. Based on CLAN analyses, it is easy to calculate measures such as what proportion of the words a learner has used are among the 50 most frequent items in the overall corpus, what proportion of words are unique to that particular learner, what is the average overall frequency of all the words used by a particular learner, and so on. With the help of the functions described in the *How to* sections at the end of the book, you can count a large number of lexical and grammatical variables in your text, and import those to your spreadsheet or statistics software.

How to create a lexical profile is explained in *How to* Section 2.4 (p 154).

Table 1 gives an overview of all the variables that we will be looking at in the texts of this advanced writer. Note that the definitions must be very specific in order to identify these variables consistently. The definitions below have been taken from Verspoor and Sauter (2000).

The above overview demonstrates that the number of variables to be considered in our analysis is quite large. Given that our corpus is limited to 22 texts of about 200 words each, it might still be feasible to code all of these by hand. However, linguistic corpora usually contain more and longer texts, where such a coding procedure would be extremely time-consuming at best, and impossible at worst. The purpose of the following section and related *How to* sections is therefore to demonstrate to what degree the processes of coding and analysis can be automatized in order to make them more efficient.

Table 1. Overview of variables to be traced in the case study of the advanced writer

General sentence complexity	Average number of words per utterance	Number of words in the text divided by the number of utterances.
	Finite-verb ratio	Number of words in the text divided by the number of finite verbs in the text.
Sentence complexity	Simple	Sentence contains one finite verb (may include non-finite structures)
	Compound	Sentence contains two main clauses, each with its own subject and finite verb (other compound structures are ignored)
	Complex	Sentence contains at least one finite dependent clause.
	Compound complex	Sentence contains at least one dependent clause and compound structure at the sentence level or clause level.
Dependent clauses	Finite Nominal	Clause functioning as subject or object (also a clause after a preposition)
	Finite Relative	Clause functioning as post modifier of a noun (also an appositive clause)
	Finite Adverbial	Clause functioning as adverbial
	Non-finite (all)	Non-finite constructions functioning as nominal, adverbial or modifier
Lexical measures	TTR	The number of Types divided by the number of Tokens
	D	A randomized Type Token ratio
	Unique lexical items	The proportion of unique words per text
	Average length of lexical items	The average length of content words (all function words are ignored)
	Frequent lexical items	The proportion of very frequent items

3. Coding and analyzing the data

To code our data, we have availed ourselves exclusively of tools and programs which are either widely available (such as Microsoft Office) or can be freely accessed and downloaded from the internet. First, we will make use of the CHILDES (Child Language Data Exchange System) project described in MacWhinney (2000), which provides a standardized system for the transcription and analysis of data. It emerged from the desire among researchers on child language to be able to share and exchange their data. The CHILDES internet resource (http://childes.psy.cmu.edu) contains, among other things, a substantial database of transcripts as well as audio and video files from a large number of language acquisition contexts, the manuals for both CHAT and CLAN, the CLAN program and a set of tools for morphological analysis. All of these resources are free. Since extensive and detailed documentation is available at this location, the description of the CHAT transcription system and the use of the CLAN program is kept to a minimum in this chapter and the *How to* sections in Chapter 8, but they should help the novice CHAT learner on the way.

In *How to* Section 2.1 (p. 129), we introduce a set of conventions for the formatting and coding of data, known as the CHAT format.

When you are transcribing and coding data in CHAT format, there is a relatively limited set of coding operations which you have to perform multiple times in each file. For example, let us assume that you want to code the different sentence types and the different types of clauses. You will then have to insert two new lines, called dependent tiers, to put the information in, for example, an %xsen tier, where each sentence will be coded as simple, compound or complex and an %xcla tier, where you classify the clauses as nominal, adverbial, relative, non-finite or other. There are two options for performing such coding operations. The first is to transcribe and code your data directly in CLAN, that is, to use the program as your text editor. In this case, you can create your own coding files and enter the dependent tiers in the Coder mode. The steps which are necessary to do this are described in the CLAN manual. Doing so can be convenient, as it will help you prevent all kinds of problems that may be created by converting text files created with other text editors to text-only format.

Another option is to use Word as your text editor (but saving your files in text only format) and create your own set of tools with the help of this program. While this may lead to a set of its own problems, the advantage is that you can automatize many of the coding procedures. Which of these two options you decide to use is a matter of personal preference. As the CLAN program and the Coder mode are described in some detail in the CLAN manual, the *How to* sections related to this chapter will focus mainly on how to create tools with the help of Word.

In *How to* Section 2.2, (p. 136) we explain how several of the coding operations described in the first *How to* section can be achieved automatically with Word macros.

Once all transcriptions have been prepared in text-only files according to CHAT conventions, the data can be analyzed in the CLAN program, which can be downloaded from the CHILDES website and installed on your computer. Before you can analyze your data, however, you have to make sure there are no errors in your files.

In *How to* Section 2.3 (p. 148) we will give instructions on how to first check for formatting errors. Section 2.4 (p. 154) explains how to create a lexical profile and 2.5 (p. 161) explains how you can recalculate values to 0–1.

4.   Tracing development

Our main research question from a DST perspective is how development took place: Which variables seem to develop at the same time (connected growers), which variables seem to compete (competitors), and which variables seem to have developed prior to other ones (precursors)? Our assumptions and questions will be as follows:

1.   Sentence constructions will go from simple to more complex.
      How does complexity emerge?
      Are there any competing variables?

2.   Lexical items will go from more frequent to less frequent.
      Is it true that the proportion of highly frequent words decreases as the writer becomes more proficient?
      Is the increase in vocabulary size as the writer becomes more proficient reflected in an increase in TTR-based measures, such as D?
      Does the proportion of unique words increase as the writer becomes more proficient?
      Can average word length provide insight into lexical development?

3.   There may be some kind of interaction between the lexicon and sentence complexity.
      Is there any particular relation between a general complexity measure (such as number of finite verbs per 100 words) and a general lexical measure (such as the use of frequent words or average word length)?

Below, we will briefly show how the data pertaining to these questions can be explored by means of visualizations. In the next chapters, we will look at statistical procedures which can establish how likely it is that any patterns we may find are merely coincidental, or whether there is a high probability that they are actually indications of change through development.

4.1   The development of complexity in syntactic constructions

Our assumption above was that the proportion of simple sentence constructions would decrease and a higher proportion of more complex constructions would be visible in the course of language development. As simple sentences and compound sentences consist of main clauses only, they are simpler than complex or compound-complex sentences, which have finite dependent clauses. Even more complex than finite dependent clauses are non-finite constructions, such as *to induce their incidental attention to some specific linguistic forms when processing either input or output*. An increase in complexity may furthermore be indicated by longer noun phrases as in *one of the major purposes of these tasks for learners.* To test our assumption that sentence constructions develop from more simple to more complex, we can look at the development of the following variables:

a.   proportion of simple and compound sentences
b.   proportion of complex and compound-complex sentences
c.   the number of words per finite verbs (total number of words divided by the number of finite words)

Figure 1 shows how these three variables develop over time. We have also added a polynomial trend line to the finite verb ratio (FV) line to see what the general trend is.

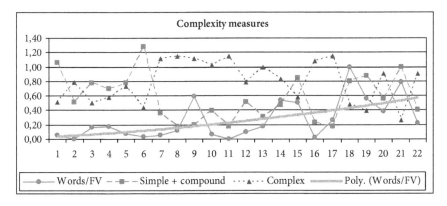

Figure 1. Development of sentence complexity measures

   Figure 1 shows that up to Text 5, the writer used both simple and complex constructions to a similar degree. After this point, a marked dip of simple and compound sentences occurs, accompanied by an increase in complex sentences. Meanwhile the Words to Finite Verb ratio remained relatively low, except for a few small peaks. This means that sentences were made more complex by means of finite dependent clauses. After Text 16 the Words to Finite Verb ratio increases perceptibly, while at the same time the distribution of simple/compound and complex constructions evens out again. This indicates that at that stage, non-finite constructions and longer noun phrases contribute to overall complexity to the same degree as dependent clauses.
   One of the questions is how this complexity emerged. Did all dependent clauses develop at the same time? Did some occur before others? Are there some constructions that compete with each other? To find an answer to these questions, we plotted the types of finite dependent clauses (adverbial, nominal, rela-

tive) and non-finite clauses (not separated for different kinds), first separately and then together in different combinations. Here we will show the development of the proportion of adverbial and relative clauses, each with a polynomial trend line (Figure 2).

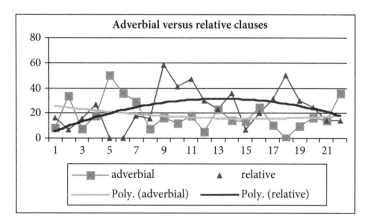

Figure 2. The development of adverbial and relative clauses, each with a polynomial trend line

Figure 2 shows that the number of adverbial clauses first increased somewhat and then decreased and leveled off until the last few texts. Relative clauses, on the other hand, increased at the same time as adverbial clauses decreased. The trend line seems to show typical U-shaped behavior, which means that as learners are trying to acquire a new construction they may overuse it for a while. When we looked at the development of nominal clauses versus relative clauses, a very similar pattern emerged. These patterns suggest that relative clauses develop somewhat later than adverbial and nominal clauses, and at one point seem to compete with them. In Figure 2 we can see that adverbial clauses and relative clauses compete. If one is used, the other is not, and vice versa. We will explain how to test this assumption in Chapter 5.

To summarize, this advanced writer was still developing in terms of complexity measures. She moved from simpler constructions to more complex ones. To make her sentences more complex, she first used finite dependent clauses and later longer noun phrases and other non-finite structures. In the development of dependent clauses, the relative clauses showed a typical U-curve, suggesting overuse, and a competitive relationship with the adverbial and nominal structures.

4.2   The development of the lexicon

As far as vocabulary is concerned, one would expect beginning learners to use highly frequent items and then proceed to acquire less frequently used words as they become more proficient. We would also expect the use of vocabulary to become more creative (with less repetition of the same items) and more sophisticated. To test these assumptions we calculated the lexical diversity measure D, the *frequent word* measure (for each text, we calculated the percentage of the total content words belonging to the 50 most frequent items in the overall corpus) and the *unique word* measure (for each text, the percentage of words which were only used once in the entire corpus). A final measure of lexical sophistication is the average length of content words in each text. We would expect D, average word length and unique words to increase and the percentage of frequent words to decrease. Figure 3 shows the development of the frequency measures.

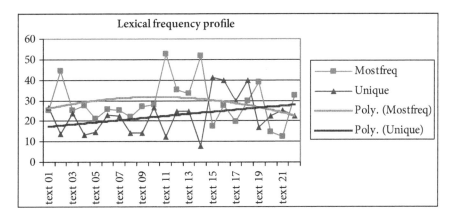

Figure 3. Development of lexical frequency profile

It is evident from Figure 3 that our assumptions concerning lexical frequency are met. The number of unique words increases and the number of very frequent words decreases. After Text 15, there seems to be a balance between the two measures. Figure 4 then shows the development of D, the proportion of unique lexical items, and average word length.

In Figure 4 we compare D, unique words, and average word length. To be able to represent the development of these three variables within the same graph, we normalized the data.

In *How to* Section 2.5 (p.161), we explain how to recalculate data to values from 0-1.

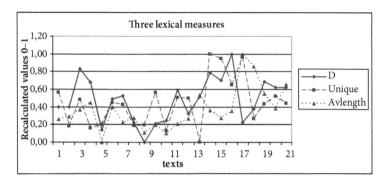

Figure 4. Development of lexical diversity (D), unique words, and sophistication (average word length)

Our assumption that lexical diversity (D measure) and sophistication (unique words and average word length) increase over time is met. But do they measure the same things? Even though one would expect unique words and lexical diversity (D) to correlate strongly because they measure essentially the same thing, the correlation between them is not very strong (0.38) and their relationship changes over time, especially around Text 19. Also average word length, a very general measure of lexical sophistication, does not measure exactly the same thing as lexical diversity because the correlation is even lower (0.20) and the measures diverge after Text 15. We may conclude that these measures tap into slightly different aspects of lexical development. In the Chapters 5 and 6, we will explain how to measure whether these patterns are meaningful or random.

Another question we had was if the TTR and D would show the same picture, and as Figure 5 shows, they do. The two measures show a strong correlation (0.83). (Note that for the present corpus, this is not a surprising finding, since all our texts are of the same length and relatively short.)

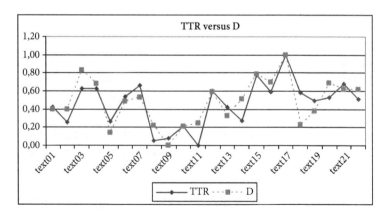

Figure 5. Development of TTR versus D

4.3   Interaction between sentence complexity and the lexicon

Finally we wanted to establish whether there is an interaction between lexical sophistication and sentence complexity. It is possible that these two measures develop hand-in-hand because if you use more complex sentences, you are likely to use less frequent and more sophisticated words such as *induce,* and these words in turn occur with more technical language, which is usually more complex. On the other hand, it is possible that a more advanced vocabulary (comprising less frequent words) needs to have been acquired before more complex language can be used, and in that case vocabulary would be a precursor for sentence complexity. This is a reasonable assumption for L1 acquisition as well as early L2 learning, but we do not know how these variables might interact in data from a more proficient learner. Another possibility is that a learner may have trouble focusing on two different aspects of language at the same time because both require cognitive resources. To discover the relation between lexical sophistication and sentence complexity, we looked at the most general complexity measure, the average distance between finite verbs and the ratio of unique words.

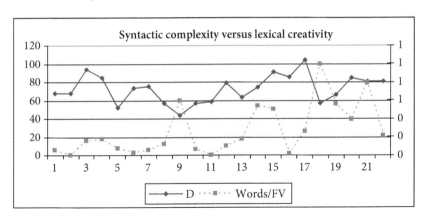

Figure 6. The interaction between sentence complexity and lexical diversity

Figure 6 shows that after Text 5, the two variables seem to compete quite strongly until Text 19, where they seem to go hand in hand again. Both variables furthermore appear to show a dip in Text 09, which raises the intriguing possibility that at that point some other variable was in a state of strong development. We may conclude that for a part of the developmental process these two measures compete. Again, in the next chapters we will discuss how to measure whether these observations are meaningful or not.

5.   Conclusion

At the beginning of this chapter we argued that for a usage-based DST perspective on second language development, it is best to use longitudinal, naturalistic data (spoken or written) and to look at how many different linguistic variables develop over time. The reason is that we do not only want to see if they develop, but also when they emerge, how they develop, and how different variables may interact.

The assumption underlying the DST interpretation that there can be a trade-off between different skills in SLD is that learners have to make some kind of choice as to which component of the message they will allocate a larger proportion of the finite cognitive resources to. Such trade-offs will, by necessity, be less pronounced in written texts than in spoken data: The written data we used were produced without time limit, and presumably re-written several times in the process. During such revisions, the author had the option to focus on different components of her linguistic repertoire each time she read and changed the text. Nevertheless, the linguistic subcomponents clearly emerge as competing with each other, in particular at certain moments in her development. It is therefore reasonable to assume that such effects would be more pronounced in a longitudinal corpus of spoken learner data.

The main purpose of this chapter was to show you how you can use dedicated linguistic software, but also widely available text editing and spreadsheet software, specifically CLAN, Word and Excel, to code a range of different variables consistently and efficiently. Lastly, we showed how the data may be explored through charts, and which observations and assumptions could be made on the basis of this visual presentation of the data. Our main concern was not so much to show specifically how we coded and analyzed the data at hand, but to provide you with templates which you might apply and use in the exploration of your own data.

In the next chapter, we will focus on how to interpret longitudinal case data and how to test whether the patterns found are meaningful or random.

Variability and DST

Marijn van Dijk, Marjolijn Verspoor & Wander Lowie

1. Introduction

Variability in development has been at the core of SLD research: Not only are there great differences between language learners, but also their language may be very different from moment to moment. In traditional thinking, these differences have often been seen as unwanted by-products of the real data. The reason for this is that it is implicitly assumed that the "underlying" development must be a rather smooth, linear process and that a description of such processes must be able to generalize across language learners. On the other hand, much SLD research in the 1980s has focused on finding out what the causes of variability are. The fact that variability may have different causes is readily acknowledged from a DST perspective, but it is not the main focus of study. In DST and other process-oriented research agendas, the degree of variability in any particular subsystem is seen as an intrinsic property of the developmental process. For example, a learner who has not fully mastered a particular subsystem yet will be "thrown off" more easily by small contextual changes and will therefore show the highest degrees of variability at that time. Thus, DST recognizes the context dependency of developing behavior and stresses the complex interactions between internal and external sources of variability.

The main purpose of this chapter is to provide an introduction into analyzing variability in individual development and to demonstrate several descriptive techniques that can be used in order to visualize these phenomena and test variability centred hypotheses. We will begin by providing a short overview of earlier research on variability in SLD, point out how a DST approach differs from traditional approaches and explain why it may be useful as an additional perspective. Then we will re-examine a classic study in SLD and show how several findings can be interpreted in line with current studies in developmental psychology.

Note that in *How to* Sections 3.1–3.3 (Chapter 8), we explain in detail how we created our Excel graphs, resampled the data and detrended it. Practice files 3.1–3.3 on our web site SLD_Methods (DOI:10.1075/lllt.29.website) contain the actual data we used and most of the figures we present in this chapter.

2.   Traditional versus DST approaches to variability in SLD

According to Rod Ellis (1994: 119), there are several approaches to variability within the field of SLD. On the one hand, Chomskyan linguistics paid relatively little attention to variability because the main object of study was a speaker's "competence" rather than "performance". The general claim was that one had to abstract away from individual instances to find out what learners "know" rather than "do". Competence can be defined as the ideal speaker-hearer's intrinsic ability and performance as an individual's language use with all its variability, hesitations, false starts, repetitions, slips of the tongue, and so on. Competence may be seen as the abstraction of someone's linguistic knowledge that could be achieved under "ideal" circumstances. However, this definition is problematic, as it is not clear how "ideal" should be interpreted. In language research it is often assumed that a grammaticality judgment test comes closest to ideal performance, but grammaticality involves complex aspects. For example, if native English speakers are asked to judge whether the sentence "That ain't true!" is grammatical or not, a variety of responses can be expected, not only depending on the participant's place of birth, place of residence, level of education, gender, and ethnicity, but also depending on the context in which the interview takes place, and perhaps the previous questions he or she has just dealt with. Grammaticality judgments may widely vary and will also change over time. What was grammatical in Chaucer's English, is no longer considered grammatical today. Since determining competence is problematic it is doubtful if this notion contributes to our understanding of SLD.

In contrast to the universalist approach to acquisition, two other streams in SLD research have focused on variability: These are sociolinguistic theories inspired by Labov and psycholinguistic theories inspired by Levelt. Both were mainly interested in discovering the systematicity and the causes for the apparently arbitrary variability. Many factors were considered, such as interlocutor (L1 or L2 speaker), situational context (formal, informal), task (speaking, writing), form-function relations (e.g. certain types of article errors occur with certain types of nouns), and so on, and many of these factors turned out to contribute to the variation between learners. For instance, Young (1988), who used a multi-factor analysis, found that there were different types of variability for learners of high and low proficiency. Performance was also affected by linguistic context. According to Rod Ellis (1994: 153), even though variability is enormously complex, it is possible to explain a substantial proportion of it by using the appropriate statistical procedures, recognizing that a great deal of variability remains unexplained.

Another group of linguists, including Ellis himself, looked at variability not so much to discover its systematicity, but to discover what variability could tell us about the developmental stages in the acquisition of the L2. After eliminating factors that would contribute to "systematic" variability, they found that there was still some degree of "free variability", variability that could not be attributed to any known linguistic, situational or psychological factor. According to Rod Ellis, an especially clear example of free variability is given by Cancino, Rosansky, and Schumann[1] (1978), who found that their subjects made use of a variety of forms to express negation at each stage of their development. Ellis states that a general finding of these studies is that free variability occurs during an early stage of development and then disappears as learners develop a better organized L2 system (Ellis 1994: 137). Unfortunately, this line of thought was not pursued much further in the field of SLD.

In developmental psychology, variability has become a focus of study in its own right since the early 1990s. For instance, in his overview article, Siegler (2006) summarizes the main findings of 105 microgenetic studies which aim to analyze change by means of high density observation of learning individuals. We will point out several findings that are also relevant for SLD research.

A first important finding of these microgenetic studies is that within-subject variability in strategy use is substantial at all ages from infancy to adulthood, during all phases of learning and at every level of analysis. For example, Adolph (1997), who studied the strategies infants use to go off a slide, found that each of the 5- to 15-months old infants use at least five different strategies to descend down relatively shallow ramps and six down relatively steep slopes at different occasions. Thus, infants slide on their belly or on their behind, sitting or lying, or head or feet first, depending on the specific circumstances of the situation. Microgenetic studies on learning in adulthood also report interesting patterns of variability in problem solving strategies. For instance, an experiment by Dowker, Flood, Griffiths, Harriss, and Hook (1996), looking into problem solving strategies, showed that even when all variables are controlled for, an adult's use of strategies, even an expert's, will vary, albeit to a lesser extent than the nonexpert's. Dowker et al. (1996) examined different mathematical strategies that adults use to estimate the solution to some multiplication and division problems. The subjects were 176 adults with different levels of mathematical expertise: mathematicians, accountants, psychology students and students of English, who were asked to multiply and divide multidigit numbers. The researchers found that all four groups, including the more experienced mathematicians, used on average five different kinds of strategies when they tried to solve these problems. Not only did strategies vary among individuals and type of problem, but they also varied when the same problems were presented to participants a second time. What is surprising is that the experts, the mathematicians, used a different strategy on exactly the same problem in 46% of the items.

---

1. This study will be used as an extended example later on.

A second important finding of the microgenetic studies, as reported by Siegler (2006), is that learners do not progress neatly in acquiring a skill or strategy but may show periods of regression and progression. Regression tends to be greatest during periods of rapid learning, but substantial variability is present in relatively stable periods as well. This pattern also tends to be cyclical, with periods of lesser and greater variability alternating over the course of learning. Children may use more advanced approaches on one occasion and then regress to less advanced ones on the next, but these regressions are temporary as the general trend of change was upward in all the studies. However, at early stages, development involves a back and forth competition between more or less advanced strategies (Siegler 1995 in Siegler 2006). Thus learning often includes short-lived transitional approaches that play important roles in the acquisition of more enduring approaches.

A third central finding is that high initial within-subject variability tends to be positively related to subsequent learning and such learning reflects addition of new strategies, greater reliance on relatively advanced strategies already being used, improved choices among strategies, and improved execution of strategies. For example, on number conservation and sort-recall tasks, children who used more and different strategies on the pretest used the more advanced strategies on subsequent tasks (Coyle & Bjorklund 1997; Siegler 1995 in Siegler 2006). Interestingly, small differences in initial conditions seem to have a great effect on subsequent development. Subjects who start with more advanced strategies are likely to progress to yet more advanced approaches more rapidly than children whose initial rules are less advanced (Siegler 2006).

Siegler concludes that studying within-subject variability is important to (a) predict change, (b) analyze change, and (c) understand change mechanisms (481). As Siegler (p.c) points out, language has great potential for such studies because there is variation galore at all different levels, from pronunciation to vocabulary and syntax. In the field of language development, however, very few studies are specifically directed at analysing patterns of variability (cf. Verspoor, Lowie & van Dijk 2008).

In different fields of research, ranging from studies into climate change to motor development, short term variability is associated with long term change. For instance, high intraindividual variability implies that qualitative developmental changes may be taking place (Lee & Karmiloff-Smith 2002). The cause and effect relationship between variation and change is difficult to interpret and is probably multilateral. On the one hand, variation permits flexible and adaptive behaviour and is a prerequisite to development. This is what we observe in evolution: Without variation, there is no selection. On the other hand, free exploration of performance generates variability. Trying out new tasks leads to instability of the system and consequently an increase in variation. Therefore, it can be assumed that stability and variation are indispensable, interrelated aspects of human development.

If we accept the position that variability is an important developmental phenomenon, we may ask ourselves why it is also relevant for the field of L1 and L2. Applied
to language development, the assumption is that a high degree of "free" variability
occurs at the early stages of development because the learner is trying out different
forms to express meaning. In other words, the learner, using whatever resources he or
she may have, is trying different strategies to communicate a certain meaning. Once
a learner has discovered the most effective strategies, he or she is likely to eventually
settle for those. In this respect, the variability is highly functional in that it provides
opportunities for discovering the more effective strategies. Of course, the learner will
not learn all subsystems of a language at one time and therefore there will be periods
of rather free variability in different subsystems of the language. For example, there
may be free variability in almost all subsystems in the language at the very first stages
of learning an L2. Then once the learner has discovered how to form short simple
sentences, there may be a high degree of variability in the use of verb forms (e.g.
subject-verb agreement). Once the learner can form short simple sentences, usually
with a simple present tense, he or she may start experimenting with different verb
tenses and then a degree of free variability may occur in using these tenses correctly.
Later on, there may be variability in the formation of more complex sentence constructions, and so on.

By looking at when the different periods of variability occur in the different subsystems, we can discover how the acquisition patterns of the different subsystems interact.
By looking at different trajectories (learning paths) we may discover different types of
learning processes. A pattern that consists of clear stages, for instance, might indicate
that certain rules are acquired, and these rules generalize instantly across contexts. For
example, when a learner acquires the regular plural "-s" suffix, this might result in a
rather instant application of it to a wide collection of nouns in different utterances. A
gradual, slow trajectory, on the other hand, might reflect a more fragmented learning
process, where elements are acquired and applied one by one. A likely candidate for
such a shape of change is for instance lexical growth. In this case, there is no "switch"
where the learner "gets the trick", but elements are added one by one.

It is also known that individual learners may have distinct learning styles. While
certain students "jumpstart" easily and start experimenting with language instantly,
others take a more cautious approach. These differences in styles may also be expressed
in the shape of their developmental processes. While the experimental learner is likely
to show a more irregular trajectory, with a large proportion of errors, the cautious
learner might have a more gradual learning curve.

To summarize, whereas some SLD approaches have ignored variability because
they were interested in finding universal patterns of language development and other
SLD approaches have been mainly interested in discovering the external causes of
variability, a DST approach is interested in variability to discover when and how

changes take place in the process of development, how different subsystems develop and interact, and how different learners may have different developmental patterns. The purpose of the next sections is to show the differences between traditional and DST approaches to data and several techniques to make the variability visible and to determine whether the variability is meaningful or not.

3.   Variability: Sound or noise?

As we have argued before, traditional approaches to analysis of SLD data have predominantly focused on describing general trends. To make clear the differences between the two approaches to data analysis, we will first focus on why traditional approaches have been so preoccupied with trends.

Rather than looking at individual growth curves, traditional SLD analyses are usually concerned with mean scores, standard deviations and normal distributions that represent the effect of one or more isolated factors affecting the developmental process. The measurements in traditional SLD research are mostly the product of an implied developmental process and do not focus on the process itself. The main merit of this type of research is that it enables us to generalize about trends, such as how do two similar groups behave after having received two different types of instruction. If one group has significantly better scores on a posttest than the other, then we may infer that one of the methods is more effective than the other. Most SLD research has employed traditional statistics and has contributed a great deal to our knowledge of such general trends. However, in traditional statistics, variability is smoothed out to find general trends, based on the assumption that random variability should be ignored because it distorts the "true" or "general" picture of development. In other words, these analyses aim at providing a description of average ("representative") language development that is assumed to be generalizable to the population of language learners. In this vein, variability is considered "noise" that should be omitted from the data. An equally problematic reason for ignoring variability is the argument that it is the result of a "measurement error" or "environmental error". Again, this is a matter of definition. What exactly are measurement errors? Should we ignore every day fluctuations and should we try to avoid environmental factors that may influence performance or can fluctuations and variability tell us something about the developmental process?

Because this is such a crucial issue we will illustrate this with an extended fictitious example: Imagine that you are first learning to throw a ball from a certain position through a basket, and you practice for an hour every day for several weeks until you are able to throw the ball into the basket about 90% of the time. Chances are that your first attempts are quite erratic. Let's say that you are given a score of 10 each time you have thrown the ball into the basket and a score of 1 to 9 depending on the distance the ball is from the basket: the further away, the lower the score. A measurement error would occur if you do not measure consistently with the same tape stretched tight from the centre of the basket to the point the ball fell on the floor. A measurement error could also occur if you were not consistent in attributing scores to the distances; for example, 15 cm receives a score of 8 one time and a score of 6 the next time, or if on one occasion you take the centre of the basket as the point of reference and on another occasion the rim. But suppose that you measure everything accurately and consistently and your scores in the first session are rather erratic (1-5-7-3-4-5-6-1-2-1), does that mean your actual "performance" is "noise" and we must average them out to a 4.5 to assess your real "competence" that day, or does it mean that your scores are so erratic because you are in the middle of the learning process and you have not acquired a more steady toss? From a DST perspective, such data is not "noise" but "sound", i.e. valuable information about the stage within the developmental process. In other words, a degree of variability may tell us that the learner is in the middle of the learning process and has therefore not stabilized yet.

In traditional SLD analyses, variability is also often attributed to environmental factors. Environmental factors could be internal or external. Examples of internal factors are that we may be tired one day, we may not feel like practicing another day, or we may be upset on yet another day. External factors could be variability in distance or context. Suppose, for example, you have learned to toss the ball into the basket from a four-meter distance and you have reached a rather stable performance of about 80%. It is likely that this score will change when the distance changes, but after extensive training, you may be able to reach the 80% hits mark again. But then when the context is changed slightly, and for instance the shooter has to play against the wind, the score will drop again for some time and the conditions will be such that the 80% mark is no longer attainable for a given player. In other words, different environmental factors may affect the scores, but it is reasonable to assume that these different environmental factors have a greater effect on someone who is in the process of moving from one stage to the other and less on the individual who has reached a more stable state. As an illustration to this point, Thelen and Ulrich (1991) showed that infants, who were learning to walk, became less and less sensitive to perturbations caused by a steeper slope or a moving path as they grew older. In other words, external influences caused less variability as the infants became more skilled. The authors therefore conclude that variability caused by sensitivity to the environment provides information about the actual process of development.

In both traditional SLD analyses and DST approaches, real measurement errors (errors in attributing values) will pollute the data and analyses and should therefore be avoided at all cost. However, in DST, the fluctuations caused by internal and external factors can also be looked at as a source of information. From a DST perspective, variability is inherent in any complex system and reflects actual data that should not be ignored but looked at closely to detect how a system changes from one phase to the next and how it behaves when it is in a stable state. Essential to the DST approach is that variability is elevated, both within and between individuals, into a central element of a developing system (Thelen & Smith, 1994: 343). Thus, intra- and interindividual variability are important features that should be treated as data and be analyzed.

4. Longitudinal and dense developmental data

In this chapter we argue that if we really want to know how an individual (or group) develops over time we need data that is dense (i.e. collected at many regular measurement points), longitudinal (i.e. collected over a longer period of time), and individual (i.e. for one person at a time and not averaged out). Not many SLD studies have been set up that way, but there is one notable exception, the study by Cancino, Rosansky, and Schumann (1978). This specific study has been discussed extensively in the SLD literature and was one of the first to point out the large degree of variability at the early stages of acquisition. Therefore, we will use the data from this classic study (which we will refer to as the CRS study from now on) to illustrate some nonstatistical, visual techniques that describe the data to test possible hypotheses. We will first make clear what this study was about and what the findings were at the time.

The CRS study is one of the first longitudinal studies that looks specifically at age differences in the rate of acquisition of language forms. Inspired by the UG approaches of the time, it aimed at describing the general developmental stages of L2 learners of different ages and discovering if these stages are similar to those of an L1 learner. The authors describe the natural untutored acquisition of English negative construction by six native Spanish speakers who had been in the US for less than three months, but we do not know exactly how long each had been in the US. There were two young learners, Marta (5) and Cheo (5), two teenagers, Juan (11) and Jorge (13), and two adults, Dolores (25) and Alberto (33). The children were all from upper middle-class families and attended US public schools, where they interacted with English peers on a daily basis. The adults were from different sociocultural backgrounds: Dolores had a middle-class background and was exposed to English on a daily basis as she babysat English speaking children, and Alberto had a lower-class background and worked in a factory where some of his input was from other nonnative speakers of English. All subjects spoke Spanish at home. The goal was to interview each subject twice a month in their homes for about 10 months, but not all subjects were followed that long. Even though we have no further data on them, we will assume that the four young learners are likely to eventually attain native-like fluency because they are enrolled in English medium schools, but that the older learners may have fossilized because of their more limited interaction with native speakers.

One of the main questions in the CRS study was whether the developmental stages in forming negative verb constructions in L2 development were similar to those reported earlier in L1 development by Klima and Bellugi (1966). The latter study found that in L1 children usually go from the *No-V*, and *don't* constructions to target-like negative constructions. The question was whether L2 development shows the same general stages as those described for L1 development. These stages were operationalized (by the predominant constructions) as follows:

1. *No-V* constructions, where the negative particle is sentence-external: e.g. *no singing song, not the sun shining, Carolina no go play* (a nontarget construction)
2. *Don't V* constructions, where the negative is placed within the sentence: e.g. *I don't hear* (whether this strategy is grammatical depends on the subject of the verb. For instance, while the sentence "I don't swim" is perfectly correct, "He don't swim" is not target-like. In other words, the use of this strategy includes *both* correct and incorrect uses of this strategy)
3. *Aux-neg* constructions, where auxiliaries are used to form the negative (especially *isn't* and *can't*). For instance, *You can't tell her* (a target construction)
4. *Analyzed don't* constructions, where grammatical constructions of "do" are used to form the negative (*do not, doesn't, does not, didn't, did not*). For instance *One night I didn't even have the light* (a target construction)

In order to tally the developmental data, the authors catalogued the various negating devices (no, don't, can't, isn't etc.) and for the samples shown below determined the proportion of each negating device used with a verb to the total number of negatives in any construction with nouns, adjectives or verbs. Because the CRS study did not focus on the variability but on finding universal trends in language acquisition, the main conclusion was that the general L2 stages of acquisition were quite similar to those in L1 development: Each subject would go through stage one before proceeding to stage two, and so on. What we found striking about the researchers' discussion of their analyses are repeated comments about how difficult it was to describe the developing grammar of the learners because of the great amount of variability.

> Writing "grammars" for a *dynamic system* [italics ours], however, is not only difficult, but is also not suitable as a developmental descriptive technique. [.....] Our attempts to write rules for the negative proved fruitless. The constant development and concomitant variation in our subjects' speech at any one point made the task impossible.   (Cancino et al. 1978: 209)

This quote stresses the finding that there is – in fact – very little systematicity in the developing second language. What is also interesting is the fact that the CSR study did not only show the general trends but also the truly messy individual data with their great amount of variability. We have transferred the information from the original CRS figures to the Excel format and will use those in subsequent sections to illustrate how one can make variability more visible, discover general patterns, and test whether the patterns are meaningful. In the current section we will first show and discuss the "raw" data as they were originally presented in the original article and describe what we see.

The Excel sheets with the raw data and Figures 1–6 can be found in practice file 3.1 on our web site SLD_Methods (DOI:10.1075/lllt.29.website).

In Figures 1–6, it can be observed that each learner shows variability in the use of the construction and each learner shows somewhat different patterns. The first two figures show the data of the two youngest learners, Marta and Cheo.

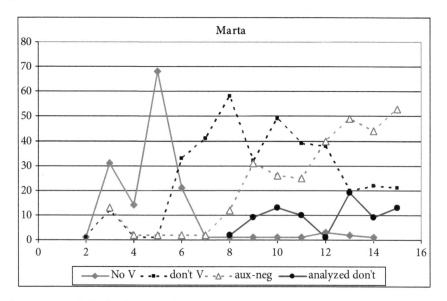

Figure 1. Marta's (5) development of negative constructions

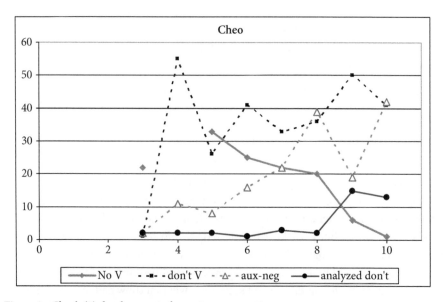

Figure 2. Cheo's (5) development of negative constructions

The two five year olds have in common the fact that they do not speak English with the interviewer at all during the first two sessions. Such a "silent period" is a common occurrence with young learners. Especially Marta seems to show classical patterns in development. She first uses the *No-V* construction predominantly, and even though she also uses the *don't V* construction, the *No-V* construction shows a clear peak before the *don't V* construction takes over in Session 6. Then the *don't V* construction shows a few peaks before the *aux-neg* construction takes over. Even though the analyzed *don't* construction already appears in Session 8 it does not really take off until Session 14.

After breaking through his "silent period", Cheo also shows a peak of *No-V* constructions in the third session. In Session 4, however, the *don't V* construction peaks. It seems as if the *aux-neg* construction is taking over the *No-V* construction by the time the last recording takes place (unfortunately, there are no data beyond Session 10). The two young learners have in common that they both show peaks in the same order and that the nontarget forms remain until the end (although they occur not very frequently). The difference between these two young learners is that Marta's *No-V* stage is longer and more pronounced than Cheo's. This might have different reasons, for instance due to age (we do not know exactly when exactly the first taping sessions took place), duration of exposure to English (it may have been that Cheo had been in the US a few weeks longer than Marta), or learning speed (Cheo is a faster learner than Marta).

The second set of figures show the data of the two teenagers, Juan and Jorge. Unlike the younger children, these teenagers use all four strategies in combination (both target-like and nontarget-like constructions) from the very beginning (although the frequencies in which they occur vary).

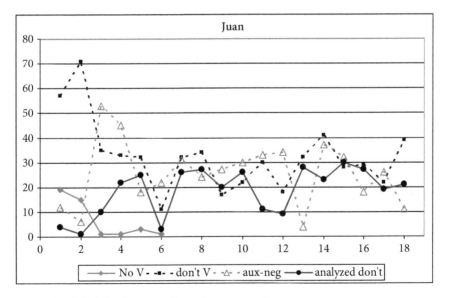

Figure 3. Juan's (11) development of negative constructions

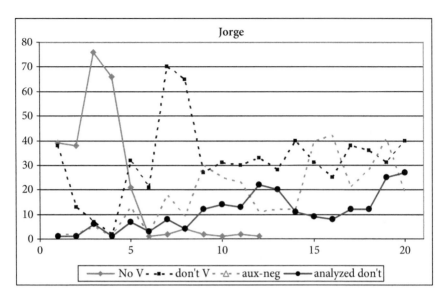

Figure 4. Jorge's (13) development of negative constructions

Like the younger children, they show peaks in nontarget construction (*don't V* for Juan and *No-V* for Jorge), but the use of nontarget forms seems to diminish faster. This is especially the case for Juan (see Figure 3): In Session 2 there is a peak in the *don't* constructions. At taping Session 6, we see the last vestige of nontarget *No-V* constructions and after that Juan shows a natural distribution of the target forms: We can see he no longer overgeneralizes the *don't V* construction because he uses an almost equal number of target-like *aux-neg* and *analyzed don't* constructions. Jorge (see Figure 4) first shows a strong peak in the *No-V* construction in Session 3 and then in the *don't V* construction in Session 7. The *No-V* construction disappears after Session 12, but the *don't V* construction still seems to be overgeneralized somewhat until the end because the *analyzed don't* constructions seem underrepresented until Sessions 18 and 19.

The third set of figures presents the data of the two adults: Alberto and Dolores. Even though the two adults differ considerably in how well they acquire the English negative constructions in the end, they do have one thing in common: They show the least amount of variability.

Alberto (see Figure 5) has two ways of forming the negative, the *No-V* construction and the overgeneralized *don't V* construction. He does not use any other forms in this time period of 10 months. In general, we might observe a slight increase of the *don't* construction over time, but this is mainly caused by one very low frequency in the first recording. Dolores (see Figure 6), on the other hand, uses only three constructions at first with a slight peak in *aux-neg* construction, then in the *analyzed don't* constructions. What is also interesting is that rather than using the constructions in a

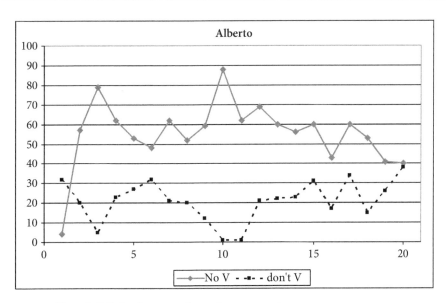

Figure 5. Alberto's (33) development of negative constructions

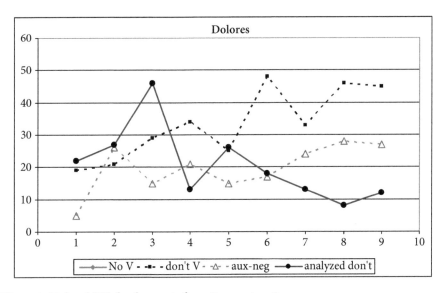

Figure 6. Dolores' (25) development of negative constructions

more balanced distribution at the end, like Juan who uses *don't V* and *analyzed don't* within a range of 20 to 40 percent, Dolores still probably overgeneralizes the *don't V* construction until the end.

What the individual data have shown is that indeed there seem to be very general "stages", in the sense that in certain periods, certain constructions are more frequent.

This is especially the case for the children in the study. As was pointed out in the CRS study (1978), L2 learners of different ages go through similar paths as L1 learners: *No-V, don't V, aux-neg* and *analyzed don't.* The raw data show that even though the learners will go through construction one before two, two before three, three before four, not all learners use construction one and not all learners eventually use constructions 3 and 4. What is remarkable is the fact that the stages are not "discrete". In fact, the development seems to be rather continuous and variable, instead of displaying clear "cut off points" between consecutive stages. There is a high degree of intraindividual variability. Even though all subjects have Spanish as their first language and have been in an English speaking country for about three months, each individual subject shows a different pattern, but what is also interesting is that both members of each age group show strong similarities in their developmental patterns.

5.   Descriptive techniques for time serial data

In the previous section we presented the raw data as provided in the CRS study. We plotted the percentages of different constructions and used line graphs to make these visible.

In the following sections, we will discuss how developmental data can be presented using various simple descriptive techniques, some of which are also discussed in van Dijk and van Geert (2002). We will assume a very basic knowledge of spreadsheet programs (such as Microsoft Excel), for instance how to enter data and how to make simple charts and graphs, but we will explain in more detail the techniques that are particular to variability studies.

All the techniques shown below are explained in detail in *How* to Sections 3.1–3.3.

5.1   Plotting group data

In the literature, it is common practice to display results of a group of learners in a single line graph. Moreover, analyses are often performed on a so-called "average group development". In the following paragraph we will show the possible effect of this practice.

Figures 7, 8 and 10 can also be found in practice file 3.1 on our web site SLD_Methods (DOI:10.1075/lllt.29.website).

Figure 7 shows the results of all learners averaged for each observation, and the consecutive measurements are connected by drawing a line or trend. Figure 7 displays the use of the so-called *don't V* strategy, where the verb is preceded by the word "don't". What we would expect is that the distribution of this form changes over time. At first, learners will "overshoot" or overgeneralize the *don't* construction because they will use it in almost all contexts. After they advance, they will start using the *aux-neg* construction and the *analyzed don't* construction, which implies that the use of the *don't V* construction will decrease.

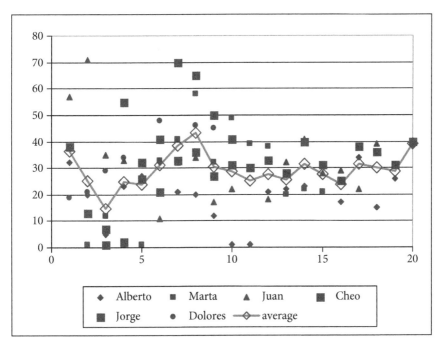

Figure 7. The use of the *don't V* strategy in the CRS study, including the average group development

In Figure 7, the grey line connects the group averages and therefore shows an "average group trajectory". Visual inspection of this line should give an impression of how the "average learner" uses the *don't V* strategy across time. When we perform such "eye-ball statistics" onto this figure, the impression is that there is an initial decrease of this use, followed by a short increase. After point 10, the use of this strategy remains roughly the same as time goes by. This result is unexpected, and seems to contradict what we had predicted beforehand. On the bases of this "average learner", our initial hypothesis of "overshooting" of the *don't V* strategy is not supported by the data.

However, if we inspect the data more carefully and look at the individual trajectories, we observe that *none* of the learners follow the trajectory of the "average learner". For instance, when we look at the data of Juan and Jorge (the data of the two adolescents), we see that both show large peaks and lows (see Figure 8). We observe, for instance, that while Juan starts out with a very high frequency of this strategy, this use of it quickly drops and remains stable around 30 instances per session. Jorge, on the other hand, starts out with around 35 instances per session, and then becomes highly variable, first decreasing to around zero, and then sharply increasing his frequency up to 70 instances of *don't V* use. After this peak, he also drops off again to around 30–40 instances per session.

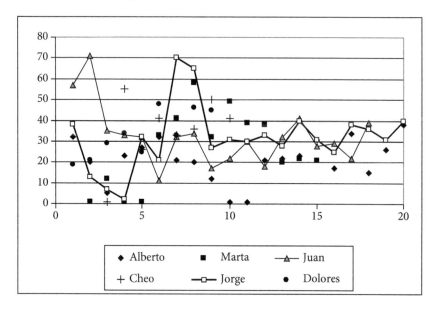

Figure 8. The use of the *don't V* strategy in the CRS study with data of both adolescents (Jorge and Juan) highlighted

What is even more interesting is the fact that although the trajectories of the two teenagers seem very different, they are also similar to a certain extent. Let us see what happens if we shift Juan's data a bit to the right. This is illustrated in Figure 9. Now, the similarity between the two learners becomes clearer. Although we have no way of knowing what happens before the first observation of Juan, both adolescents show a peak in the use of the *don't V* strategy, followed by a decrease and a relatively stable period of around 20–40 uses per session. These observed peaks also correspond to this prediction of "overshooting" of the *don't V* strategy, and suggest an important development characteristic: The variability shows a moment of transition and might be needed for the learner to progress.

If we contrast this pattern of the two teenagers with the learning trajectory of Alberto and Dolores, we see a very different picture. Although the use of the *don't V* strategy is somewhat variable, and seems to be used somewhat less in the middle of the graph, the general impression is that there is limited growth. Roughly speaking, the frequency of the use of this strategy is of the same magnitude in the beginning of the trajectory, as it is at the end. More importantly, it is clear that Alberto's pattern of acquisition does not show a peak that might represent this phenomenon of overshooting (see Figure 10 for Alberto's data).

Thus, in summary, we have seen that whereas Juan and Jorge show peaks in correspondence with the expected phenomenon of overshooting, Alberto shows no such evidence. We might speculate on the reasons for this difference. One of these might be that Alberto's input was primarily from other nonnative speakers in the factory where he worked. In this way, his input is quite different from Jorge's and Juan's, who

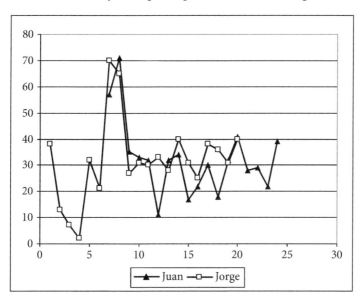

Figure 9. The use of the *don't V* strategy for both adolescents (Jorge and Juan). Here, the data of Juan are shifted 6 positions to the right

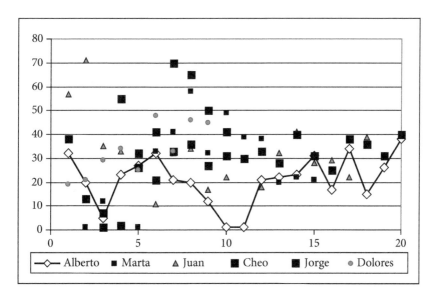

Figure 10. The use of the *don't V* strategy for Alberto

interacted with their (middle-class) English peers on a daily basis. Because the learning of these subjects takes place under very different circumstances, it is not surprising that their learning curves are very different.

Although it seems unreasonable to use group averages on data of only six subjects, it is not uncommon in the literature (see for instance the study of Furrow, Nelson & Benedict 1979, on the relation between mothers' speech and child language). However, even with bigger sample sizes, the principle remains the same, which is that when using group averages, individual irregularities and differences get lost. In our illustration, the differences between the learners were large, both qualitatively (because the learning took place under highly dissimilar circumstances) and quantitatively (as expressed in the individual trajectories). Because of these differences, the use of a "group average development" presents a picture of development that does not characterize any of the individual learning processes. Thus, as an important first step, we have been able to show that an individual curve is quite different from a group curve.

5.2   The use of smoothing techniques

When we look at the individual raw data as in the figures above it is sometimes difficult to find out whether there is any general improvement or change in the data. We can use smoothing techniques, just as in more traditional approaches to statistics, to see whether there is a general trend or not. The purpose of a smoother is to "sketch" the general trend of the data and leave out many of the irregularities of the actual data. Smoothers are therefore very well suited for representing a direction, i.e. a motion vector. This can be seen as the simplest possible general trend or direction over time, in a way similar to a meteorologist's representation of the direction of the wind by a single arrow. As such, the smoother simplifies the developmental pattern and gives an impression of the general pattern of development. However, as we argued in the previous section, we should avoid considering the smoothed lines as a *replacement* of the actual data because that would in our view be like disregarding essential elements in discovering the developmental process.

As an illustration of how a smoother works, see Figures 11 and 12. We used the *don't V* constructions again as examples. First, we created a XY-graph of the data to represent the development over time. The simplest possible way to smooth data is to add a "trend line" to the observed data. Trend lines are built-in functions in Excel that can be applied by simply right-clicking the data line.[2] Excel provides six types of trend

---

2.   It should be noted that the illustrations provided in this paragraph are very simple and suitable for the 'beginner'. For the more advanced user, there are more sophisticated procedures, such as offered by the software program Table Curve 2D (Systat Software Inc.).

lines. It takes some experimenting and experience to select the trend line that best fits the data curve. In this example we have used a polynomial trend line to the second order. This trend line gives a rather broad generalization of the data.

Figures 11 and 12 are also in practice file 3.1 on our web site SLD_Methods (DOI:10.1075/ lllt.29.website).

As Figures 11 and 12 illustrate, the higher the order of the polynomial function, the more closely the trend line fits the curve, but the less smoothing is applied. As can be seen in both cases, the smoother "averages out" all irregularities and provides a line of the selected type that has "the best fit" to the original data. The figure is therefore suggested to provide a good "general impression" of the data.

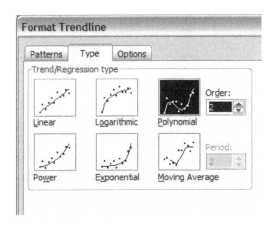

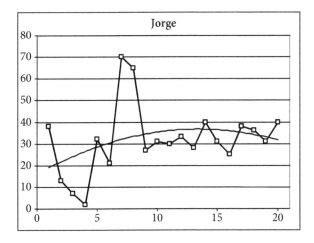

Figure 11. The use of Jorge's *don't V* strategy in the CRS study with a polynomial trend line (2nd degree)

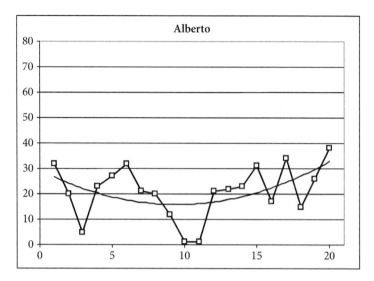

Figure 12. The use of Alberto's *don't V* strategy in the CRS study with a polynomial trend line (2nd degree)

As expected, the general trend lines help us see that Jorge's use of the *don't V* construction decreases over time, but Alberto's use of the *don't V* construction actually increases. Also adding the smoothing line helps us see that in the case of Jorge there are strong outliers especially at data points 4 and 7. As Figure 13 below shows, we can also use a polynomial function of a higher degree (in this case the 6th degree), which does help us visualize the peaks better, but shows less what the general trend is.

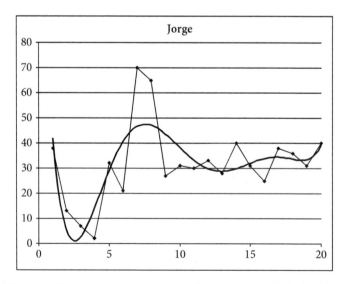

Figure 13. The use of Jorge's *don't V* strategy in the CRS study with a polynomial trend line (6th degree)

To summarize, adding smoothing lines is useful not only to discover general trends in the raw data but – depending on the degree of fit and *in combination with* the original data – also to discover local fluctuations. If the data show peaks and dips, then it is useful to see if these are meaningful or not for the developmental process. It should be stressed that the smoothing functions we have shown in this paragraph are very simple and can be used as a starting point, but that more advanced software offers the possibility of more elegant smoothing functions (such as Loess functions or splines).

5.3   Min-max graphs

As we have argued so far, there is always a certain degree of variability in any complex system, even one that is rather stable. To help us discover more about the developmental process, we need to find ways to distinguish random variability from "developmental" variability. In this section, we will demonstrate the application of a *simple, descriptive* approach to take when analyzing time serial data. This first step is important because a thorough description of the data is the groundwork for generating hypotheses that can be tested later on. We will therefore illustrate a descriptive technique that can be used to look at developmental data (from SLD) in a dynamic fashion.

As we showed in the preceding section, standard smoothing techniques eliminate much information from the actual data, but in simple plot lines, the degree of variability in the actual data may also be difficult to see. To solve this problem, van Geert and van Dijk (2002) developed several techniques that help us visualize the degree of variability. One of these techniques is the moving min-max graph, which highlights the general pattern of variability, while keeping the raw data visible. This method uses a *moving window*, a time frame that moves up one position (= one measurement occasion) each time. Each window largely overlaps the preceding windows, using all the same measurement occasions minus the first and plus the next. For instance, for every predetermined set of consecutive measurements we calculate the maximum and the minimum values. This is done by way of a predetermined moving window, of for instance 5 positions, such that we obtain the following series:

min(t1..t5), min(t2..t6), min(t3..t7), etc.
max(t1..t5), max(t2..t6), max(t3..t7), etc

Technically these values are very easy to plot. Any commercially available spreadsheet program offers functions such as min and max that can easily be computed over moving data windows.

For step-by-step instructions to make a min-max graph see *how to* Section 3.1 p. 163.

Figures 14 and 15 are also shown in practice materials 3.1 on our web site SLD_Methods (DOI:10.1075/lllt.29.website).

Essential to this way of presenting development is that the min-max technique shows the *bandwidth* of observed scores. Once this bandwidth is plotted, one can visually inspect whether they too show considerable fluctuations over time and they should again be contrasted with the eventual long-term changes in the minima and maxima. The greatest merit of this technique is that it displays the amount of variation in relation to developmental "jumps". The wider the bandwidth, the greater the amount of variation.

In Figures 14 and 15, we have applied this procedure to the data of Jorge and Alberto, to contrast it with the smoothing approach. What we would expect is the following: If indeed intraindividual variability is a developmental phenomenon, it would decrease when a learning process is reaching its end point. Thus, if maximal achievement is reached for a (first or second language) learner, we expect scores to stabilize. It should be noted that we do not expect a disappearing bandwidth. Although fully competent adults probably display a significantly smaller bandwidth than learners, their output is still variable to some degree. Nevertheless, the bandwidth of scores of a competent individual should be considerably smaller than that of someone who is still in the learning process.

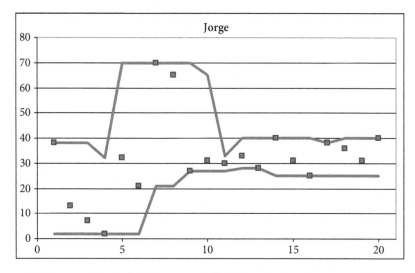

Figure 14. The use of Jorge's *don't V* strategy in the CRS study in a min-max graph

In Jorge's case (Figure 14) we see three main stages, a rather wide bandwidth of variability up to data point 4 (from 0% to 40%), a much wider bandwidth of variability between data points 4 and 11 (with a jump from 0% to 70%) and then from data point 11 on a rather narrow bandwidth (25% to 40%). These ranges of variability could be interpreted as follows: At first Jorge uses the *don't V* construction rather randomly ("free variability"), then he overuses the construction ("overgeneralization"), and then he uses the construction in a more regular pattern, assumingly in a target-like manner. In Alberto's case (Figure 15) we can also see some variability, but as the min-max graph

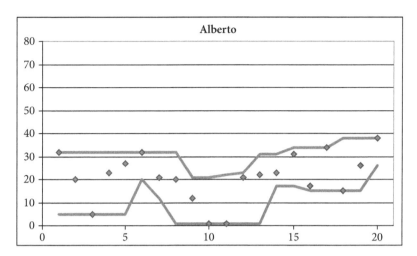

Figure 15. The use of Alberto's *don't V* strategy in the CRS study in a min-max graph

shows, there is not as strong a difference in the bandwidth over time, even though the band itself moves down between data points 7 and 13. From these two min-max graphs, we can thus hypothesize that the variability in Jorge's data might be meaningful in the developmental process, but in Alberto's case the variability might not. We can test these hypotheses by resampling the data. How to test these hypotheses will be made clear in the next section.

5.4   Resampling techniques

The methods discussed above are exclusively descriptive in nature. However, due to for instance resampling procedures (Efron & Tibshirani 1993; Good 1999), it is also possible to test the observations against chance (see van Geert & van Dijk 2002).

In the previous section, we observed that Alberto's score range in the min-max graph seems to be smaller than Jorge's. From this observation, we speculated that it might be the case that – in general – the teenagers are more variable than the adults. However, up to this point, this is just a qualitative observation, which has to be tested against chance. In order to perform such a test, resampling methods are especially well suited. This method consists of randomly drawing a large number of subsamples (e.g. 5000) from the original sample. We start out by defining a variable of interest, which functions as our testing criterion. In an analysis of variability this might be a range, difference or any of the measures that we discussed before. In our case, our question is whether Jorge is more variable than Alberto. The second step is to set up a resampling model based on a reasonable null-hypothesis. In other words, we use the original data and we randomly reshuffle it 5000 times. In each of these resampling simulations, we compare the criterion of the original set with the resampled criterion.

In this way, we get a fairly good estimation of how the original values in the original order compare to the original values in a randomized order.

A resampling analysis can easily be performed in Microsoft Excel, for instance by means of the statistical add-in Poptools (Hood 2009) (see *How to* sections for detail). The advantage of resampling procedures is that they are simple and flexible. For a general discussion of the use of these techniques, we refer to Good (1999).

As an illustration to this approach, we take a very simple case study and show the application of a resampling (bootstrapping) procedure in order to test the hypotheses, as formulated before. Here, we limit ourselves to the comparison of only two participants in the study: Alberto and Jorge.

The step-by-step instructions for the analyses are given in *How to* Section 3.2 on p. 168.

The starting point of each analysis is describing the data as thoroughly as you can. The methods we described earlier in this chapter are well suited for this purpose. On the basis of this description, a set of hypotheses can be formulated. For instance, based on the qualitative descriptions of the acquisition pattern of negation in the CRS study, we have set up the following testable hypotheses. These are:

1. Jorge is generally more variable than Alberto.
2. There are significant peaks in the use of *don't V* by Alberto and Jorge.

In the following paragraphs we will test these two hypotheses by going through the procedure step by step[3]. For transparency, the consecutive steps are presented next to each other on a single Excel Worksheet. They are also described in much greater detail in the *How to* sections.

5.4.1   *Hypothesis 1: Jorge is generally more variable than Alberto*

To confirm hypothesis 1, we will have to reject the 0 hypothesis (Jorge is not more variable than Alberto). In order to test this hypothesis, which deals with comparing variability between participants, we first need to define what we mean by "more variable in general". The first step is thus to quantify this definition of variability.

Here, we have taken *the average distance between two consecutive observations* as a working definition. This was calculated by taking the difference between each observation and its previous observation. For example, Alberto had 32 instances of *don't V* strategy at time 1 and 20 at time 2. The difference is 12 (cell E-4). Then all distances for each participant were averaged. The average (approximate) distance for Alberto was 9.895 (see cell E23) and for Jorge 12.526 (see cell F23). It therefore looks as if Alberto was less variable than Jorge, but our question is if this difference could have occurred by chance. Because we are interested in the difference between Jorge and Alberto, we now compute

---

3.   We thank Paul van Geert for helping us set up the resampling models.

the difference between the average distance of Alberto and the average distance of Jorge, which is 2.632 (see cell F24). This difference will be used as our testing criterion.

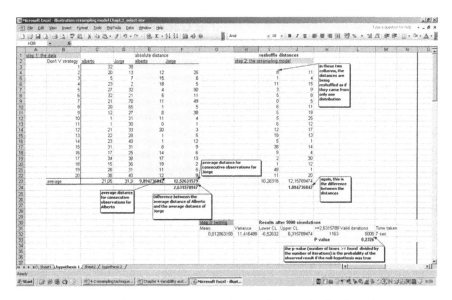

Figure 16. Screen shot of the resampling procedure used to test the first hypothesis (Jorge is more variable than Alberto).

 The files from which the screenshots are given can be found in practice materials 3.2 on our web site SLD_Methods (DOI:10.1075/lllt.29.website).

We now proceed to the second step, which is to set up a resampling model. The resampling model takes the original data in columns E and F together and reorders it randomly (see columns I and J). If you compare the individual columns F (Jorge's original data) and F (Alberto's original data) with column I and J (the reshuffled data), you will see that the numbers are completely the same, but just reordered in different sequences and across both columns. Thus, the null-hypothesis is that these differences stem from *one* single distribution (and not two, as our alternative hypothesis states). In other words, the two sets of data are added together to form one set and then shuffled. Note for example that Alberto's second value (E5:15) occurs as Jorge's third value J6:15). At the bottom of these columns (cells I23 and J23) are the new average distances and in cell J24 is the new difference between these averages. By means of the Monte Carlo Analysis in Poptools, it is possible to reorder the data in columns I and J as often as needed and every time the data are reordered a new number appears in cell J24.

The third step is to reshuffle the data in Columns I and J automatically 5000 times, i.e. simulate 5000 resampling simulations in a so-called Monte Carlo Analysis. This means that 5000 times we have a new number in cell J24. By comparing our testing criterion (which is the original distance in cell F24) with the newly calculated distance (cell J24), we can test our null-hypothesis. To interpret the results of the simulations, we have to calculate the p-value by dividing the number of times the newly calculated distance was the same or greater than the testing criterion divided by the number of iterations (see cell L33). The value in this cell gives us the frequency with which the original difference between Jorge and Alberto (cell F24) was replicated in the 5000 randomized simulations. Only if this frequency is very low (below 5%, which corresponds to a p-value of 0.05), can we reject our null-hypothesis.

In our extended illustration, the p-value is 0.2326, which means that roughly 24% of all simulations produced values that were similar to the original data. This means that we cannot reject the null-hypothesis and must conclude that on average, Jorge is not more variable than Alberto[4]. So although, by means of visual inspection, we thought that generally there might be more variability in the data of Jorge, this was not confirmed by this analysis.

5.4.2   *Hypothesis 2: There are significant peaks in the use of don't V by Jorge and Alberto*

We now want to zoom in at the data and focus on the local peaks. When visually inspecting the data previously, we had observed that the peaks in both teenagers are large, and the question is whether the peaks are more than just coincidental variation. We therefore want to find out, in this illustration, what the probability is that the peaks in the data of Alberto and Jorge are the result of chance. We will go through three steps again as in testing hypothesis 1.

We start again by defining what we mean by a "peak". In this case, we stipulated that if there is a real peak, it should not be just one isolated jump. In order to be able to ignore isolated, one-time fluctuations, we started out with a simple moving average over 2 observations[5]. For example, if you look at cells B6 and B7 in Figure 17a, you can see that Alberto used the *don't V* 32% of the time at data point 1 and 20% at data point 2. In D6 and D7, the average of these two, 26% is given. We continued on the basis of this new data set in columns D and E. We then formulated our working definition of a peak as the distance between the minimum and maximum observation in a given data set.

However, before we can look at the peaks in this data set, we first have to check whether there is a general increase in the dataset. If there is a general linear trend

---

4.   We have also performed several somewhat more complex definitions and criteria (including a sequence effect and looking at relative variability), but the results remained roughly the same: the resampling model was able to reproduce the data in 20–25% of all cases.

5.   The assumption is that our sampling frequency is slightly higher than the duration of the peak. Although this is a reasonable assumption, it is possible to formulate a different definition of a peak depending on what you are interested in.

upwards, this upward movement itself would also create peaks, not due to degree of variability but due to general increase. If this were the case, we would have to detrend the data, which is basically substract the slope from the data points. However, in the case of Alberto and Jorge, there were no significant slopes, and we were able to continue with the data from the moving averages in columns D and E.

> Even though we did not need to detrend data in this set, we have given more detail on when detrending may be necessary and step-by-step instructions in *How to* Section 3.3. p. 177.

Because we wanted to see what the maximum distance was between any of the data points for each learner, we calculated the differences between data points in several steps. We first subtracted consecutive observed values (e.g. the difference between data points 1 and 2), then with a delay of 2 data points (the difference between data points 1 and 3), with a delay of 3 data points the difference between data points 1 and (4), 4 data points, etc. Below each column (in row 27) we wrote down the maximum positive distance for each learner. As the screenshot shows, the maximal positive differences between any data points in the set were found in step 5 for both Alberto (26) and Jorge (63). This maximal positive distance will be used as the testing criterion in the resampling model.

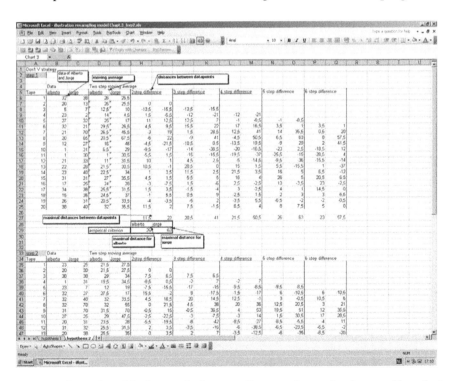

Figure 17a. Screenshot of the first step in the resampling procedure testing the second hypothesis (significant peaks).

In step 2, (see Figure 17a) we formulated our resampling model, i.e. we defined *what* has to be resampled. In this case, we took the null-hypothesis that by reshuffling the original data, we will get the same maximal distance as in the observed set. It is important to note that we resampled our data with replacement, which implies that in each simulation, a new set is randomly drawn from the original pool, and not all observations are necessarily selected in each simulation. Because we are looking at the individual trajectories, we compared the maximal simulated distance for Alberto with the maximal distance in the data. After that, we did the same for Jorge.

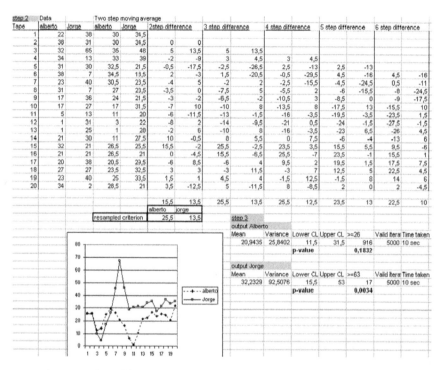

Figure 17b. Screenshot of the second and third step in the resampling procedure testing the second hypothesis (significant peaks).

In step 3 we ran two separate Monte Carlo Analyses, one for Jorge and one for Alberto, with 5000 simulation steps. After this, we calculate the probability that the peak that we observed in the dataset is produced by the random model and is just random fluctuation. Only if this probability is small (below 5%), can we reject the null-hypothesis that the peak is caused by random fluctuation.

Figure 17b shows that for Alberto, the resulting p-value was 0.1894, which means that in almost 19% of all simulations, the random model was able to reproduce the peaks in the order of magnitude of those of Alberto. Therefore, we cannot reject the null-hypothesis for the data of Alberto. For Jorge, on the other hand, the result turns out to be highly significant (p = 0.0028)[6], and we can safely conclude that the peaks are not likely to be the result of coincidental fluctuations.

In summary, in this illustration we have shown the possibilities of testing variability centred hypotheses using resampling procedures. As a general conclusion from this illustration, we have seen that in general Jorge is not more variable than Alberto. However, when we zoom in at the local variability, we have established that while the peaks for Alberto cannot be distinguished from random fluctuation, there is a significant peak in the data of Jorge, which is not likely to be the result of coincidental fluctuation. The illustration we have just provided is very simple and suited to the data at hand. Obviously, these analyses can be extended with more data and additional assumptions and null-hypotheses. We stress the fact that any such procedure should start with a thorough description of the data and a well considered resampling model. It is important to carefully formulate a procedure suited to each data set and research question.

6. Conclusion

In this chapter, we have tried to show that variability has been observed in many SLD studies, but the focus has usually been on identifying the causes of variability. Only some authors discussed the so-called "free variability", the variability that could not be attributed to any direct cause and was thought to have something to do with development. Moreover, in many SLD studies the focus has been on universal trends and group averages, mainly because individual case studies are regarded as random and not generalizable. However, we have shown that no individual behaves as the average person, and that all individuals have their own patterns. Each individual shows degrees of variability, but individuals may show disproportional amounts of variability when they move from one stage to the next. In our re-examination of the CRS data we showed that smoothers can indicate the general trend and that min-max graphs can show where transitional phases might be occurring. These are descriptive techniques that rely on visual exploration and that help us discover interesting patterns. To test whether the patterns we have observed are random or not, we can use resampling techniques (e.g. a Monte Carlo Analysis). We have shown that even though Jorge's data are not necessarily more variable than Alberto's, he does show significant peaks and Alberto does not. We may surmise that Jorge's peaks in the *don't V* constructions

---

6.　In an additional calculation – where we also included negative peaks – these findings turned out to be relatively robust (p-values of Alberto and Jorge were 0.1450 and 0.0044 respectively).

help him develop the negative constructions, whereas Alberto does not really seem to develop any new constructions.

From a DST perspective we would expect different kinds of variability patterns to show different kinds of development. A smooth, rather linear pattern is expected in learning items that are not rule governed, such as lexical development and jumpy patterns in items that are rule governed such as syntactic or grammatical rules, where a learner discovers a rule, experiments with it and then settles in a new attractor state. Only a few case studies focusing on the variability patterns in SLD have been conducted so far (Verspoor, Lowie & van Dijk 2008; Spoelman & Verspoor, 2010), and more longitudinal dense case studies are needed to discover the possible developmental L2 patterns for individual learners and groups of learners. For instance, the data in this chapter seems to suggest that there are different developmental patterns for learners of different ages: The younger ones take longer to produce the peaks in the non-target forms than the teenagers and the adults do not show peaks to the same extent as the teenagers. Another application of the methods presented in this chapter is to trace learners in different conditions such as naturalistic versus instructed L2 settings.

Visualizing interactions between variables

Marjolijn Verspoor & Marijn van Dijk

1. Introduction

So far we have argued that language should be seen as a complex system and that language may be viewed as a collection of many elements or components. These components are related to each other and will all affect each other. This implies that when one component changes, another component will change too, and the other way round. If we consider the fact that language in itself is a component of a complex environment with which it interacts, the task of deciding which interacting components to study is difficult. It is important to stress that we will have to limit ourselves and make informed choices, inspired by theoretical insights, about which developmental variables to study.

Looking for the way different variables interact will help us focus not on the final outcomes, but on the process itself. First we will discuss the different types of interactions various components may have and discuss what has been found in different L1 and L2 studies up to now. Then we will revisit the data that were presented in Chapter 3 and subject our previous findings to analyses to determine whether the interactions suggested by inspecting the raw data are worth testing further. To test hypotheses about interactions, we have to simulate the data in a model. This chapter focuses on the analyses that are needed before we can finally proceed to modeling (in Chapter 6).

2. Defining growers

The description of the developmental system as a dynamic ecological system is based on the following general assumptions (cf. van Geert 2009). First, development is defined as the growth or increase in level of more developmentally advanced or complex variables and the decline or decrease of less developmentally advanced variables. For example, in the previous chapter, development was observed in the growth of the more advanced *analyzed don't* constructions and the decline of the nontarget *No-V* construction. As the growth of a variable depends on the level already attained, it is a so-called auto-catalytic process.

Secondly, in an ecological system, growth or change depends on the availability of resources, which are limited. For instance, a resource factor for lexical growth is the language spoken in the environment, but also the learner's language aptitude or motivation. The assumption of limited resources is commonly expressed by the well-known and basic logistic or Verhulst equation for population development, which will be discussed in more detail in Chapter 6. If applied to knowledge-related variables, it basically states that the growth of knowledge depends on what one already knows and on what one does not know yet, given what there is to know in the current context of the particular person in a particular environment. A related concept relevant for SLD is the "carrying capacity". Since growth is resource-dependent and resources are limited, growth is by definition limited. The carrying capacity refers to the state of knowledge that can be attained in a given participant's interlinked structure of resources (van Geert 1994b).

The minimal developmental system we could study would consist of one single variable or component, for example a learner's lexical knowledge. Such a single-variable system is then automatically assumed to be part of an environment (in the abstract sense of the word), which consists of any other component that may affect this lexical knowledge, such as the learner's syntactic knowledge or the language of the instruction in his L2 class. However, none of these would be addressed explicitly in our data analysis.

However, for a description of development it would be more meaningful to see how various components interact over time. For instance, it is relatively obvious that a learner's vocabulary acquisition may be related to acquiring new syntactic patterns. We may assume that the learner needs to know more difficult words to be able to produce longer sentences with more complex structures. In other words, we want to describe the ecological relationships that can hold for any couple of components or variables, which we will call "growers". It should be noted that this approach makes sense only if the variables that are studied in combination have a meaningful relationship to each other.

Growers may have relationships of different kinds:

–   Supportive: Growers develop in unison because they support each other
–   Competitive: Growers develop in alternating patterns (when one goes up the other goes down) because they compete with each other
    Conditional: A minimal level of one grower is a necessary precondition for another grower to develop, also referred to as a "precursor" interaction.

An additional point is that the relationship may be asymmetric, meaning that the relationship changes over time. For example, one may first need to be able to use words actively before one can make more complex sentences, so the number of words is at first conditional before more advanced syntax can develop. However, after the syntax has begun to develop, the number of words may keep on growing too, which indicates a supportive relation from then on. An example of a competitive relation may be the use of certain constructions in making English sentences more complex, such as longer noun phrases, different types of dependent finite clauses and dependent non-finite constructions.

Several studies so far have looked at possible interactions between growers. The study by Bassano and van Geert (2007) illustrates the process of the emergence of syntactic complexity by looking at how one word (W1), two word (W2), three word (W3), and four or more word (W4+) utterances developed over time. For one of the two learners, W1 utterances were at the top level at the beginning of the observation (14 months) and declined until they leveled off after the 30th month. Both the W2 and W3 utterances presented an inverted U-curve with a dip around the 21st month and a peak at around the 26th month (half of the utterances during a session), and began to stabilize after the 32nd month. From the W2–3 peak on, the W1 and the W2–3 frequencies were very close to one another. The W4 + utterances showed an S-shaped increase: They started off around the 23rd month, began to dominate upon the W1 and W2–3 utterances around the 28th month and reached a maximum level at around the 31st month (more than half of the utterances during a session). By assuming a series of precursor relationships between the less and more advanced developmental structures, which are characteristic of the development of qualitatively more complex forms out of qualitatively simpler ones, Bassano and van Geert (2007) were able to model these interactions by means of asymmetric support–competition dynamics.

Robinson and Mervis (1998) report a clear interaction between the lexicon and syntax in L1 development. This study shows that when multiword sentences start to emerge, the lexical growth starts to decline. The presumed reason for this is that in the one-word phase, the child can use available resources to develop the lexicon but in the more advanced phase, more and different resources are needed to develop the grammatical system, which goes at the expense of learning new words. Thus, in this case, it seems as if multiword utterances have a competitive relation with the lexicon, in the sense that they compete for growth. However, it might even be the case that at the same time there is a conditional relation between the two, in the sense that lexicon has to have a certain minimal size in order for multiword utterances to emerge.

Verspoor, Lowie and van Dijk (2008) looked at the development of an advanced Dutch learner of English (the one also discussed in Chapter 3 and below). They also examined the relationship between the learner's lexicon and syntax in academic texts and found an asymmetrical competitive interaction between the development of the average SL in words (a sentence complexity measure) and the TTR (a lexical creativity measure). The growers showed an oscillating pattern with a slight – but clearly distinguishable – upward trend. At the earliest and later stages of development, the two variables show a weak to moderate positive correlation, but in the middle (Texts 4–15) they showed a negative correlation, which indicates that these two indices of language fluency share a competitive relationship to each other during that time. Thus, when academic writing proficiency increases, there seems to be a trade-off between a more varied word use and longer sentences at different stages in the developmental process.

Again we might speculate towards the existence of a conditional relation that changes into a competitive one.

Finally, Spoelman and Verspoor (2010) examined the development of different complexity measures of a beginning Dutch learner acquiring Finnish. They examined the development of complexity at the word, noun phrase and sentence level. As word complexity increases, both noun phrase and sentence complexity increase, so there might be a symmetrical supportive relation, but noun phrase complexity and sentence complexity alternate in developing and can therefore be considered symmetrical competitive growers.

In the remainder of this chapter we will revisit data from the study we discussed in Chapter 3. As mentioned earlier, it is also the data used in Verspoor, Lowie and van Dijk (2008), but because we have used different coding techniques and looked at different variables, the analyses will not be the same.

 Some of the techniques discussed here are explained in more detail in *How to* Section 3.1 (Chapter 8) and several figures and analyses that occur in this chapter are also presented in practice file 3.1 on our web site SLD_Methods (DOI:10.1075/lllt.29.website).

3.   Analyzing interactions in time serial data

The purpose of this section is to show how dynamic patterns of interacting variables can be made visible before they can be tested for meaningfulness in simulations. Here we will demonstrate the use of a series of simple steps to analyze possible interactions. In this illustration, the steps will be applied to our own data set on the development of sentence complexity, dependent clauses and lexicon in more detail to see which patterns emerge. It should be stressed, however, that analyzing interactions only makes sense in cases where there is clear theoretical or empirical motivation to do so. Although a more exploratory approach ("fishing" for interactions) also seems to be a possibility, such an approach would present some danger in the sense that the results only present a *description* of patterns and not necessarily an explanation of the phenomena at hand.

The procedure – suited for analyzing rather global interactions between variables- is as follows. First the raw data are visually inspected for their trend and patterns of variability. Then, in order to capture the general tendencies and the way they relate to each other, a *smoothing function,* in this case a Loess function with a fit of 32%, is used. These smoothed trajectories were estimated with the software Table Curve.[1] However, similar analyses can also be performed with other – less sophisticated – smoothing methods (e.g. moving averages) with a standard spreadsheet program. Often, it takes some time to find the right balance between erasing too much of

---

1.   Because this software is not widely accessible, we have not included such analyses in our How to sections.

the interesting variability (see Chapter 3) and still obtaining an adequate representation of the global trend in the data.

Often, the variables that are expected to influence each other's development are not presented on the same scale. While some variables are best expressed as a ratio (such as TTR) or average (e.g. MLU), others simply count the frequency of a certain construction in a given sample (e.g. the absolute frequency of prepositional phrases). In order to compare trajectories with data that are not presented on the same scale, the smoothed data can be *normalized*. In Chapter 3 we discussed how data can be presented as percentages and further normalized by scaling them between their own minimal and maximal value, to fit the same scale (between 0 and 1). This means that for each data series, the minimal value will always be "fixed" at 0, and the maximal value at 1.

> In our example, we have used the following formula: (x-min)/(max-min)), which is explained in more detail in *How to* Section 2.5 on p. 161.

Finally, the association between variables is expressed by a correlation coefficient. In those cases where there seems to be a general relation between two variables across the total trajectory, one general correlation coefficient can provide information on a possible interaction between both. However, in some cases, the association seems to be more temporal because it changes over time. In those cases a "moving" correlation coefficient can be applied to the time series, and the resulting values are plotted in a simple line graph and inspected for local changes.

> *How to* Section 4.1 (p. 180) explains in detail how to create a moving correlation.

3.1 Development of sentence complexity

In Chapter 3 we explained the details for our constructs. Just as Bassano and van Geert (2007) assumed a series of asymmetric relationships between the less and more advanced developmental structures, we assumed that our Dutch university learner of English during her three years of study would use more complex constructions as she developed. The constructions we examined are ordered in a hierarchy from simple to more complex:

a. *Simple and compound* sentences (consisting of main clauses only)
b. *Complex* sentences (sentences containing one or more finite dependent clauses)
c. *Words to finite verb ratio*

The first two measures are expressed as relative values and are thus each other's complement, so when one goes down, the other goes up and vice versa. The third measure, *words per finite verb* overlaps with both sentence types. In a short simple sentence such as *The cat is out of the bag* there is one finite verb with 7 words, so the ratio is 7:1. In a complex sentence, the ratio can still be low, as in *Because the cat is out of the bag, he no longer has to hide*. The *words to finite verb ratio* is again 7:1. In English though, an even more complex structure would be one without a finite verb, as in *The cat out of the bag, he no longer <u>has</u> to hide.* In this sentence, the *words to finite verb ratio* is 12:1. This ratio will indirectly give us insight into complexity other than shown by the number of finite dependent clauses in simple and complex sentences, such as non-finite constructions and longer noun phrases.

Our assumption was that the proportion of simple sentences would decrease and be taken over by a higher proportion of complex sentences. Then we would expect a decline in complex sentences (which have finite clauses) and a rise in so-called simple sentences because relatively more non-finite constructions would be used, which would result in a higher *words to finite verb ratio*. As Figure 3 in Chapter 3 (repeated here for ease of reference as Figure 1) shows, our expectations were met.

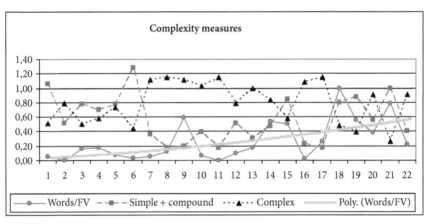

Figure 1. Development of sentence complexity measures

Figure 1 clearly shows that there is a lot of intraindividual variability in all three variables. However, despite this variability, there is (1) a clear increase in the numbers of *words per finite verb,* with a certain degree of stabilization near the end, (2) an initial decrease of simple/compound utterances, followed by an increase again (and by definition the exact reverse for complex utterances).

Because we are interested in relatively global interactions between the three measures of complexity, we start by smoothing the raw data with a Loess-function (in this case we have used 32% fit). Here we focus only on Words/FV and single/compound utterances (because complex utterances are the inverse of the latter). The resulting trend lines are shown in Figure 2.

The analyses in Figure 2–4 are given in practice materials 3.1 on our web site SLD_Methods (DOI:10.1075/lllt.29.website).

As can be seen more clearly in this representation, the simple and compound structures first decrease, and then increase, forming a classical u-shaped development. This is also what is expected, since the rather short main clauses with finite verbs are made longer and more complex by means of non-finite constructions. On the other hand, Words/FV shows a rather straightforward increase, with a slight 'dip' near the end, showing that indeed sentences steadily become more complex.

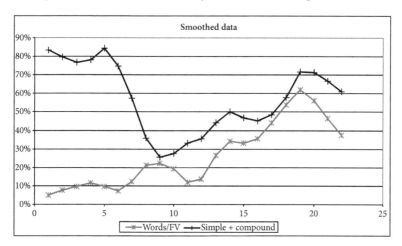

Figure 2. Smoothed trajectories of sentence complexity measures

Although the scales are already similar, we have also normalized the data, to show the relative changes of both variables even more clearly. The result of this is shown in Figure 3.

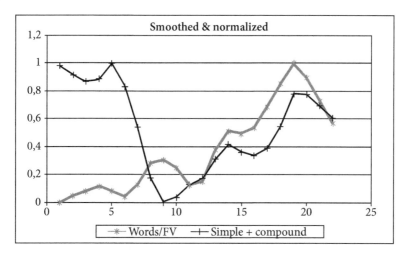

Figure 3. Smoothed and normalized trajectories of sentence complexity measures

What is interesting in Figure 3 is that although initially, there seems to be a negative relation between both variables, this seems to change in a rather high correspondence between them from Text 9 onwards. The fact that there is no "overall" association between them is also confirmed by a (nonsignificant) correlation coefficient of almost zero (r =-.076, p=0.736). However, when we zoom in at the temporal association, by computing a moving correlation coefficient (with a window of 5 measurement), we obtain the following picture (see Figure 4).

See *How to* Section 4.1 p. 182 for more detail.

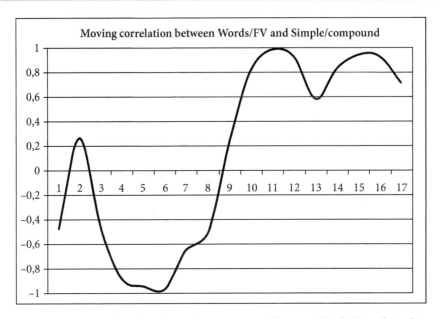

Figure 4. Moving correlation (window of 5 measurement) between Words/FV and simple/compound sentences

Figure 4 confirms our initial observation. Initially, there seems to be a negative (or competitive) relation between the two: Higher frequencies of simple and compound sentences go together with a lower ratio of *words to finite verbs*. However, after the simple constructions have decreased and thus more complex sentences have emerged, the Words/FV starts to increase too. From that point onwards, the relation seems to be supportive: A higher proportion of simple and compound sentence goes together with higher levels over Words/FV. In other words, the so-called simple sentences are becoming internally more complex by means of longer noun phrases and other non-finite constructions. Initially, both variables seem to have a negative preconditional relation: The proportion of simple/compound to complex sentences has to be a certain "low" before the ratio of words to finite verbs in simple sentences emerges and both measures of complexity grow hand in hand.

3.2 Development of different types of dependent clauses

The sentence complexity measures in the previous section are rather global measures of complexity, but at a more detailed level we can look at the development of different types of complex sentences. Complex sentences may have different kinds of finite dependent clauses: those that function as an adverbial, as a nominal or as a post modifier of a noun (relative clauses). Again we will assume a series of asymmetric relationships between the less and more advanced developmental structures during development. At the end, once a writer is really proficient and advanced, the writer should show flexibility and balance in the structures used, resulting in a good mix of these structures.

a.   Adverbial clauses are easy to form: Add a subordinate conjunction before the clause and put it before or after a main clause. (e.g. *He is sick > because he is sick)*

b.   Nominal clauses are also easy to form: Add a subordinate conjunction before the clause and embed the clause in the main clause. (e.g. *I know something. The cat is out of the bag. > I know (that) the cat is out of the bag)*

c.   Relative clauses are more difficult to form: Substitute a noun with a relative pronoun and put the clause after the noun that it modifies. (e.g. *You saw the boy. He did not go to school > The boy whom you saw did not go to school)*

In Chapter 3 we showed the development of the proportion of adverbial and relative clauses. In Figure 5 we have plotted the same data again, this time including the nominal clauses.

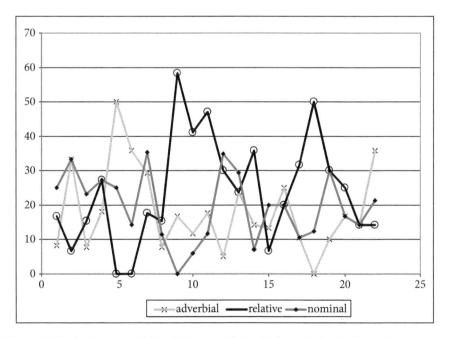

Figure 5. The development of the relative uses of adverbial, nominal and relative clauses

In Figure 5, we can see that there is a rather high degree of variability in all three variables. Also, it seems as if the adverbial and nominal clauses are fairly frequent from early on, and the relative clauses "peak" somewhat later. Also, in the end, all types of clauses are roughly equally frequent, which indicates that the speaker seems to "find a balance" in mixing these different types of clauses.

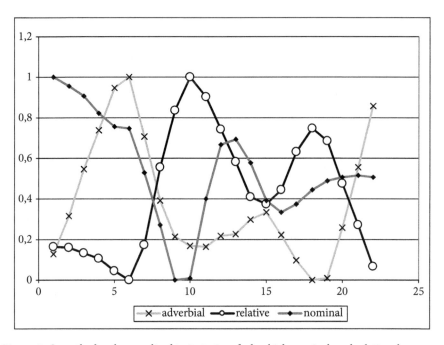

Figure 6. Smoothed and normalized trajectories of adverbial, nominal, and relative clauses

In Figure 6, we smoothed (with the same Loess function as in the previous illustration) and normalized the data again. We can now compare the global tendencies and relations of all three variables more clearly. When visually inspecting these curves, we can first see a negative association between the adverbial clauses and the relative clauses, each time the adverbials go up, the relatives go down, and vice versa. This relation is also confirmed by a significant correlation of $-.779$ ($p < 0.001$). Secondly, although less pronounced, there also seems to be a negative association between the relative and nominal clauses. The correlation between these two variables is $-.714$ ($p < 0.001$), confirming this negative relation. Finally, the relation between the nominal and adverbial clauses was less clear. Although in some parts of development, they seem to "grow together", this is not always the case. The correlation turned out to be positive ($.343$) but not significant ($p = .118$).

When we look at the more local correlations, in this case with a moving window of 5 values, presented in Figure 7, it seems there are clear differences in the relations among the three growers. The most pronounced and stable association is the negative interaction between adverbial and relative clauses. The relation between adverbial and nominal clauses, on the other hand, is also relatively stable, and tends to be positive. Finally, the relation between nominal and relative clauses seems to be quite erratic. Please note that when we use a moving correlation, the resulting coefficients are based on small sets (in this cases 5 values of each grower), which means that the values can be overestimated and cannot be tested for significance. Therefore, a moving window of correlations should merely be seen as a descriptive technique to make the interaction between the variables more visible.

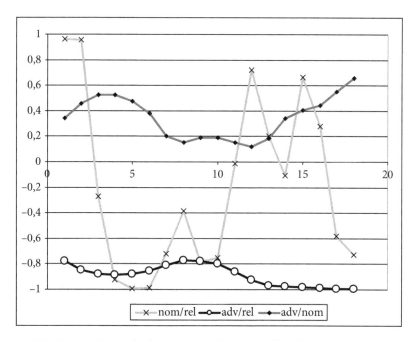

Figure 7. Moving correlation plot between adverbial, nominal and relative clauses

Thus, in summary, the analyses so far have shown that the relative clauses seem to have a clear, competitive relation with the adverbial clauses over the entire trajectory. There are also indications for a generally competitive interaction between relative and nominal clauses, although the local interactions seem to be much more complex. Finally, the relation between the adverbial and the nominal clauses seems to be more support-ive, although the influence on each other is probably less strong. We may conclude that our advanced learner, as we assumed, showed asymmetric relationships between the less (adverbial and nominal) and more advanced (relative) developmental structures.

4.   Interaction between lexical sophistication and syntactic complexity

In Chapter 3 we mentioned that different lexical measures such as frequent words, unique words, lexical diversity (TTR or D) and lexical sophistication seem to measure somewhat different types of lexical development as their developmental measures do not show high correlations. In this section, we want to look at the interaction between lexical sophistication and syntactic complexity more closely. We have decided on the lexical sophistication measure because the lexical creativity measures (TTR or D) may not really distinguish between easy and difficult words (see Chapter 3).

Lexical sophistication, operationalized as *average word length* of content words (see Chapter 3 for more detail) is a very general measure of lexical complexity and/or frequency effects, as both less frequent words and more complex words with different affixes tend to be longer than frequent and morphologically simple words. For sentence complexity we have decided to use the *words to finite verb ratio*, which has shown to be an insightful general complexity measure for this advanced learner.

We have speculated earlier about the relationship between these two measures over time, but since no such longitudinal studies have been conducted for L2 learners, we have to base our hypotheses on what we know from L1 development. In L1 development several studies (Robinson & Mervis 1998; Bassano & van Geert 2007) have shown that lexical development is a precursor for syntactic development. Our learner, though, differs in two ways from L1 subjects: Our L2 learner already has a developed L1 system and she is an advanced L2 learner. On the other hand, almost all developmental measures we have looked at so far in this learner have shown quite a bit of development over the three years. We do not have a particular hypothesis at this point, but would like to discover whether there is a conditional or supportive relation between these two measures.

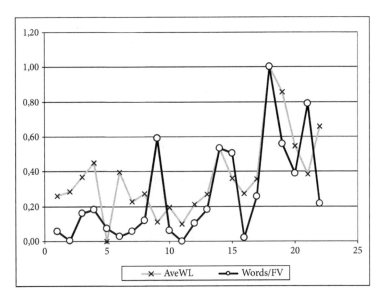

Figure 8. Normalized raw data of *average word length* and *words over finite verbs*

Figure 8 shows the development of lexical sophistication – *average word length* – and syntactic complexity – *words over finite verbs*. Visual inspection of these raw data already points at a clear correspondence between the two measures. However, we can also see that there is high variability in both variables and that these *local* fluctuations also seem to correspond. For instance, in Texts 14, 15 and 18, there are clear peaks in both *average word length* and the *words over finite verbs*. This might point at relatively local context effects (such as fatigue, topic difficulty, etc), and we thus want to see the more global interaction between these two variables. Therefore, we have smoothed the data again to compare the more global trends and relations between them.

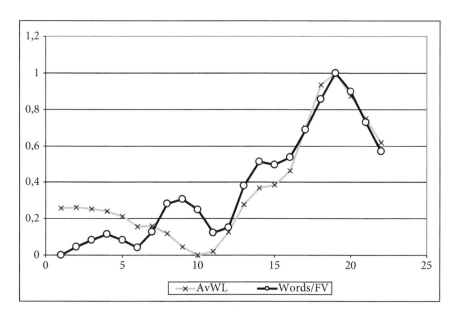

Figure 9. Smoothed and normalized trajectories of *average word length* and *words over finite verbs*

As can be seen in Figure 9, the shape of development of these two measures (*average word length* and *words to finite verb ratio*) is highly similar. The overall correlation coefficient is also positive and highly significant ($r = .876$, $p < 0.001$), confirming this correspondence. It is also interesting that the syntactic measure seems to increase *before* the lexical does (already in Text 8). To look at this interaction more closely, we created a graph with a moving window of correlations.

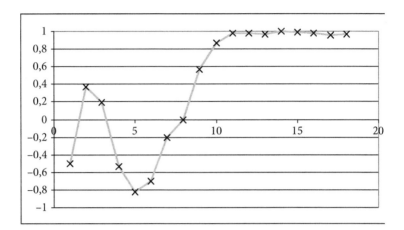

Figure 10. Moving correlation (window of 5 values) between *average word length* (avWL) and *words over finite verbs* (Words/FV)

Figure 10 shows indeed that the "support" between the two measures "drops" around this point in time. This might mean that during the first increase of the *words over finite verbs*, it is at the expense of lexical complexity, while later on they support each other's growth. However, we cannot be sure until we test this by modeling the data.

5. Conclusion

The function of this chapter was to show how different variables in a complex, developing system, called growers, may influence each other over time. In SLD, we do not expect a learner to develop all measures at the same rate. For example, a level of lexical sophistication may be needed before syntax can develop, or simple structures are learned before more complex structures. We have stressed, however, that our search for interacting variables should be based on some theoretical insights. On the other hand, our close examination of related measures such as lexical sophistication and syntactic complexity has given us some insight that might feed into theoretical issues.

The methods and techniques presented here were basically ways to make the various interactions more visible. In the previous chapter, we were able to test our findings concerning variability statistically by running Monte Carlos to see if the patterns found were below chance level or not. These statistical types of tests cannot be used to determine whether the interactions such as support or competition found between two variables are meaningful or not. To do so we have to simulate the data and see if we find similar patterns. That will be the topic of our next and final chapter.

Modeling development and change

Wander Lowie, Tal Caspi, Paul van Geert &
Henderien Steenbeek

1. Introduction

In the previous chapters, we have seen how variation in SLD development can be investigated and how this procedure can help reveal processes that underlie development. The purpose of Chapter 4 was to show how developmental patterns can be made more visible. It also showed how hypotheses based on a visual display and inspection of the data may be tested in single case studies. In Chapter 5, we saw how we may trace the development of different subsystems in a learner's language over time and how they may affect each other. Although these variability analyses can provide valuable information about the process of language development and the way in which the different variables in the data affect one another over time, they cannot tell us whether our theoretical assumptions have been met.

One way of testing our theoretical assumptions is by simulating the developmental process. In other words, after data collection, data description and data exploration, such as variability analyses, we can use modeling to test our theory. For instance, in the vocabulary acquisition case study reported in this chapter, we started off with hypotheses based on theoretical insights gained from the literature on the topic, then collected our data and then after applying variability analyses as explained in the previous chapters, we tested our theoretical model by simulating it.

Since there are many different types of models and different ways of applying them, we will first explain what the differences are between traditional deterministic models and dynamic stochastic models. Then, after discussing our basic model and the possible adaptations that can be made to it, we will show how we applied dynamic modeling to L2 vocabulary developmental data.

2. Types of models

Before explaining the differences between different types of models, we need to define the term "model". A *mathematical model* is defined as "a representation of the essential aspects of an existing system (or a system to be constructed) which presents knowledge of that system in usable form" (Eykhoff 1974). The actual model is therefore the set of functions that describe the relations between the different variables. Similar to the way in which an architect creates a scale model of a building to see what it will look like and to test the strength of certain constructions, we can create models at a more abstract level to help us understand phenomena in nature, including human development and language acquisition. As we will show in this chapter, a model can be expressed by means of an equation or the corresponding plot in a graph.

Models can be characterized according to their behavior. The types of models that are relevant to us can be divided into three dichotomies that partly overlap: static versus dynamic models, linear versus nonlinear models, and deterministic versus stochastic models.

2.1   Static models

Static models describe the state of a system as it is at a given moment without taking the time dimension into consideration. They are like snapshots of events. The main purpose of a static model is to provide the concepts and terms needed to describe actions; in other words, they can make clear what the essential aspects of the system are at one point of time. In addition, a static model can take time into consideration by plotting the development at different times additively. However, the components themselves do not interact and change over time. In contrast, a dynamic model plots the development at different times based on a recursive principle, which we will explain in detail below.

2.2   Linear versus non-linear models

A linear system is a system in which the whole is the sum of its parts, and a nonlinear system is one in which the sum is not the whole of its parts. Mitchell gives an illuminating example in her clear introduction to complexity. If you add two cups of flour and one cup of sugar, you will have three cups of a flour/sugar mix. However, if you have two cups of baking soda and add one cup of vinegar, you have an explosion (the interaction between vinegar and baking soda creates carbon dioxide). The difference between the two is that flour and sugar do not interact, but baking soda and vinegar do (Mitchell 2009: 23). In other words, in a nonlinear system the results are not just a sum of the parts. An SLD example would be as follows: Suppose a learner is very motivated to learn a new language. Then he takes a test and fails miserably, so his motivation goes down, which in turn affects the way he will study for the next test.

2.3   Deterministic models

Traditional models in SLD usually hypothesize a linear relationship between the components, and are deterministic. In a deterministic model, the assumption is that every action causes a fixed reaction, and every reaction causes the next reaction, so that it is possible to predict exactly where the system will be at any moment in time. For example, a group of L2 learners may be tested before and after a vocabulary instruction intervention. If the learners' vocabulary knowledge increases significantly more than that of a control group, then the improvement is assumed to have been caused by the instruction (a linear cause and effect result) and the implication is that if you do the experiment again, you are likely to have very similar results.

We will illustrate the deterministic model with a fictive example of vocabulary learning. Suppose an ideal L2 learner with perfect memory has decided to learn 10 new L2 words per week for 10 weeks in a row, the trajectory of her development will then look as illustrated in Figure 1.

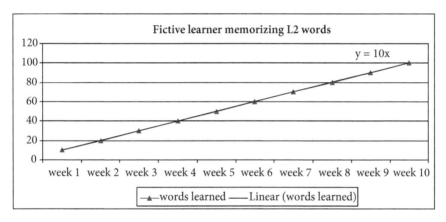

Figure 1. Hypothetical example of a L2 learner's vocabulary development

Figure 1 is the simplest static and deterministic model to express development over time. Basically it shows the relation between two variables, time (on the X axis) and total number of words learned (on the Y axis). Vocabulary size is seen as a direct and fixed influence of time, and as any spreadsheet program can calculate for you, the mathematical equation is y = 10x. In other words, the linear development is captured by the fixed relationship between two variables, in which one changes as a function of the other: $y = f(x)$.

In real life learners may have less time in a particular week, or some words may be more difficult to remember, or the motivation to learn may vary. So let's suppose our fictive L2 learner is like a typical learner and for some reason or other is able to learn fewer words at the beginning, after week 4 is able to learn more (because once you know a few words, it may be easier to remember new ones) and around week 8, once she knows quite a few, the learner finds it difficult to memorize new ones because she has had less time to practice them all (See Figure 2.).

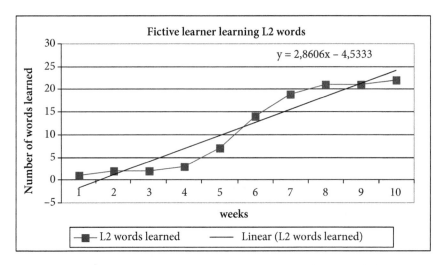

Figure 2. Hypothetical example of an L2 learner's vocabulary development. The linear trend line and formula have been given in an Excel spreadsheet

The trajectory of actual vocabulary development in Figure 2 is not a straight line, but the trend line is. The trend line has averaged out all the fluctuations, and vocabulary development is still expressed in two terms, x and y, with x being time and y being the current value of the number of words at a given point on x (x_n). The model also specifies the relationship between x and y as fixed: if we know what x is, we can determine the value of y exactly. In this case, as the spreadsheet shows us, the equation to determine the value of y is more complex than in Figure 1.

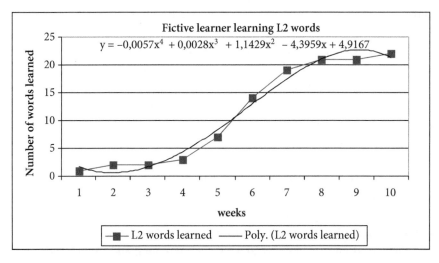

Figure 3. Hypothetical example of an L2 learner's vocabulary development. The trend line here is a polynomial to the 4th degree

In Figure 3 we see the same fictive learner again, but now the trend line (the model) follows the real learning curve better because it is a polynomial to the 4th order (cf. Chapter 4 for details on polynomials). Even though this model shows a closer approximation of the actual learning curve, it is still deterministic because it specifies the relationship between x and y as fixed: if we know what x is, we can determine the value of y exactly. In this case, the formula to determine the value of y is more complex than in Figure 2, but y is still defined only in relation to x.

The curves found in Figure 3 are more likely to resemble the real data in vocabulary learning than the straight line in Figure 1 because in real life our fictive L2 learner, however motivated, would not be learning exactly 10 words a week in isolation. As we saw in the previous chapters, there will always be some degree of random variation in her behavior. Moreover, she may read a lot in the L2, take grammar classes, and have interactions with her peers or native speakers, or perhaps she has acquired a new interest in fixed expressions, which comes at the expense of remembering isolated words. Because the outcome of such a process can never be fully determined, her language development is likely to behave in a less predictable or *stochastic* manner.

2.4   Dynamic, non-linear and stochastic models

The models in Figures 2–3 are static, linear and deterministic as they are based on an additive formula. The models take the same starting position (e.g. the number of words known in week 0) for each subsequent calculation.

A model is dynamic when it is recursive. A model is recursive when it describes a process in which the same components are described at subsequent moments in time. For example, once our fictive learner knows 10 words in week 1, the starting point for week 2 is not 0 words, but 10, and the starting position in week 3 is not 0, but 20 words, and so on. For this learner, the outcome might be quite similar if it is calculated with an additive or a recursive formula because our ideal learner does not forget any words and the number of words learned is fixed. However, if the number of words memorized each week were different, the two models would give different results.

The simplest way of including recursiveness can be seen in Equation 1:

$$\text{Equation 1: } y_{t+1} = f(y_t)$$

This general dynamic model entails that the next time-step of a value y, written down as y_{t+1} varies as a function (f) of the previous one (y_t). By including related terms (t and $t+1$) on the left hand side and the right hand side of the formula, the model becomes recursive (or iterative). Translating this equation to a vocabulary example, we could say that the number of words our learner knows at this moment is partially dependent on how many words she knew the moment before. Even though Equation 1 is dynamic, it is still linear. To become nonlinear, a random factor needs to be incorporated. When we include a random factor, the model becomes stochastic. Randomness can be incorporated by adding a growth rate that may fluctuate over time. For example, for different reasons, a person's vocabulary can grow a bit faster in week 1 than in week 2 and then again a bit slower in week 3.

Probably the best known example of a *dynamic, nonlinear and stochastic* model is that of the logistic map, which is generated by the *logistic equation*. This equation was discovered by Pierre François Verhulst in 1838, and was originally used as a demographic description to account for population development. In 1976, Robert May discovered that iterating this equation with initial values that changed continuously and gradually produces discrete (sudden) changes, which reproduce the seemingly-chaotic behaviour of dynamic systems. The logistic equation is given in Equation 2:

$$\text{Equation 2: } x_{t+1} = r * x_t(1-x_t)$$

In Equation 2, the x in x_t is a number between 0 and 1 and x_t represents the population size at time t. So 0 is the minimum population and 1 the maximum population (or any other phenomenon that can be quantified and changes over time). r represents the growth rate of x, which is the difference between the number of births and deaths in a particular time frame. The left term (x_{t+1}) of the equation predicts the population size in the following year, and the following, and the following, and so on. The recursiveness of the formula expresses iterative change. The "iteration" is that x_{t+1} is (partially) based on x_t. Each iteration changes as a function of the previous iteration.

The value of r determines the behaviour of the logistic map. When r is between 0 and 1, x will eventually diminish (the population will become extinct). When r is between 1 and 2, the value of x stabilizes. But the most interesting development occurs when r is between 3 and 4 because then the population development happens to start behaving chaotically by constant fluctuations (*oscillation*). This behaviour is demonstrated in the bifurcation diagram in Figure 4.

In Figure 4, the x-axis denotes the growth rate r and the y-axis denotes the range of values produced for x in the equation as r increases gradually. Until the growth rate reaches 3, we see almost linear growth, but at 3 there is a bifurcation: x takes on one of two possible discrete values. If the growth rate increases even more, the bifurcation again diverges and rediverges and continues to split until a wide range of potential x values is covered by chaotic oscillations.

Bifurcation is difficult to imagine for an individual L2 learner, but in language development, we often see that a seemingly discrete and sudden jump is in fact the result of ongoing gradual change in the growth rate, even though it does not appear

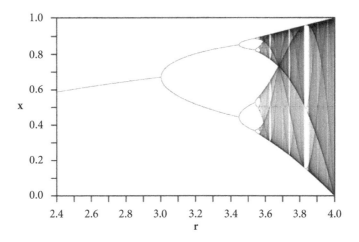

Figure 4. Bifurcation diagram for the logistic map[1]

that way to the undiscerning eye; also, we can see instability and seemingly random fluctuation, which again may simply be a part of the growth process.

The logistic map is a frequently used example of dynamic development, but there are many other models that show dynamic and stochastic behavior. The key feature of all those models is their recursiveness and randomized growth rate. To describe the real-life unpredictable development of dynamic systems most accurately, we will have to use models that are dynamic, stochastic and nonlinear, which we will call *dynamic models* for short.

2.5   Specifications of dynamic models

The basic dynamic model in Equation 2 can be specified by adding a wide range of additional terms. The more terms added, the more complex and specific the model becomes. Terms that can be included in dynamic models are expressions of the initial state, the growth rate, the maximum value that can be attained, and all the internal and external factors that affect the system. Each of these requires a brief explanation before we can continue.

---

1.   This copy was found at en.wikipedia.org. This picture and similar ones are widely available on the Internet. Also numerous Java applications are available to create simulations of the logistic map.

The initial state of a model can have important consequences for its development. The most famous example of the effect of the initial state has been referred to as the "butterfly effect", in which the flap of the wings of a butterfly in Brazil could hypothetically cause a tornado in Texas (Lorenz 1963). The sensitivity to initial conditions varies strongly from model to model, but can indeed be dramatic. For L2 learners the initial state may be related to age (previous experience with language), L1 (to what extent it is similar or different to the L2), other languages known, language aptitude, and so on.

The growth rate is a crucial term in all growth models. We have seen the relevance of the growth rate in our example of the logistic map. It is important to realize that the growth rate could be both positive and negative, as in dynamic terms decrease is also a type of growth. The growth rate is a baseline, just as the 10 words per week in the vocabulary example; it changes in accordance with the resources and carrying capacity and development itself, and of course interactions with other developing aspects of the language of the individual.

The maximum value that a dynamic system can attain in its most optimal conditions is commonly referred to as its *carrying capacity*. In terms of population growth, this means that given the availability of a certain amount of food, water, and other essential resources, the population eventually maintains a particular size. This same principle can be applied to vocabulary development. The carrying capacity would then be the maximum number of words that can be known under ideal circumstances by a particular learner, which is dependent on the sum of underlying factors, such as attention and working memory capacity and other factors, such as the learner's native language background in the case of L2 learners.

All factors that may affect the system are termed *resources*. A distinction is sometimes made between internal and external resources. An example of an internal resource in language development is motivation. An example of an external resource is a factor like instructional input. Clearly, all these factors may affect one another differently over time, a fact which will have to be incorporated in the model to be selected.

2.6   Summary types of models

Before we start describing how we can model vocabulary growth in dynamic systems, let us summarize the different types of models we have discussed in this chapter. A static model describes the components of a system at one point in time. Linear development can be captured by the fixed relationship between two variables, in which one changes as a function of the other: $y = f(x)$. We can say that linear development of a system is the same as the development of the sum of all its components. When the eventual development of a system can be predicted, this development is called deterministic. Development is considered dynamic if the model contains a recursive component. In that case, the development of a factor is described as the factor itself at different moments in time: $y_{t+1} = f(y_t)$. When one of the components is a random factor, the eventual outcome cannot be predicted, and we speak of stochastic development. The basic dynamic, nonlinear, stochastic model, which we have called *dynamic model* for short, can be specified with many different terms such as the limit to how much a person is capable of learning in ideal circumstances and the rate at which this happens (*carrying capacity*), the opportunity to encounter new words (*external resources*), the mental ability to remember words (*internal resources*), and the difficulty of encountering new words when you already know quite a few (*dampening factors*), a factor that van Geert has sometimes included in his models.

Different types of models can be combined. Although linear models are by nature deterministic, dynamic models can be deterministic or stochastic and linear or nonlinear. In the next section we will discuss the specific dynamic model we have used for our data.

3.   Our basic dynamic growth model

Equation 1 is a basic equation that expresses the dynamic nature of development. Just as we saw with regard to the population, this equation specifies growth as a joint product of a component's current growth level (the iterative principle), and the overall available resources (without specifying the resource types). The terms in this equation can be specified and adapted for particular situations. In this chapter, we will take Paul van Geert's models on L1 acquisition as our starting point. Van Geert (1991) modeled data of early L1 vocabulary development collected by Dromi (1986) on the basis of the following logistic equation:

$$\text{Equation 3: } L_{t+\Delta t} = L_t + L_t {}^*r_{\Delta t} {}^*(1 - L_t/K_t)$$

Equation 3 describes the current value of a learner's Lexicon ($L_{t+\Delta t}$), which is based on the value at the preceding point in time L_t. The Δ symbol is a general symbol that stands for difference or change. Hence, $t + \Delta_t$ means the current time t plus some amount of time added. (Instead of using Δ_t you can also use the number 1, to specify any arbitrary time addition.) As in Equation 2, the growth rate r is the proportional increase in one unit of time. Unlike Equations 1 or 2, the model explicitly addresses the resources available to the system through the K parameter. K signifies the carrying capacity – the maximal obtainable value given the limitations on the resources available for growth. In other words, the different resources are not configured separately in this model, but are treated as a general construct incorporated in K. Since the availability of resources is dynamic, the time-dependent index is added to K in the equation as K_t. The final term in the equation, $(1-L_t/K_t)$, is very similar to Equation 1 and shows that this is indeed a logistic equation and implies that L_t/K_t will be a value between 0 and 1. The bigger the carrying capacity (K), the higher $(1-L_t/K_t)$ becomes and so the bigger the resulting lexicon can maximally become.

Figure 5 compares the real data and the model, which is the result of a computer simulation of *n* iterations based on Equation 3. It is clear that while the model is somewhat similar to the actual data, its fit is not optimal. To improve the fit, additional factors would need to be included in the model.

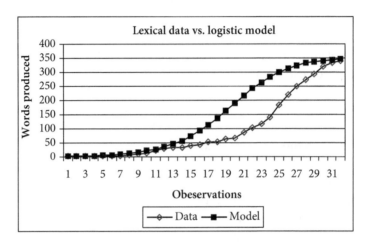

Figure 5. Lexical data (Dromi 1986 in van Geert 1991) vs. logistic model curve. Based on van Geert (1994b)

For example, to successfully simulate real-life data, van Geert (1993) points out that it is often necessary to add a feedback delay as a damping factor on the growth rate *r*, which determines the steepness of the S-shaped curve. We will not replicate this adjusted equation here, but it is important to realize that any model can be fine-tuned to accommodate additional factors that affect the system.

4.   Connected growers

In the previous section we showed a basic growth model for one variable, in this case the early lexicon. However, in language development different variables may affect each other over time, for example the lexicon and syntax. In dynamic terms, each developing variable is called a *grower*. Two growers can be referred to as *coupled* or, more generally, as *connected growers*.

As we pointed out in Chapter 5, growers may affect each other both positively (support) or negatively (competition), and this relationship may change over time. To model the interaction of different variables over time, we will first have to define a set of connected growers, such as the lexicon (operationalized as the number of words known) and syntax (operationalized as mean length of utterance). To describe their growth in relation to each other, we can couple their equations as in Equation 4.

Equation 4:
$$A_{t+1} = A_t * \left[1 + r_A - \frac{r_A * A_t}{K_A} - c_A * (B_t - B_{t-1}) + s_A * B_t \right]$$
$$B_{t+1} = B_t * \left[1 + r_B - \frac{r_B * B_t}{K_B} - c_B * (A_t - A_{t-1}) + s_B * B_t \right]$$

Equation 4 illustrates one option for modeling a simple system consisting of two connected growers, A and B, using coupled equations. The parameters in the equation are K = carrying capacity, which is specified separately for A or B; n = time; r = growth rate; c = (level of) competition; s = (level of) support. Note that in each equation, the first half is basically the logistic growth equation we saw earlier, but the second half specifies the interaction with the other grower. The interaction between the growers is expressed in the amount of competition (C) the grower experiences from the other grower (at the previous moment in time, t−1) and the support (S) the grower will invoke on the other grower. In this example, the equations are identical. Therefore, if their parameters have the same values, they will yield simultaneous and identical growth curves. However, any differences in any of the parameters will yield different patterns for each grower. The connection of two growers, expressed in coupled equations, will create more powerful models compared to single grower models. In fact, an infinite number of growers can be coupled to create network simulations. In our own simulation, we limited ourselves to 4 growers.

One specification of this coupled growth model that is particularly well suited to modeling language development is the *precursor* model. In a precursor interaction, one grower's development is prerequisite for that of another. For example, a child needs to know a certain number of words before her utterances can become longer as they turn into short sentences. The first grower (in this case lexicon) is therefore defined as a *precursor*, and the other (in our case the mean utterance length) as a *dependent*. The precursor needs to reach a threshold value before it can enable the development of the dependent. This can be added to the equation of the dependent as an additional parameter P, which has a binary (on/off) value. $P = 0$ until the precursor reaches its threshold value; $P = 1$ from then onwards, so the dependent only starts to grow after the precursor has reached this threshold value.

Various versions of the precursor model can be configured, with one-way or bi-directional support, or increasing or decreasing competition. A typical precursor interaction is graphically represented in Figure 6.

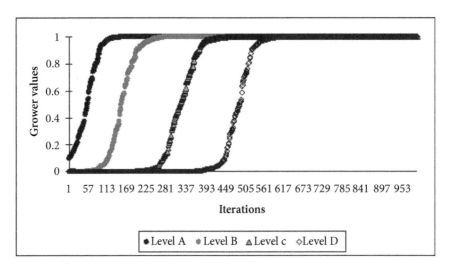

Figure 6. Four growers in a precursor interaction

The model in Figure 6 is idealized, but it illustrates well the interdependency of variables in a dynamic system. In this example, all the parameters in the equations of connected growers are the same (equal growth rates and equal carrying capacity) but the threshold values for each grower are different.

In a more complex and realistic example, van Geert (1993) addresses a hypothetical study of the emergence of cognitive rules at Levels A, B, and C, which have a developmental hierarchy ranking. His model assumes that these rules will compete with each other. In other words, the more rule B is used, the less rule A, and the more rule C, the less rule B and so on.

Figure 7 depicts such a model of a precursor interaction with increasing competition between four growers, Levels A, B, C and D. Beginning at A, each grower is a precursor to a dependent, which is in turn a precursor to its successor. The competition increases in accordance with the growth of each grower. The model produces an identical result: Within 1,000 iterations, Level A will decline to a minimum, Level B will decline as well but not as much, and Levels C and D will rise in turn to their carrying capacity (set as 1 in this model).

The simulations show that if the competition between the strategies is strong, there is a stepwise growth pattern (see Levels C and D). However, if the competition between the strategies is weaker, the growth patterns are not smooth (see Levels A and B). Van Geert concludes that growth patterns involving weak competition.

> ...will contain performance regressions (or U-shaped growth, if one prefers the alternative term) as well as normal stepwise growth characteristic of stage-like development, dependent on the values of the parameters involved. If a

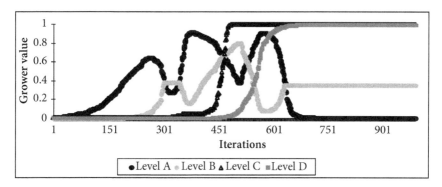

Figure 7. A precursor model of four connected growers with increasing competition

> performance dip occurs (which is in so many cases) it always occurs just before
> a stronger strategy overgrows a weaker one. In this case the dip is typically
> pretransitory.   (van Geert 1993: 305)

Modeling studies that have applied the DST approach to L1 and L2 development have
suggested that language development can best be described by a prototypical dynamic
precursor model. For instance, a study by van Geert (1991) investigating the development of syntax and vocabulary in L1 acquisition showed that the lexicon can be seen as
a precursor because syntactic development can only start once a minimal vocabulary
size has been attained. Over time, the interaction between lexicon and syntax shifts to
support. In other words, after a certain amount of lexical items have been acquired,
the lexicon enables the comprehension and production of grammar. By configuring a
mathematical model of lexicon and syntax in a precursor interaction, Robinson and
Mervis succeeded in replicating the growth curves of indexes denoting those categories (1998). In Chapter 5 and in Verspoor, Lowie and van Dijk (2008), the detailed
variability analyses clearly hint at dependency relations between the lexical and syntactic components, suggesting precursor interactions. To test this assumption, the data
can be simulated.

In sum, by using models of connected growers, we can test whether the assumptions we have made about different interactions in the actual data are reasonable. We
can test the effect of the growth of one variable on the growth of another variable
(components of the system may be each other's *precursors*), we can test the effect of the
initial value of the different components of the system, and we can test external and
internal resources of the system. In other words, we can test whether all our underlying assumptions based on the actual data hold when we simulate the data.

In fact, we could develop a network system of numerous coupled growers and
simulate the interaction of as many meaningful components as we wish in a dynamic
network simulation, but that is beyond the scope of our chapter. In the next sections

we will demonstrate how four connected growers can be used to model vocabulary growth in an L2 learner of English.

Details on data fitting and modelling can be found in *How to* Sections 5.1 and 5.2 (Chapter 8) and in the related practice materials on our web site SLD_Methods (DOI:10.1075/lllt.29.website). We have chosen to use different data than presented in the chapter in order to simplify the instructions.

5. Modeling vocabulary growth

The data we will use are taken from a case study on academic English vocabulary development. The participant in the case study is a 24 year-old female, a native speaker of Portuguese who started a year-long academic degree program taught entirely in English. This was her first immersion period in a language other than her native language. Data about her vocabulary development were gathered during a period of 36 weeks.

From the literature, we know that vocabulary knowledge can range from reception (recognizing words) to free production (using words correctly and appropriately). There are various intermediary degrees across the receptive-productive range of knowledge levels (Melka 1997). Studies of before- and aftertreatment effects on L2 learner populations have shown that there are varied rates of development for these different lexical knowledge levels. For example, these studies have noted that little transfer takes place from lower and more-receptive knowledge levels into free production, and only limited growth occurs in controlled production – while recall and recognition grow significantly over time (Laufer 1998; Laufer & Paribakht 1998; Schmitt & Meara 1997). Also, the influence of external or environmental factors such as word frequency, overall learner proficiency, and learning context varies between receptive and productive knowledge (Schmitt & Meara 1997; Laufer 1998; Laufer & Paribakht 1998). The discrepancy between productive and receptive vocabulary has commonly been referred to as the *receptive-productive gap*.

Because we were dealing with an advanced learner in an academic environment, this study focuses on the development of academic vocabulary, as defined by the University Word List (Xue & Nation 1984) and Academic Word List (Coxhead 2000). Based on the literature, four levels of vocabulary knowledge ranging from more-receptive to more-productive have been specified: (A) recognition, (B) recall, (C) controlled production, and (D) free production (Laufer, Elder, Hill & Congdon 2004; Laufer & Goldstein 2004; Laufer & Nation 1995, 1999). As in van Geert's hypothetical study (see Figure 7), these levels were assumed to be hierarchical; in other words, one first needs to be able to recognize and recall words before they can be produced in a controlled or free situation. It is important to mention that "active" in this case should not be confused with "productive" and simply refers to the activation of the word form, rather than its meaning.

The levels of recognition, recall and controlled production of academic vocabulary knowledge were tested by using the Longitudinal Academic Vocabulary Test (LAVT) (Caspi & Lowie 2010). *Recognition*, the lowest knowledge level, was operationalized as the ability to recognize the correct form of a word from a multiple choice of four alternatives, when being presented with its definition and initial letter as cues. *Recall*, the second knowledge level, was operationalized as the ability to recall a word when only its initial and definition are given as cues. *Controlled production*, the third knowledge level, was operationalized as the ability to produce the word in a controlled context of a gap fill or "cloze" exercise with its initial given as cue. Data for the fourth knowledge level, *free production*, were gathered by giving essay assignments from which free production was calculated as a score. This score was based on the ratio of correct academic word families to total academic word tokens, divided by the total number of correct content words multiplied by the general family/token ratio.

5.1   Results

After having collected the data for 36 weeks, we conducted various variability analyses on the data (as described in Chapters 4 and 5) to find out whether there are changing interactions between the four knowledge types. The analyses, which are not presented here, revealed alternating growth patterns that suggested complex interactions between the lower (more receptive) and higher (more productive) levels in the hierarchy. Before modeling the data, we first inspected the developmental patterns in the actual data. Figure 8 contains the scores of the four levels plotted along the 36-week study period, as well as the linear growth trends for each knowledge level.

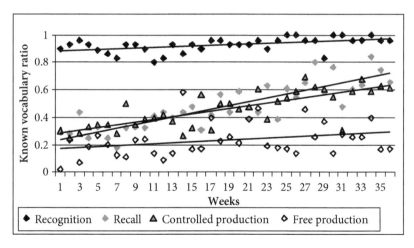

Figure 8. Development of academic English vocabulary knowledge levels over 36 weeks' immersion in the case study data

If we look at the trend lines, we can see that recognition, recall and controlled production all increased. A correlation analysis on the data shows strong and significant positive correlations (up to around 0.8) between all these three lower vocabulary knowledge levels and time, indicating significant growth during the immersion period. However, free production, the fourth and highest level, was the exception. Although free production also increased and showed a significant correlation with time, this correlation is weak. In addition, the correlations between the three lower knowledge levels are significant, but not between any of these knowledge levels and free production.[2]

Table 1. Correlations between different levels of vocabulary development and time (weeks)

Correlation	Spearman's rho value
Recognition-Weeks	.628 (p < 0.01)
Recall-Weeks	.849 (p < 0.01)
Controlled production-Weeks	.769 (p < 0.01)
Free production-Weeks	.347 (p < 0.05)
Recognition-Recall	.599 (p < 0.01)
Recall-Controlled production	.658 (p < 0.01)
Controlled-Free production	Not significant
Recognition-Controlled production	.439 (p < 0.05)
Recognition-Free production	Not significant
Recall-Free production	Not significant

5.2   Modeling the data

Based on previous research findings about receptive and productive vocabulary knowledge, our inspection of the raw data and variability analyses, we formulated the following three expectations.

1.   Although all knowledge levels would increase during the study, their growth rate would not be parallel. In other words, the receptive-productive gap would continue to manifest, but its size would fluctuate over time.
2.   With regard to the nature of the interactions between these knowledge levels, we expected to find precursor interactions between the lower, more-receptive levels of the continuum and the higher, more-productive levels. This means that a certain amount of receptive vocabulary would be a prerequisite for production, and that the interactions between lower and more-established receptive knowledge

---

2.   Since individual growth data are unlikely to be normally distributed, we calculated Spearman's *rho* coefficient, which is a nonparametric measure of correlation.

levels and higher, less-established productive levels would reflect simultaneous support and competition.

3. Finally, we expected that a model configuring these interactions would achieve a good fit with the data. In other words, we postulated that the *precursor* model could account for vocabulary development across the continuum of receptive-to-productive knowledge levels.

To test our assumptions we used a model of precursor interaction that van Geert (2003) developed in Excel-VBA code. It utilizes the MS Excel spreadsheet program to iterate combinations of the equations similar to those presented in this chapter. The program, which is provided in practice materials 5.2 on our web site SLD_Methods (DOI:10.1075/ lllt.29.website:10.1075/lllt.29.website), enables the user to configure various versions of the precursor model. Here we will discuss which values we entered and how to interpret the results.[3]

We specified four growers, active recognition, active recall, controlled production, and free production, which correspond with the four knowledge levels in the data. We first defined the parameters of initial growth rate, initial value, developmental delay, level of environmental support, and amount of random variation for each grower. In the program, the values are entered with nominal values (such as *high, moderate, low, strong,* or *weak*), but to be able to do the configurations, these nominal values are given numerical values, which range between 0–1 (for example, 0.8 as a high and 0.6 as a moderate value). The worksheets in the model show the numerical values we assigned to our parameters. On the left hand side are the number of growers, their names and the control parameters. See Table 2.

Table 2. Growers and the numerical values given to control parameters in the Excel worksheet

4	Rate	Initial	Delay	Support	Variation
Active recognition	0.04	0.85	10	0.9	0.06
Active recall	0.06	0.35	20	0.7	0.09
Controlled production	0	0.35	20	0.7	0.09
Free production	0.5	0.15	70	0.2	0.5

We defined the interactions between the growers in the following manner:

1. A medium value of recognition is a conditional precursor for recall,
2. A medium value of recall is conditional for controlled production,

---

3. In our how to sections and practice materials we have given examples with fewer variables.

3. A high value of controlled production is conditional for free production.
4. Once the precursor value threshold is crossed,
    a. recognition moderately supports recall,
    b. recall weakly supports controlled production,
    c. controlled production weakly supports free production,
    d. free production, in turn, competes weakly with controlled production.

All of these interactions are determined *by change*, meaning that they are relative to the change in the values of the growers that generate them. To the right of the information given in Table 2, the worksheet shows the control (relational) parameters within the hierarchy we have specified. Because we have not specified every possible combination of interactions, some cells are 0. See Table 3.

Table 3. Relational parameters and numerical values in Excel worksheet

by level	to Active recognition	to Active recall	to Controlled production	to Free production
from Active recognition	0			
from Active recall		0		
from Controlled production			0	
from Free production				0
by change	to Active recognition	to Active recall	to Controlled production	to Free production
from Active recognition	0	1	0	
from Active recall		0	1	
from Controlled production		−0.5	0	0.5
from Free production			−1	0
Precursor	to Active recognition	to Active recall	to Controlled production	to Free production
from Active recognition	0	0.5		
from Active recall		0	0.5	0.8
from Controlled production			0	0.8
from Free production				0

Once we have specified all our control parameters and change parameters, we can start simulating our data. By clicking on the "simulation" tab in the menu of any of the worksheets in the workbook (see Figure 9), and choosing "calculate model", we can obtain the outcome of 300 iterations of the equations we configured and their graphic representation.

Figure 10 shows the result of our simulation after 300 iterations. Because random factors were incorporated, each simulation shows slightly different results. That is why there are so many dots around each trend line.

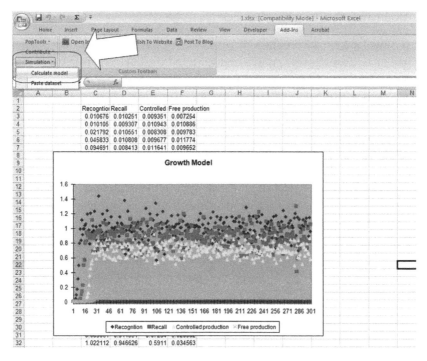

Figure 9. Screen print of simulation data

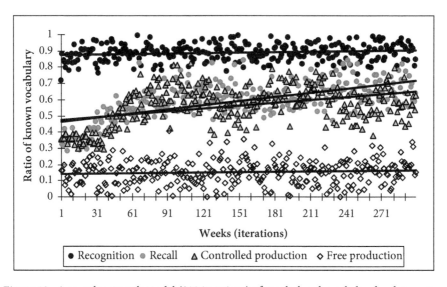

Figure 10. A complex growth model (300 iterations) of vocabulary knowledge development

5.3   Evaluating the theoretical model

Now it is time to evaluate our theoretical model. To do so, we evaluate the simulation outcome on two aspects: the growth over time and the interactions between knowledge levels. If our model is adequate then it should be able to replicate both of these data dimensions. In other words, validating the model does not rely only on the correlation between the model and the data, but also on comparing the internal interactions between the model's levels to those found between the data levels.

A comparison between Figure 10 (the model) and Figure 8 (the actual data) shows that they are quite similar: first in the range of outcomes obtained and second in the linear regressions of the model and the data, seen in the trend lines. To confirm this visual impression, we correlated the model values with the data, treating the difference between the number of observations in the data and the number of iterations in the model as missing values, thus effectively correlating only the first 36 model iterations with the data. We found similarities between the model and the data, as manifested in the correlations of the level in each with the number of weeks (or iterations in the case of the model).

Table 4. The two left columns: nonparametric correlations (Spearman's rho values) between knowledge levels and time and within the knowledge continuum levels in the data and in the model. The two right-hand columns show the correlations between the levels of the model and those of the data ($* = p < 0.05$; $** = p < 0.01$)

CORRELATION	MODEL	DATA	DATA-MODEL	MODEL-DATA
Free production-weeks	.352*	.374*	–	–
Controlled production-weeks	−.177	.769**	–	–
Recall-weeks	.432**	.849**	–	–
Recognition-Weeks	.656**	.628**	–	–
Free -Controlled production	.025	.188	−.128	.324 (p = 0.54)
Controlled production-recall	−.160	.658**	.485**	−.111
Recall-Recognition	.334*	.599**	.249	.283
Free production-recall	.261	.233	.258	.296
Free production-recognition	.170	.210	.279	.119
Controlled production-recognition	-.110	.439**	.196	−.029
Free production-free production			.299 (p = 0.77)	–
Controlled production-controlled production			−.030	–
Recall-recall			.351*	–
Recognition-recognition			.330*	–

The "data-model" column in Table 4 refers to correlating the first knowledge level in the pair, derived from the data, with the second, derived from the model. The "model-data" column refers to the same procedure, in which the first variable was derived from the model and the second from the data. While general similarities between the model and the data are shown in similar growth patterns, linear trends, and correlations, not all aspects of the data are replicated by the model. For example, the correlation between controlled production in the model and in the data is not significant, and neither is the controlled production-time correlation in the model, as it is in the actual data. However, considering that we have also configured random variation in our model, we can still regard the outcome of our simulation as capturing the basic premises of our developmental data.

We could attempt to find the optimal values that would enable us to still maintain the configuration that tests our expectations of hierarchal precursor interactions between receptive and productive vocabulary knowledge level. Such a step, however, requires procedures that are beyond the scope of this chapter.

5.4   Discussion

Although it is quite likely that fine-tuning the numerical values in the model would have yielded a better fit to the data, the model still verifies our hypothesis regarding development along the vocabulary knowledge continuum. In other words, the disparate development between receptive and productive knowledge reported in the literature and also found in our case study is successfully replicated by a simulation that involves a hierarchy of precursors and dependents. In this simulation, each developing precursor must first reach a threshold value, after which it supports the development of its dependent component.

To sum up, using a model based on precursor interactions between receptive and productive vocabulary knowledge levels has allowed us to simulate the growth patterns in the data, although not all of its correlational patterns. The model confirms our findings and the reports of nonlinear growth of vocabulary knowledge levels, manifested specifically in a robust gap between reception and production (cf. Melka 1997). This model can be used to test similar hypotheses or investigate the potential influences of changes in variables such as amount of input (background support) or longer delay in onset of specific growers.

At this point, the statistically inclined reader might ask why this study uses such an overly complicated model to explain such simple growth curves, namely four very simple linear curves. The reason is that the goal of the model is not to describe but to test theoretical assumptions. In the behavioral sciences, the usual approach is to find the simplest statistical description. In our vocabulary case, the simplest possible model would be a model of four unconnected linear regression models with time as the independent variable. However, such a model aims at providing the simplest possible statistical description of the data, not at referring to an underlying theory of change.

Dynamic models, on the other hand, are not meant to be the simplest possible statistical descriptions of data. They are intended to be mathematical models of theories of growth or change. The theory underlying the current dynamic model postulated conditional, changing and complex interactions between the variables and also defended the position that growth of a variable takes the form of an iterative process, which is also resource-dependent. The model that we have presented here is a formalization of these conceptual decisions, and thus should be evaluated, first with regard to how successful it is in instantiating the underlying conceptual model, and second with regard to its achievement in generating an outcome that corresponds with the empirical observations.

6.   Conclusion

Designing a model relies heavily on theory and empirical evidence. One cannot model any phenomenon without relying on theory or research, or preferably both, in defining the terms involved and setting their values and the directionality and strength of their interactions. Since the field of linguistics is rife with often conflicting theories, using a model can also help us determine which theory is preferable and which is most likely to benefit from revision.

This chapter has illustrated the rich potential of the dynamic approach, in our case of the testing of theoretical findings in studies which identified a continuum of receptive-productive knowledge levels and claiming a nonlinear transfer between these levels (Laufer et al. 2004; Laufer & Goldstein 2004; Laufer & Nation 1995, 1999). We have seen that a dynamic model based on coupled nonlinear or logistic equations can replicate patterns found in empirical data, and confirm or dispute theory explaining these findings.

The model in this chapter illustrates the possibilities that dynamic modeling offers us in terms of hypothesis testing. However, by means of simulations we can also speculate on the outcome of the model in different learners at different stages, with different sizes of vocabulary at a given knowledge level, or on the impact of increased input (in the general form of "support") on overall vocabulary growth.

Adapting and adjusting such models to specific data requires identifying the internal hierarchies in the data (if they exist), and the interactions between the levels or components that comprise these hierarchies. Since the notion of dynamic growth and interaction is not unique to L2 acquisition, or indeed to any one area of research, we are able to generalize models of development (for example of populations) and use them to corroborate a specific linguistic theory.

Although the modeling in this chapter has focused on unraveling theoretical issues, other applications such as teaching are certainly worth considering. As van Geert and Steenbeek (2005) argue:

> By combining dynamic model building with empirical studies, insight can be obtained in the dynamics of problematic learning and teaching trajectories. These insights can hopefully be transformed into functional rules-of thumb that may help teachers to optimally support learning in this particular group of pupils, through scaffolding that reckons with the particular dynamics of the learning process in question (127).

We hope that you will adopt and explore the possibilities that DST in general and the additional tool of dynamic modeling has opened for applied linguistics. The *How to* section and examples on the web site should give you the tools to try out some simple modeling yourself.

Epilogue

Kees de Bot

The main aim of this book is to provide the interested researcher or student in applied linguistics (AL) with ways to do research from a dynamic perspective. In the first chapter, some of the basics of this approach have been presented; in the other chapters, various techniques and approaches have been discussed and laid out, hopefully allowing other researchers to start their own research. In this final chapter, we want to bring the different lines together again.

1.   What's new?

One question we hope to have answered in this book is what makes research from a dynamic perspective different from more traditional research. This question can be answered at two levels. The first level concerns the basic assumptions behind the traditional and the dynamic approach. The second level refers to the methodology and paradigms used.

At the first level, what makes the dynamic approach different is the focus on change and development. Of course, a lot of research in AL has been focused on language acquisition, which does imply change, but the theorizing behind it has been based on fixed and stable units as reflected in terms such as "end state", "ultimate attainment", "interlanguage" and even "lexical storage" and static models. In such a view, language use is the processing of fixed and stable units such as "phonemes", "words" and "syntactic rules". The dynamic view differs fundamentally: All components and subsystems that play a role in language use are constantly changing and interacting with each other over time because of use. Language use is language development, and therefore measuring the state of the language system at a given moment in time is only meaningful when we realize that such a state is no longer the way it was milliseconds after our measurement. Of course, such thinking can easily lead to nihilism: What is the point of studying a system when it evades us the moment we tap into it? It could be argued, though, that the Heisenberg principle applies here. The language system cannot be studied independently of the way it is studied: We see the state of the language system through the lens of the way we study it. We fixate a system in time that by definition is in flux. The state we observe is not "the" state, but one of many possible states.

At the second level, the level of methodology and paradigms, the approach we use to study language follows from the assumptions mentioned. If the focus is on change, we should use methods that allow us to study exactly that. There are basically two levels at which we can study language development: language as a system of communication in a community over time (historical linguistics), and language as it develops in individuals (first or second language development). In this book the focus has been on the latter, though we assume that the basic principles of development are largely the same at the diachronic level and the individual developmental level; they are just at different timescales.

For the study of language development, we can study change over time by means of analyzing longitudinal data and by creating or simulating time through modeling. Longitudinal is used in the broadest possible sense; it implies all timescales from years (lifespan development) to milliseconds (in motor programs in speech articulation) and everything in between. In the chapters in this book, we focused on timescales of weeks and months, but we did so while acknowledging that data at that timescale interact with data at other timescales, like the online assembling of words and written text.

This leads us to another difference we want to discuss here: the issue of explanation of causality. In a dynamic way of thinking, the distinction between description and explanation more or less evaporates. A full discussion of the problems and issues in causality and explanation is well beyond the scope of this book, but it may be useful to discuss briefly some of the most relevant issues here. If a football player hits a ball and it moves, there is good reason to believe that the kick caused the movement of the ball. Even though we can never be absolutely sure (there is a rather remote possibility that the earth moved and the ball remained in place), the likelihood that the kicking caused the movement of the ball is rather high. However, in most cases, we cannot make a direct link of causality. For example, in a traditional approach, single cause studies are the rule rather than the exception: A particular approach to teaching vocabulary is compared with another approach and the differences between the experimental and the control groups are interpreted as being caused by the differences between the methods. There is a vast literature on the problems of methods comparison, and there is no need to dwell on that here. For our present purposes it suffices to say that the assumption of direct causality in such studies is highly problematic, not just because there are so many differences between individuals, groups, teachers, settings and so on that can have an impact, but also because the application of a new vocabulary teaching method has implications at many other levels over time, and may affect other subsystems of the language, besides the lexicon, too. The point is that causality relates to the likelihood of alternative explanations and is therefore ultimately subjective. Explanation of development is notoriously difficult: Many variables may have an impact on the learning of a foreign language, the variables are likely to interact over time, and some variables may be effective during one stage of development but not during another stage.

In a dynamic approach the goal is not to list possible causes for change and development but to describe the process of change and development itself by means of tracing the iterative change over time: Which components in the system change from one moment to the other and how they influence each other over time. In a dynamic approach the multitude of influences is acknowledged and no claims about the unique contribution of single factors are made. Devising a theoretical model about how variables may interact over time, validating the model with empirical longitudinal data and then testing our theoretical claims by comparing the simulated data to the empirical data is the optimal strategy. However, quantifying a relationship between variables is not an explanation of cause, but the models used can elucidate how variables combine to shape development. The focus is more on description than on explanation, and various ways to visualize development are used to help us understand what is going on, even when the why of these developments evades us.

One of the criticisms that the dynamic approach has generated is that it focuses on the detail of individual development with all the variation that it entails, and that therefore the findings cannot be generalized. This raises the issue of what generalization is. In traditional statistics, generalization refers to the applicability of findings on the sample level to the population that the sample is assumed to represent. Inferential statistics are used to estimate the likelihood that what was found on the sample level applies to the population level in general. There are two problems: One is that drawing a representative sample from a population is very difficult, since for most characteristics of the population we have no reliable indicators that can structure the sampling. It would be difficult for any study on Chinese learners of English as a foreign language to claim to have drawn a representative sample from the population: What do we know about time invested and individual differences such as variation in attitudes, motivation, aptitude, and so on. In fact, one might wonder whether there is any research in AL that would rightly claim to be generalizable beyond the sample it is based on. This certainly restricts claims about generalizability in this tradition. Of course, a series of studies on the same population with different samples will enhance the chance of findings that apply to more than a single sample, but the literature is rife with contradictory findings.

The second issue is that even if the sample is representative of the population, the data used are often not suited to the statistical procedures applied. One issue is random sampling, which is difficult to achieve in instruction based studies in particular and indeed we may wonder whether for many studies random sampling is appropriate. Other issues relate to the constraints on data that certain statistical procedures pose. Analysis of variance in different forms is now one of the standard statistical procedures in our field, but few studies use data that allow the application of that type of analysis.

In a dynamic approach, the aim is not to generalize from a sample to a population. A basic assumption is that individual differences shape development and that individuals vary in how such differences work out. The approach chosen is what might be called "theory-based generalization". Data are checked against theoretical notions and the theory will be strengthened by data supporting it. This implies a soft approach towards falsification in which single cases are not assumed to refute a theory completely, since there will be individual variation that comes into play. The specific interaction of variables in an individual may lead to behavior and data that do not conform to, or at any rate, cannot be predicted by the theory.

As the literature on CT/DST and language learning shows, one of the most important tools in research from a dynamic perspective is modeling. In this book, Chapter 6 especially provides information about the thinking behind modeling and presents a number of examples on language development. Modeling language development has certain advantages and disadvantages: As mentioned earlier, it allows us to simulate processes that we found in real life. However, to do so we have to quantify general conceptual notions because we need numerical values for the equations. For example, if we claim on the basis of previous research that motivation plays a role in SLD, then for our modeling we need to indicate exactly how strong we think that relationship is. If we then also claim that success in language learning has an impact on motivation, we need to quantify that relationship too, which means that the traditional correlation coefficient that expresses how strongly the two variables are related does not fully cover what we are interested in: A coefficient of .40 does not mean that the relation is that strong in both directions. In addition, and that is where we cannot do without modeling, the two factors interact over time but not necessarily equally strongly all the time: High marks for language tests may first enhance the motivation to study and invest time in learning, but when marks continue to be high, the learner, particularly in an instructional and examination setting, may feel that a little less investment will do as well. Also when the learner has reached a very high level of proficiency and encounters no problems in using the language anymore, the motivation to work on it may also decline. All of these relationships need to be modeled and quantified and ideally the outcomes of the modeling should be compared to real learner data to see whether the assumptions applied are valid.

Modeling is not without its own problems, though. One thing is that it requires at least some basic mathematical knowledge that not all researchers or students in AL necessarily master. If we want to take the dynamic approach seriously, we will need to develop this knowledge and include training of such skills in our teaching programs. A problem at another level is that there is in a way a *contradictio in terminis* in using modeling in a CT/DST approach: While one of the basic tenets is the embeddedness and interconnectedness of subsystems, modeling inevitably implies a limitation on the number of variables we want to look at, which is a form of reductionism that a dynamic kind of thinking opposes. It should be added that the programs used in modeling do not by themselves limit the number of variables that can be studied, but adding more than 4 or 5 variables makes the model basically uninterpretable.

2. A step forward?

Whether the dynamic movement will in the long run be more than a fad remains to be seen. Overlooking the recent literature, we can see two streams of research emerge: a "soft" approach that links up with an existing way of thinking in the social sciences that could be labeled as "the ecological approach" which includes the work of leading researchers such as Leo van Lier and Claire Kramsch. In this approach, which is qualitative and interpretative in nature, the metaphors from theories on complex dynamic systems are used. The present book is a representative of the other approach: Here the approach is more hard-science like and mathematical, based on models and tools from other sciences and characterized by the use of different ways of quantifying data. For the ideas on language as a complex system to take root and to become established as a serious addition to our theorizing about SLD, we need to come up with research that is both scientifically sound, conceptually convincing and interpretable for researchers that have been involved with mathematical modeling. The ultimate test will be whether we can involve our students in our research and provide them with topics and approaches that are within their grasp. But we also need to extend that grasp: If DST is to stay as a theory of SLD, at least some basic mastery of its tools will be necessary as part of students' skills when they enter the field.

It is our hope that this book will at least lead to more students taking up the challenges of this perspective on language development because without generating involvement of young researchers and students, the dynamic movement is bound to fail.

How to sections

Marjolijn Verspoor, Wander Lowie, Paul van Geert, Marijn van Dijk & Monika S. Schmid

1. Introduction

Chapters 3–6 in this book have presented methods and techniques in applying DST to second language analysis that are not commonly known yet. Therefore, we decided to include a very practical *How to* chapter in which we explain each method and technique in detail. Some of these *How to* sections contain instructions for those who have little or no experience with Excel and others are quite advanced. For most of the *How to* sections, we put practice materials on our web site SLD_Methods (DOI:10.1075/lllt.29.website), containing the actual files we used in our explanations and analyses in both the theoretical chapter and the How to section. We will direct the reader to those in the text. The main idea of these files is that you can look more closely at the actual formulas and programs we used.

However, a crucial warning is necessary. As everyone knows, computer software is subject to change all the time. We used an English 2003 version of Excel and Windows XP. We realize our readers will have many different versions of Excel or different programs, but we assume most of our instructions can be "translated" into other programs, even though it will take some time and determination to figure these out. We feel in no way responsible for solving programming problems, but we do invite our readers to share their experiences on a blog to learn from each other.

2. How to section – Chapter 3

To code our data, we have availed ourselves exclusively of tools and programs which are either widely available (such as Microsoft Office) or can be freely accessed and downloaded from the internet. We will make use of the CHILDES (Child Language Data Exchange System) project described in MacWhinney (2000), which provides a standardized system for the transcription and analysis of data. The CHILDES internet resource (http://childes.psy.cmu.edu) contains the manuals for both CHAT and CLAN, the CLAN program and a set of tools for morphological analysis. All of these resources are free. Since extensive and detailed documentation is available at this location, the description of the CHAT transcription system and the use of the CLAN program is kept to a minimum in the *how to* sections, but they should help the novice CHAT learner on the way.

2.1   Formatting in CHAT

Chapter 3 dealt with coding for many different variables. This *How to* section gives details on how data are coded according to the formatting conventions known as the CHAT format. Once the data are formatted, they can be read and analyzed by the CLAN program. Many of the standard texts and codes can be inserted rather automatically by means of macros, which will be discussed in the next *How to*. This particular section outlines the most general principles for formatting CHAT files.

CHAT files are text-only files which contain linguistic data in a format that the CLAN program can read and analyze. For researchers working with audio files, CLAN may be used in what is referred to as "coder mode" from the start. This will ensure that all transcriptions conform to the CLAN standards, and eliminate many potential problems. However, if you are working with files which were written using a different text editor, such as Microsoft Word or WordPerfect, you will have to convert those files to CHAT format and text-only mode. This conversion can result in a number of problems, since many text editors introduce automatic formatting to texts, for example replacing straight quotation marks or apostrophes (") by what they sometimes refer to as "smart" quotation marks ("or"). When the file is converted to text-only, these and other symbols (especially the diacritics used in many languages) can be changed so that they are not recognizable to CLAN or other programs. These problems can be further aggravated if the software used by the original writer of the text is different from the one which you are using (e.g. if one is an Apple user and the other a Windows person).

The CHAT files must be formatted carefully in order to conform to certain standards which the CLAN program recognizes. Here is an example of what a CHAT-file might look like (the symbol → represents a tabulator):

```
@Begin
@Languages: → en, nl
@Participants: → XYZ 301138 Student
@ID: → en, nl|corpus|XYZ|||3011||Student||
*XYZ: → i like my new school and i love my
new friends.
*XYZ: → i do al [*] lot with Shanice.
%err: → spelling
*XYZ: → she sit [*] next to me in the class.
%err: → verbagreement
*XYZ: → <with Inge, Iris have i got> [*] a lot of
fun to [*].
%err: → wordorder, spelling
*XYZ: → only the bags are very heavy to wear [*].
%err: → semantics
@End
```

At first sight, this text may appear rather complex, but once you have familiarized yourself with the CHAT coding system, you will find that it quickly becomes easy to use, as long as you observe a number of principles strictly. A CHAT-file is a text-only file with the extension .txt, .cha (this denotes a CHAT transcript) or .cex (identifying a file on which some kind of CLAN operation has been performed). If you prefer to work with a text editor such as Microsoft Word, it is important that you save the files as plain text. Each CHAT file contains data from one data collection session. Usually, these are data which were originally in the spoken form and have been transcribed, but CHAT/CLAN has also been used for the coding and analysis of written data.

CHAT files are organized in different "tiers" or layers, the three most important of which are header tiers (in the example @Languages, @Participants, @ID), utterance tiers (in the example *XYZ) and dependent tiers (in the example %err). Note that the codes for these tiers (e.g. @Languages) must be followed by a colon (:) and a tabulator (→).

In the following, you will find more detailed descriptions of the conventions, rules and restrictions applying to each type of tier.

2.1.1   *Header tiers*

Header tiers provide general information about the file (the speaker(s), the language(s) used etc.) and must start with the symbol @. This symbol helps CLAN realize that the line does not contain actual linguistic data, but meta-information.

– @Begin and @End
   CHAT files begin with a line which contains the sequence "@Begin" and end with a line which contains the sequence "@End". No empty lines are allowed either before @Begin or after @End (nor anywhere else in the file).

– @Languages:→
   Here, you code the main language of the text. If there is more than one language, you can specify this as well, as was done in the above example. In this particular case, the text is in English, which is therefore identified as the primary language. Dutch is coded as the second language because a number of texts in this corpus contain some code-switches. In the actual text, words which do not belong to the main language can be identified by means of the suffix "@s". A list of abbreviations for different languages can be found in the CHAT manual.

– @Participants
   In this line, a three-letter code must be specified for each person who participates in the interaction transcribed in the file. The code is used to identify the speakers for each utterance in the main body of the text. You may choose a code

which identifies each individual speaker, e.g. the first three letters of his/her name, but we have found it useful to pick the same code for the same type of speaker (the student, the investigator etc.) across all the files in a particular corpus. This is helpful later on, when you want to have CLAN analyze the utterances of the people you are interested in (excluding others, for example, the interviewer) for a whole set of files in one go.

One option is to choose codes symbolizing the role of each speaker, e.g. STU for student, TEA for teacher, INV for investigator, CHI for child, and so on. We prefer a combination of letters that will appear nowhere else in the text, that is, something that will definitely not be part of any word, for example XYZ. This can sometimes make automatic search-and-replace routines easier.

This three-letter code is (optionally) followed by the name or identification code of the person. In our case, it is the identification number which we have given each student. It could also be a name (note that no spaces or punctuation are allowed, so the name should be e.g. Monika_S_Schmid).

The name is followed by the "role" of this speaker, in the present case "Student". The CHAT manual lists a large number of possible roles (Child, Mother, Adult, …). Note that roles are case-sensitive, so the role "student" with a lowercase s will lead to an error message in CLAN.

@ID
The identification tier specifies slots for the following information:

@ID:→**language(s)|corpus|code**|age|sex|**group**|SES|role|education|.
The information set in bold above is obligatory, all other information is optional. In our example, the non-obligatory information has been omitted:

@ID:→en|corpus|XYZ|||3011||Student||
You may choose not to code the ID tier initially. Once you perform the command CHECK in CLAN (see below), the ID tier will be inserted, based on the information in the @Participants line, if it is found to be missing.

In addition to these obligatory headers, there are optional headers, e.g. @Coder (to enter the name of the person who did the coding, useful if several people work on the same project), @Activities (to describe the situation which was recorded), @Comment, @Date, and @Location. For a full list, and how to fill these, see the CHAT manual.

2.1.2   *Utterance tiers*

Utterance tiers identify the person who has produced this particular utterance and contain the actual linguistic (spoken or written) data. They must start with an asterisk * followed by the three-letter code identifying the speaker, which was specified in the @Participants tier. Note that the three letter code must be followed by a colon and a tabulator (strictly in that order, and with no empty spaces intervening anywhere). Every utterance consists of one sentence:

```
*XYZ: → hello mij holiday was great.
*XYZ: → i have been in Spain a beautifull country!
*XYZ: → i'ts hot in there, thirty degrees.
*XYZ: → i was every day on the beach, and now i'm brown.
```

The lexical analyses which can be performed by the CLAN program can, of course, only recognize standard spelling. Deviations, such as *mij* (instead of *my*) or *beautifull* will not be identified correctly. We may want to code these errors in the dependent tiers in order to perform an extended error analysis, but for CLAN to be able to ignore these misspellings (or repetitions, retractions, pauses etc. in spoken data) and correctly count the lexical items used, we must provide appropriate information within the utterance tiers themselves.

Errors in the utterance are identified by an asterisk enclosed between square brackets [*]. If the error extends over more than one word (as in the phrase "with Inge, Iris have I got" above), the entire error is furthermore enclosed between angled brackets. Note that it is important to ensure that each opening bracket must have a closing bracket, […] or <…. > on the same utterance tier. An error can therefore not extend across several utterances.

```
*XYZ: → hello mij [*] holiday was great.
*XYZ: → i have been in Spain a beautifull [*] country!
*XYZ: → i'ts [*] hot <in there> [*], thirty degrees.
*XYZ: → <i was every day on the beach> [*], and now
i'm brown.
```

In order to allow for more detailed coding of the errors, the utterance can be followed by a dependent "error tier" (%err: →) to be discussed below. If, in addition to marking these misspellings as errors, you want to enable the CLAN program to include the words produced here in frequency analyses, you can provide the correct alternative for a misspelling together with the error code:

```
*XYZ: → hello <mij> [* my] holiday was great.
*XYZ: → i have been in Spain a <beautifull>
[* beautiful] country!
*XYZ: → <i'ts> [* it's] hot <in there> [*], thirty degrees.
*XYZ: → <i was every day on the beach> [*], and now
i'm brown.
```

–   code-switches are indicated by the symbol @s following the word:

```
*XYZ:  I don't like cheese but I do like honing@s and
bitterballen@s very much!
```

If an entire utterance is switched to the secondary language of the text, this can be indicated in the following way:

```
*XYZ:  [- en] ik vind het heel leuk op deze school.
```

(I find it very nice at this school. – "I like this school")
In other words, a code is included at the beginning of the utterance, informing the program that the present utterance is not in the primary language of the text (the one which was specified first in the @Language tier). Should an utterance be predominantly in Dutch, and be identified as such by means of the [– en] code, but contain a few English words, then these can in their turn be marked with the @s suffix.

Note that sometimes material can be ambiguous. In the present example, the researcher has to decide whether the word *mij* (pronounced /maI/ in this student's first language) is an orthographical error (a misspelling of *my*, since in Dutch the letter combination *ij* is interchangeable with *y*) or a code-switch:[1]

```
*XYZ: → hello <mij> [*] holiday was great.
or
*XYZ: → hello mij@s holiday was great.
```

As Chapter 3 deals with the analysis of written data, these are the only codes pertaining to the utterance tiers which we need to concern ourselves with. The CHAT manual gives in-depth descriptions of a number of other codes, regarding for example to the treatment of repetitions, retractions, interruptions and self-interruptions, overlaps and so on. There are a few other important considerations with respect to the

---

1.   In our study we considered it a misspelling if the word occurred in an English context and a code-switch in a Dutch context.

utterance tier that must be observed before CLAN can perform data analysis operations on the files.

Utterance delimiters: Each line must end with an "Utterance delimiter", which can be a period (.), an exclamation mark (!) or a question mark (?). (This also implies that the utterance delimiter may not appear within an error code: verry. [*] should be verry [*].) Note that utterance delimiters may appear only at the end of the utterance. In other words, no utterance delimiters are allowed within a line and only one sentence may be used per utterance line.

Punctuation marks: All other punctuation marks, such as commas (,), semicolons (;) or brackets at the end of a code (], >), must be followed by a space. To make sure you have spaces after each punctuation mark, you might do the following. When you are finished coding your file, run a search-replace (Edit – Replace). In the "Find what" line, enter just a comma, in the "Replace with" line enter a comma followed by a space. Then do the same with the brackets] and >. This, of course, means that those symbols which were already followed by a space prior to your search-replace are now followed by two. This does not really matter, but if you want to be very tidy, you can afterwards run another search-replace, where you replace two empty spaces by one.

Abbreviations: Abbreviations may not be followed by an utterance delimiter. Since you may not use periods anywhere except at the end of the utterance, you cannot use abbreviations such as Mr. or Mrs. and these words have to be spelled out (the CHAT manual suggests Mister and Missus). Individual letters and abbreviations, such as P.E., have to be coded by following each letter with a @ and lowercase letter L, i.e. "P@l E@l" (Note that there is no space between the letter and the @ or between the @ and the l, but there has to be a space between the code for each individual letter (i.e. between P@l and E@l etc.). Acronyms, such as USA are represented as U_S_A.

Capitals and numbers: The use of capitals and numbers is restricted. For example, uppercase letters within words are not allowed. This can sometimes be an error source when there is a space missing between words, e.g. writeEnglish. Names such as McDonald would also be rejected. Numbers have to be spelled out (not 4 but *four* - note that in our data, we simply replaced all numbers with the word "numb" in order to ensure that these items would not distort lexical frequency counts). Furthermore, the program for morphological analysis available in the CLAN program automatically identifies all words which start with a capital letter as proper nouns; you should therefore use lowercase initial letters for words which are not nouns or names, even at the beginning of sentences. Titles or other stretches of text which use nondefault capitalization can be exempted from this convention by replacing the space between the words with an underscore, e.g. The_Tempest.

2.1.3 *Dependent tiers*

Each "utterance" line can have several dependent tiers pertaining to it, where additional information which you wish to analyze may be coded. These are preceded by a % symbol, plus a three-letter code indicating which information they contain, such as the %err tier included in some of the examples above, where information about the errors contained in the previous utterances is specified.

You might also have a %com tier, where you can enter comments (such as "the telephone rings"), a %spa tier where you code speech act information and so on. You may not have more than one tier of the same type per utterance, so if there is more than one error in the same utterance, they all have to be coded in the same %err-line. The CHAT manual contains a list of predefined dependent tiers. Should these not be sufficient for your own coding needs, you can add your own three-letter tier names and prefix them with the letter x.

The option of creating dependent tiers to accompany each utterance is what makes the CHAT transcription system such a powerful and useful tool for the analysis of learner data, in particular for investigations from a DST perspective. It allows the researcher to tag utterances for any number of characteristics, and then relate these to each other, without making an unreadable mess of the utterance itself. With the help of the CLAN program, frequency analyses can be extended or limited to any type of tier – the utterance tier, a particular set of dependent tiers, but also dependent tiers of a specific kind, such as a specific error code.

For example, if we do assume that in the process of development, there may be a trade-off between subcomponents of linguistic skills, such as pronunciation, syntactic complexity and lexical richness, we might create a pronunciation tier where the target-likeness of the production of each instance of a particular phoneme is coded. Each utterance might also have a syntactic tier associated with it, where we specify sentence complexity. We can then analyze these two features in relation to each other, and also identify lexical richness measures, such as type-token frequencies, in utterances of varying syntactic complexity or phonological accuracy. That is, we may trace the development of a speaker not only across data collection points, but within a particular session.

Once you have formatted your texts in CHAT, you want to make sure you have done so correctly. To do so, you need to perform the CLAN 'check' command. See *How to* section 2.3.

2.2   Creating a set of tools in Word

In the previous *How to* section we outlined the general principles involved in the CHAT coding system. To speed up the coding of different variables in your data necessary for converting your files according to CLAN standards, this *How to* section illustrates how to use your word processing program (in our case Microsoft Word and Windows XP) to create a set of tools, called Macros, which can record a string of commands and operations.

In *How to* 2.1, you saw the following text in CHAT format.

> I like my new school and i love my new friends. I do al lot with Shanice. She sit next to me in the class. With Inge, Iris have i got a lot of fun to. Only the bags are very heavy to wear.

In our research on this type of data, we had to code about 500 of such texts and we needed to add student numbers, scores, and all kinds of other information before we coded it for about 60 different variables and analyzed it in CLAN. As you can imagine, it would be a very tedious job to code all this by hand, and there is always the danger of mistyping codes, which will then not be counted correctly by the computerized analyses. It is therefore both more convenient and more reliable to have the computer do the coding work for you, wherever possible.[2] To do so, we wrote a number of mini programs (called Macros) to insert the headers and tiers and to correct errors that would cause problems in CLAN to make the text look as follows.

```
@Begin
@Languages:     en, nl
@Participants:  XYZ 301138 Student
@ID:    en, nl|corpus|XYZ|||3011||Student||
*XYZ:   i like my new school and i love my new friends.
*XYZ:   i do al [*] lot with Shanice.
%err:   spelling
*XYZ:   she sit [*] next to me in the class.
%err:   verbagreement
*XYZ:   <with Inge, Iris have i got> [*] a lot of
fun to [*].
%err:   wordorder, spelling
*XYZ:   only the bags are very heavy to wear [*].
%err:   semantics
@End
```

Once you familiarize yourself with the steps associated with creating Macros, you will find them a fantastically useful tool. In addition to inserting the CHAT codes you want, they can be used to automatically reformat the output from programs such as

---

2. In the CLAN coder mode, you can also define a set of options for each dependent tier, thereby ensuring that only the correct codes will be chosen.

CLAN or SPSS, to reformat paragraphs, tables or citations from one style to the other, and so on.

Below, we give step-by-step instructions how to create Macros to add a code after a word, mark a word as a code-switch, mark a stretch of text as an error, insert a dependent tier of the type %err after the utterance containing the error, and insert an %xsen tier of one of three types (simple, compound, complex) after an utterance. We also show how you can work even more efficiently by copying and pasting the program text for Macros that you have already created.

In this *How to* we will not be able to explain all the different Macros we wrote, but by giving a few examples, we hope you discover the general principles to write Macros and apply them to your own data when needed.

2.2.1   *Recording Macros in Microsoft Word*[3]

The Word program allows you to record a string of operations as a kind of mini-program, which is referred to as a "Macro". In other words, a Macro is basically a "recording" of every key stroke, cursor movement or mouse click which you have performed. Macros are very useful for operations you need to perform often in exactly the same kind of way. For example, in our data we want to code the proportion of finite verbs in relation to the total number of words in each text in order to get an impression of sentence length and complexity. In order to do this, we have to identify each finite verb manually in the text (unfortunately, most such identification tasks can not yet be performed reliably by computers) and then add a code after the verb. This code has to be something which CLAN will recognize as not belonging to the actual utterance, for example "[% f]". Typing this string out every time is cumbersome: First, we have to move the cursor to the correct place (which we will most likely do by means of a mouse click) and then we have to type the angled bracket, the percentage sign followed by a space and the letter "f", and the other angled bracket. It is also easy to make a mistake in typing this string. It would therefore be more convenient and reliable to either have a button that we could click on or a keyboard shortcut which will insert the code at the location of the cursor.

Before writing a Macro, you need to try and anticipate exactly where the cursor is and how it may need to move if you want the string [% f] to appear exactly one space after a finite verb. In our example below, we put our cursor one space after the verb and then click to get the string and an extra space.

---

3.   Almost all word processors provide tools to create macros, but the details may change. Newer versions of Word may also not always function exactly as described below. Therefore, if something does not work exactly as shown, try to find the keys strokes or icons that will do the job.

2.2.2 *Practicing writing a Macro (indicating a finite verb)*

1. Open a Word document and use some text you may have.
2. Put the cursor in the space directly after a finite verb.
3. Choose Tools – Macros – Record New Macro

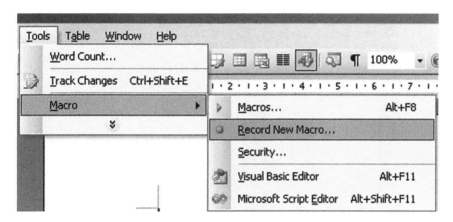

4. In the window which appears, you can specify a name for the Macro you are about to record, for example "finiteverb". (If you don't pick a name, it will simply be called "Macro1". If you are planning to make more extensive use of Macros, it is a good idea to give each a transparent name. Note that no spaces are allowed within the Macro name).

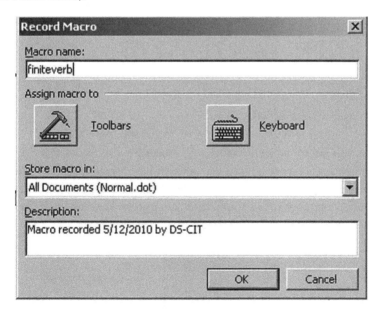

5. Click the keyboard icon.

6. Put the cursor in the window "Press new shortcut key" and press the Control, Alt and F keys simultaneously (the window will show CTRL-ALT-F). Note that a shortcut must be preceded by either the CTRL key, the ALT key, or a combination of both.

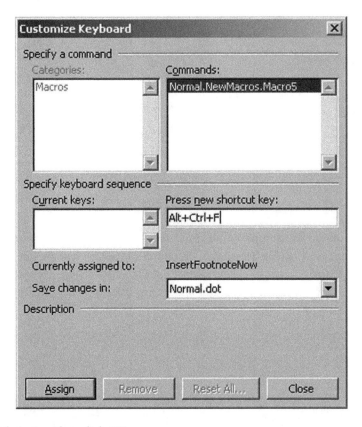

7. Click Assign, then click OK.
8. You are now taken back to your original document. In the top left corner of the screen, you can see an icon symbolizing a recorder. This means that every action (e.g. clicking the mouse button) you perform now is being recorded, and will be repeated later on whenever you run the Macro. (Note that while in recording mode, you can move your cursor only by using arrow keys and not by moving the mouse across the screen and clicking).

9. Type: space [% f] space.

10. Click the "Stop recording" button (the blue square on the left side of the recorder icon). Note that if you accidentally do not press the "Stop recording" button but the little X at the top of the recording icon, the recording icon itself will disappear, but the actual recording of the Macro will continue. You can check this by going back to Tools – Macro: instead of the option "Record New Macro" you saw under 2 above, it now says "Stop recording".

11. Now you have written a Macro that should produce space [% f] space from the point where your cursor is. Try it out, by putting the cursor behind the next finite verb and pressing Control+Alt+F simultaneously. (If this does not work properly, you may have to start all over again).

For the next illustrations of Macros, you need a bit of text in CHAT format as follows. You can retype the following in a Word document.

```
@Begin
@Languages: → en, nl
@Participants: → XYZ 301138 Student
@ID: → en, nl|corpus|XYZ|||3011||Student||
*XYZ: → i like my new school and i love my new friends.
*XYZ: → i do al lot with Shanice.
*XYZ: → she sit next to me in the klas always.
*XYZ: → with Inge, Iris have i got a lot of fun to.
*XYZ: → only de bags are very heavy to wear.
@End
```

2.2.3 *Writing a Macro to mark a code-switch*

Recall that words are marked as code-switches in CHAT by adding the suffix @s. This is therefore a fairly simple Macro: It only involves moving to the end of the word and typing in these data. In our example, the Dutch word *klas* (grade) is an example of a code-switch.

Before you start recording this Macro, determine which strokes are needed on your keyboard to move the cursor to the end of the word. For the keyboard variant which we used (input language Dutch keyboard United States international), we had to press Ctrl + right arrow (which moved the cursor to the beginning of the next word) and then the left arrow key (to go back one space) to go to the end of the current word.

1. Put your cursor before or somewhere in the middle of the word *klas*.
2. Chose Tools – Macro – Record New Macro.
3. Change the predefined Macro name (e.g. "Macro1") to "Codeswitch".
4. Assign it the keyboard shortcut Control + Alt + C, if you wish.

5. When you are back in your document window, press Ctrl + right arrow (which moves the cursor to the beginning of the next word) and then the left arrow key (to go back one space) to go to the end of the current word. (Remember that while in recording mode, you move your cursor only by using the arrow keys and not by moving the mouse across the screen and clicking).
6. Type: @s followed by a space.
7. Click on the "Stop recording" button on the recording icon.
8. Try out this Macro on another Dutch word: *de* in the last line.

2.2.4   *Writing a Macro to code an error*

To practice this Macro you will need a bit of text in CHAT format again. This Macro will change the first string into the second one.

```
*XYZ: → i do al lot with Shanice.

*XYZ: → i do <al> [*] lot with Shanice.
%err: →
```

Note that the incorrect word is now enclosed in angled brackets so that CLAN can be told to ignore this word (which means that it will be excluded from CLAN analysis), followed by a space and the string [*], which indicates that it is an error. Then an extra tier is added with the string %err: followed by a tab. This is when our recording stops. The type of error can then be filled in by hand. (Of course it is possible to extend the Macro to include the type of error, but we will not discuss that here.)

1. Select an error, either a single word or an expression.
2. Choose Tools – Macro – Record New Macro
3. Change the predefined Macro name to "Error"
4. Click on "Keyboard"
5. Click in the box "Press new shortcut key" and press the key combination you want, for example Ctrl + Alt + E, pressed simultaneously.
6. Click "Assign"
7. Click "Close"
8. The recording symbol appears at the top left of your screen, and a little cassette-icon appears next to your mouse arrow.
9. Select "Edit – Cut" in the toolbar
10. Type: < >
11. With the arrow keys, move the cursor back between the two brackets

12. Select "Edit – Paste"
13. With the arrow key, move the cursor to the right of the > bracket followed by a space
14. Type: [*] followed by a space

You have now successfully written a Macro which will enclose the text containing an error between angled brackets, followed by the error symbol [*]. If you do not wish to code specific error types on the %err tier, you may stop the recording process at this point.

Otherwise, the next step is to enter an error tier. To do so, you have to find the end of the utterance with the error, insert a new line, insert the string %err: followed by a tab.

15. Select "Edit – Find"
16. In the "Find what" window type: *XYZ.
17. Click "Find next"
18. Click "Cancel" (to close the search window).
19. With the arrow key, move the cursor to the beginning of the line
20. Type "Enter" to insert a new blank line
21. Move the cursor up one line with the cursor keys
22. Type: %err:
23. Press the Tabulator (or "Tab") button
24. Click on the "Stop recording" button on the recording icon

2.2.5   *Writing a Macro to insert a %syn-tier after an utterance*

The following is a relatively simple Macro to write, but we will use it as a starting point to copy and paste it to make new Macros, which will be dealt with later. In this example, there is one new "trick" to go to a new line.

In the previous example, *writing a Macro to code an error*, we added a new line by first searching for the beginning of the next utterance (i.e. find the next *XYZ). In this example, we will search for the end of the utterance, by giving "^p" as the find option, which will search for the next hard return (which usually indicates the end of the paragraph). There are a number of other useful search options, such as "^t" to search for the beginning of a paragraph, "^#" to search for any number, "^$" to search for any character, and so on. If you wish to search for some specific item, but do not know how to do so, click "More" in the search window, and then click on the "Special" button.

1. Put your cursor in an utterance that you want to classify as a simple sentence
2. Choose Tools – Macro – Record New Macro
3. Change the predefined Macro name to "Synsimple" and click OK.

4. Select "Edit – Find"
5. In the "Find what" window type: ^p (this indicates a paragraph end)
6. Click "Find next"
7. Click "Cancel" (to close the search window).
8. With the arrow keys, move the cursor to the beginning of the next line
9. Type "Enter" to insert a new blank line
10. With the arrow keys, move the cursor up one line
11. Type: %syn:
12. Press the Tabulator (or "Tab") button
13. Type: simple
14. Click on the "Stop recording" button on the recording icon.

2.2.6   Copying and pasting Macros

If you wish, you can now record the Macro for the "compound" and "complex" tier in exactly the same fashion as the "simple" tier. However, it is also possible to duplicate the Macro using the program code which you have just created.

If you need to write a Macro that is similar to one you have already created, it may be easier to copy and paste the actual program code which is created when you record the Macro. In order to do this, you need to perform the following operations:

1. Choose "Tools – Macro – Macros"
    A window appears, containing the Macros which you have just created. Click on the Macro SynSimple once (by double-clicking, you will cause the Macro to be run).
2. Click "Edit"

This will take you to the so-called VisualBasic Editor, where you can see the program code for all the Macros (written in the programming language VisualBasic). The code for the Macro which you have just created should look like this:

```
Sub synsimple()
"
"  synsimple Macro
"  Macro recorded 4-8-2009 by author
"
     Selection.Find.ClearFormatting
     With Selection.Find
         .Text = "^p"
         .Replacement.Text = "^p"
         .Forward = True
```

```
            .Wrap = wdFindContinue
            .Format = False
            .MatchCase = False
            .MatchWholeWord = False
            .MatchWildcards = False
            .MatchSoundsLike = False
            .MatchAllWordForms = False
        End With
        Selection.Find.Execute
        Selection.MoveRight Unit: = wdCharacter, Count: = 1
        Selection.TypeParagraph
        Selection.MoveUp Unit: = wdLine, Count: = 1
        Selection.TypeText Text: = "%syn:" & vbTab & "simple"
    End Sub
```

The first part of this code is the identification of the Macro itself: the name you have just given it, the date on which you recorded it, and which user of the computer it was who performed the recording.

After this, the actual operations you performed are described in program code. The first 14 lines describe the Search operation you performed. This may look overly complicated, but these are merely a number of standard settings, which pertain to the default options always present in a simple Search routine. Firstly, the command "Clear Formatting" removes any selections which might have still been activated from a previous search operation. Then the search text ("^p") is specified, followed by the replacement text. Again, this is present by default, even though we performed only a search operation, not a replacement operation – it is whichever text string was used last for replacement. If you wish, you may delete this line.

The line Forward = True refers to the default setting which searches in the direction of the text. (In cases where you have specified in the search window that you want to search upwards, this parameter will be set to False).

The line Wrap specifies whether the search is to be continued at the beginning of the document after the end has been reached.[4] The next six lines all pertain to the additional options you can select when performing a search operation, such as matching the format, matching the case, searching only for entire words etc. As we did not select any of these options, they are all set to False here. (If you wish, you may delete any line which is set to the default option.).

---

4. In cases where you wish to be asked about this, you can change this from `wdFindContinue` to `wdFindAsk`, and should you simply want the search to stop once the end of the document has been reached, you can enter `wdFindStop`.

The next line "Selection.Find.Execute" is the instruction to actually perform the search operation, that is, to move the cursor to the next paragraph end. After this, the cursor is moved to the next line (by being shifted one position to the right), a new line is inserted, and the cursor is shifted up again. After this, the code for this particular tier is entered.

On the basis of this program code, you can quite simply create two new Macros. You do this by marking the **entire** code (from "Sub synsimple" to "End Sub"), copying it, and pasting it again underneath. In the first two lines of the code, where the name is now given (twice) as "synsimple", you change it to read "syncompound". You then scroll down to the line

```
Selection.TypeText Text: = "%syn:" & vbTab & "simple"
```

and again change "simple" to "compound". To create a Macro for complex sentences, repeat these steps, but this time change "simple" to "complex" both in the Macro name and in the text.

If you now go back to "Tools – Macro – Macros", you will see that the two Macros "syncompound" and "syncomplex" are in the list of Macros.

2.2.7   Creating a toolbar for Macros

The previous Macros were written with a keyboard shortcut (i.e. Control + Alt + F) but if you have to code a great number of variables, it may be difficult to remember all the shortcuts and it might be handier to select the Macro from a number of options. The simplest way to choose a Macro you have created is to go to Tools > Macro > Macros (or Press Alt+F8) and then select the Macro you need and press run.

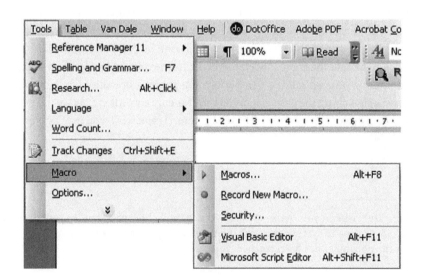

Another handy way to start a Macro is to select one from a toolbar, which you can create yourself. (Note, however, that the possibilities of creating such toolbars have been severely restricted in the 2007 version of the Microsoft Office package, so if you are using this version of the program, you will have to rely on the Macro menu we just discussed or the keyboard shortcuts.)

Let us assume that you need to use several Macros to code your texts. You now want to create a toolbar from which you can pick your Macros as required, by simply clicking on them. Such a toolbar can be created in the menu Tools – Customize. Pick the tab "Toolbars" and click "New". Give a name to your new toolbar, such as "Coding".

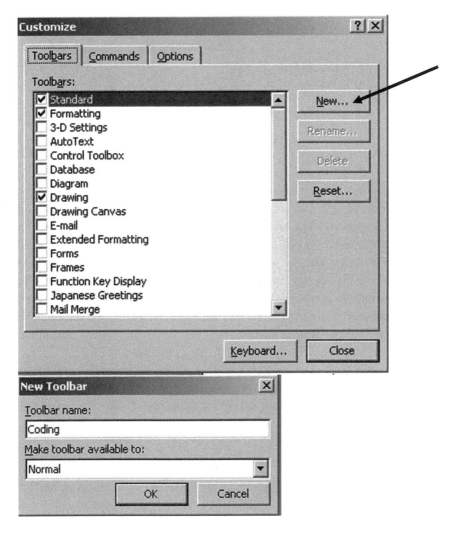

A small new toolbar will appear on your screen (which, for the moment, is empty). Pick the tab "Commands". In the window on the left, you can see the different menus.

Scroll down until you get to "Macros" and click on this. You now see all the Macros you have created in the right hand window, and you can grab them and drag them to the new toolbar. (Note that the "Command" window also contains the option "Keyboard", where you can change or assign keyboard shortcuts to your Macros – or to any other Word function).

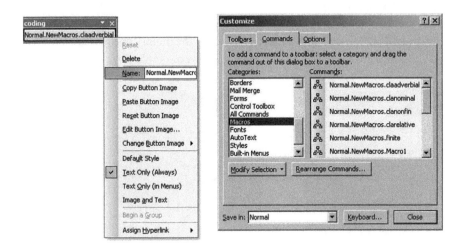

The names for the Macros that appear on this new toolbar are very long, as they contain the entire identification string (e.g. Normal.NewMacros.finiteverb), but while the "Customize" window is still open, you can right-click on the name and change it to something shorter and more convenient (e.g. FV).

We hope that the examples of how to record Macros and design Toolbars will allow you to develop your own tools for the specific coding options you require. For example, you could write a Macro to insert the obligatory headers in the file, to code retractions and repetitions and so on. Once you have the set of tools you need, you can assign keyboard shortcuts to each Macro (using the Menu "Tools – Customize – Keyboard", if you have not already assigned them in the process of originally creating the Macro) and/or place them on a new Toolbar, called, for example, "CHATTools" (or, of course, on an existing one). Once you understand the basic principles of programming Macros, you can use ever longer and embedded Macros to automatically help you get text prepared to analyze.

2.3   Getting data ready to analyze with CLAN

In the previous *How to* sections we showed what the CHAT conventions are and how you can create your own tools to code efficiently. Before you can start to analyze your text files, you have to be sure CLAN can "read" them. This *How to* section illustrates how your files can be checked to see if they conform to the CLAN standards. For this

How to, you will need to download the CLAN program on your computer, and from the web site you can download a folder called "Practice materials 2.3", which contains some files to run through CLAN.

2.3.1 *Setting up CLAN and checking your files through the CHECK command*

Once you have prepared your transcriptions in word files according to the rules and conventions explained in *How to* section 2.1, and then saved them as text-only files, you are ready to begin using the CLAN program. This program can be down-loaded freely from the CHILDES web site (http://childes.psy.cmu.edu/) and installed on your computer.

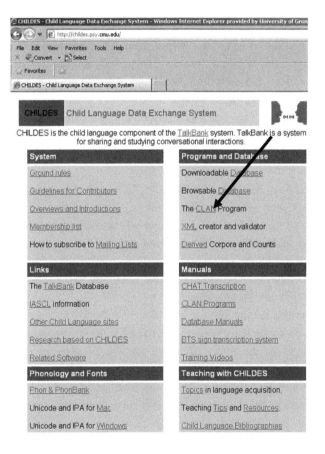

2.3.2 *Setting up CLAN*

When you start the program, you will see a screen looking more or less like the one depicted in the next screenshot.

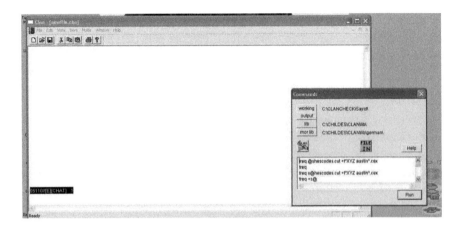

The large window is where the output from the commands will appear; in the small window, you can enter the commands. But first, you have to tell CLAN where to look for your files. Click the button "working". This will bring up a dialog box from which you can select both the drive and the directory where the files which contain your data are located. If you want a different directory for the output that will be created from the analyses you plan to run, you can specify this under the "output" button. (You will have to create an output folder first and then browse to it under the output button).

The web site SLD_Methods (DOI:10.1075/lllt.29.website) contains a folder "Practice materials 2.3" with four subfolders containing 22 text files which have been coded in CHAT. They contain files at different stages of the coding process. You can download the mother folder with subfolders and files on your own computer. For the purpose of the exercises below, set your working directory to the subfolder "initial". You also have to specify a folder on your computer as Output folder unless you want these files to be saved in your working directory.

The two buttons left are 'lib' and 'mor lib'. Here the folders for program help files are specified – files which are used as the basis for the commands that will be run. By default, 'lib' is in the folder in which the CLAN program was pre-installed (e.g. C:\CHILDES\CLAN\lib), and it contains a number of files necessary to run the program, which usually have the file extension ".cut". The most important of these files is the "depfile.cut". In this folder you can also store files which contain lists of items that you wish to be counted or changed in all of your data files (for details see the CLAN manual).

The directory specified under "mor lib" is where the files which are necessary to perform a morphological analysis are stored. CLAN offers the possibility for morphological tagging of each word in a data file for a number of languages - among others English,

Spanish, German, Dutch, Hebrew and Cantonese (see http://childes.psy.cmu.edu/
morgrams/). For these languages, other researchers have written grammars and
compiled lexicon files which can perform a morphological analysis of each word, identifying the lexicon entry form (the "lemma") from which it was derived, the word class,
and the inflectional form. If you want to avail yourself of this function, you may download those files separately and specify under "mor lib" where the directory is which
contains them.

2.3.3   *Checking your files*

Before you can begin working with CLAN, you have to verify whether there are no
problems or oversights left in your coded files. If your working directory contains a set
of files ending with the extension ".cha", as is the case in our example, the command for
checking these files is "check *.cha" (in other words: check whether all the files located
in the working directory which have the extension .cha are in compliance with all necessary CHAT transcription conventions).

   Note that if you are using a text editor such as Word for the transcription and
coding of your files, you have to make sure that all files are closed in Word before
you check them in CLAN. Word creates backup files for any open files which contain
a large amount of information pertaining to the file. This information is invisible in
Word, but it will upset CLAN. If an open file in Word is the source of an error, you
can identify this by the file name to which the message pertains. Here is an example of
such an error message:

```
From file <E:\MY FILES\Texts\~$01.cha>
*** File "E:\MY FILES\Texts\~$01.cha": line 1.
```

You can see that the filename which appears here starts with the symbols "~$". This
means that this file is the backup of a file opened in Microsoft Word. These backups
are erased when the file is closed (note that in the case of a program crash, the backup
files remain and later have to be deleted by hand).

   If you are working with files that were created with a different text editor and
then converted to text-only format, the initial results of the CHECK command can
sometimes be very discouraging with huge numbers of mistakes, but deciphering
and correcting them is not too difficult once you know what to look for. The folder
"checkfile" on the web site (or your own computer now) should contain two files
which create problems, and one which checks out okay. You can verify this by setting your working directory to this folder, and then typing "check *.cha" at the
command prompt.

There are two types of errors at this stage: "Basic Syntax errors", where the violation detected in the file refers to the basic coding conventions, so that no further checking of the actual text is performed, and ordinary errors. A Basic Syntax error is caused, for example, by the use of tabulators within utterances, or by the nonuse of tabulators after the utterance code. To illustrate this, we deleted the tabulator after the speaker code in the first utterance of the file called 02.cha, and inserted a tabulator into the second one. That is, we changed the string "the father had always prevented them" to "the father had always → prevented them" and ran the command "check 02.cha". This elicited the following output from CLAN:

```
From file <02.cha>
*** File "02.cha": line 8.
*XYZ: In her newspaper column Error, Stage left, Anna
Quindlen is accusing Actors' Equity.
Use TAB character instead of space character(s).(4)
*** File "02.cha": line 11.
*XYZ: → she says that → Actors' Equity likes it
Illegal character(s) '<tab>' found.(48)

Warning: BASIC SYNTAX ERROR - Second pass not attempted !
Warning: Please repeat CHECK until no error messages are
reported!
```

Because the second stage of the checking process was not performed, it is quite possible that the file 02.cha contains many further errors, which the program is not detecting at this point, and which will only become apparent once you have corrected the initial oversights and run the check command again.

The file 01.cha, on the other hand, does not contain any such basic syntax errors, but will produce a number of other error messages. In each case, the error message is preceded by the utterance which contains the violation, with the offending bit underlined. The first two error messages we received pertained to the fact that a number was used within the text:

```
*** File "01.cha": line 6.
*XYZ:  the story is about the relationship between a
father and his 2 daughters and about the way he influenced
them.
Numbers are not allowed inside words.(47)
*** File "01.cha": line 6.
*XYZ:  the story is about the relationship between
a father and his 2 daughters and about the way he
influenced them.
Numbers should be written out in words.(38)
```

As you can see, you may sometimes get multiple error messages triggered by the same violation, so replacing "2" with "two" here will fix both these error messages.

In the next utterance there are two sentences, each of which elicits an error message. The first one pertains to a new utterance (starting with a capital letter) and the second one to an utterance that does not have an utterance delimiter (a period) at the end:

```
*** File "01.cha": line 7.
*XYZ:   after their father's death, the two grown-up sis-
ters, Constantia and Josephine weren't controlled by their
father anymore. They also couldn't rely on him anymore.
Utterance delimiter must be at the end of the
utterance.(36)
*** File "01.cha": line 11.
*XYZ:   the story ends with a dialogue between the two
women about the question whether they should keep Kate as a
maid or fire her
Utterance delimiter expected.(21)
```

Again, these problems could easily be fixed by dividing the first utterance into two utterances (and putting *XYX: → in front of the second utterance) and adding a period at the end of the last utterance and then running the CHECK command again.

In order to keep errors to a minimum, it is important to stick to the guidelines mentioned in *How to* 2.1. The most common errors in CHAT files are:

a. utterance delimiters (punctuation marks such as ., ?, !) within the utterance
b. no utterance delimiter mark at the end of utterance lines
c. the obligatory headers are not all there, or not in the correct order
d. uppercase letters within words
e. numbers in the text (they have to be spelled out)
f. two tiers of the same kind (e.g. two error tiers) are associated with one utterance tier
g. a comma is immediately followed by the next word (there has to be a space between the two)
h. a code starting with & (e.g. & = laugh) is immediately followed by a punctuation mark (there has to be a space between the two)
i. there is an empty line after the @End line
j. there is an empty line before the @Begin line
k. there are empty lines in the text

Once your texts have no more error messages, it is time to start analyzing your data. The next *How to* section explains how to obtain data from your output files.

2.4   Creating Lexical Profile and Frequency counts with CLAN

In Chapter 3 we explained that you can create a Lexical Profile from your own corpus data. This *How to* section illustrates how to create a table in Microsoft Excel with which a large number of lexical items can be counted and analyzed. These counts and analyses will provide insight in lexical diversity, i.e. the Lexical Profile, of a group of learners. For this *How to* section you need to download the folder "Practice materials 2.4" from the web site SLD_Methods (DOI:10.1075/lllt.29.website).

2.4.1   *Creating a table for frequency counts in Excel*
Since conducting a lexical analysis on 22 files of ca. 200 words each is a rather lengthy business, the folder "Practice materials 3.4" contains a subfolder called "LFP", with the first eight texts. Download these to your computer.

Set your working directory to this folder and your output directory to a folder on your computer, e.g. "My files:\LFP". Now type the following command at the CLAN command prompt:

freq *.cha > freq.txt

This command performs a frequency count on all the files in your working directory which end in the extension .cha and places the result from this analysis in a file called freq.txt (a text-only file), which is located in the directory which you have specified as your output directory. It will look as follows:

freq *.cha

```
Thu May 06 21:00:31 2010
freq (23-Apr-2010) is conducting analyses on:
  ALL speaker tiers
*****************************************
From file <F:\HOW TO FILES\FOR WEBSITE\initital\02.cha>
  1 Anna
  3 Asian
  1 Error
```

```
 1 Quindlen
 5 a
 1 about
 1 according
 1 accusing
 1 actor
12 actors
 3 also
 1 always
 2 are
 1 around
 1 article
 1 be
 1 because
```

Now we would like to transfer all this information into Excel in order to be able to manipulate it. What we need are three separate columns, the first one with the text number, the second with the number of times used and the third with the actual item. To do so, we open Word and from there open the file freq.txt, which has just been created, and which contains the words from the eight consecutive analyses.

Use this information to create three columns: the name of the file in the left-hand column, the number of times a word has been used in the middle column, and the lexical item in the right-hand column, as shown below. You may want to devise some handy Word tools to do this rapidly. (Of course, it would also be possible to write an extended Macro to do all this in one go.) You will get a text as follows:

```
Text02    1 Anna
Text02    3 Asian
Text02    1 Error
Text02    1 Quindlen
Text02    5 a
Text02    1 about
Text02    1 according
Text02    1 accusing
Text02    1 actor
```

After you have a neat list with only the text number, tab, number and item, you can replace each single space with a tab, so your columns will look as follows:

```
text01    1    A
text01    2    About
text01    2    And
text01    1    Between
text01    1    Daughters
text01    1    Father
text01    1    He
text01    1    His
text01    1    Influenced
text01    1    Is
text01    1    Relationship
text01    1    Story
text01    3    The
text01    1    Them
text01    1    Two
text01    1    Way
text02    1    Anna
text02    1    Error
text02    1    Quindlen
text02    2    A
```

Once you have created these columns, you can copy-paste them to Excel. Open a new file in Excel, and type the headings for the three columns – e.g. "Text" – "Number" – "Item" – into the first row. Paste the columns, starting in row 2. (See Figure 1.)

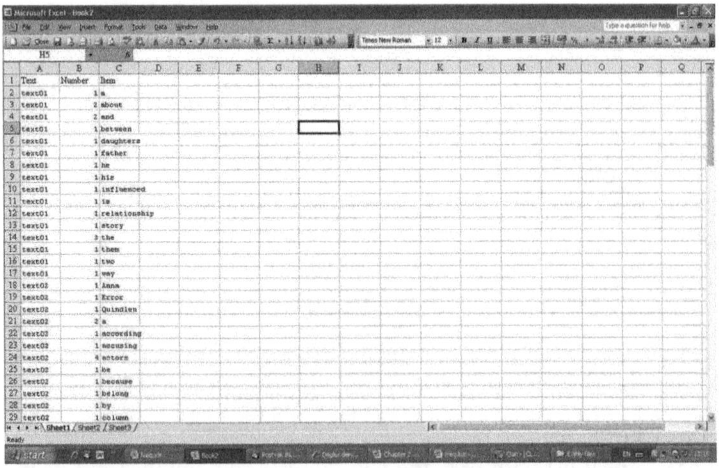

Figure 1. Columns with text, number and items pasted in Excel

Now we have a word count for each individual text. However, we would like to know, of course, how the use of the individual words develops across each text. In other words, we need a table which looks like Table 1, telling us that the word "a" was used once in text01, twice in text02 and text03, and so on. Excel allows you to create a table which can give you this information by means of a function which is called a "PivotTable".

Table 1. Table showing us frequency of items over texts

	text01	text02	text03	text04	text05	Total
A	1	2	2			5
About	2			1		3
according		1				1
Accusing		1				1
Actors		4				4
After					1	1
All			1			1
And	2					2

In order to do this, you first have to select the rows and columns that contain your data. You can select the entire sheet by clicking in the top left grey box, between the column label A and the row label 1 or you can just select the cells that actually contain data with the mouse or the cursor.

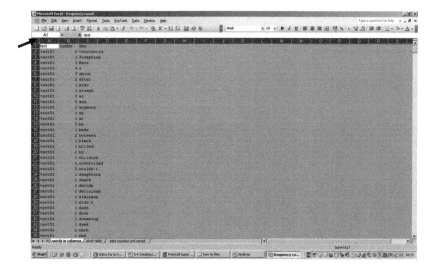

Figure 2. Select all data on worksheet

Click "Data – PivotTable and PivotChart Report"

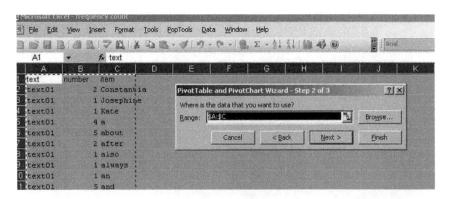

Now you have to work through a number of dialogs. The first asks you what data you want to analyze, and whether you want to have a PivotTable or a PivotChart. You can just click "Next" here, accepting the default selections. In the next window you are asked where your data to be analyzed are, the area that you have selected is displayed in the box called "Range".

Since this is where the data you want to analyze are indeed located, you can again just click "Next".

In the next dialog, you are asked whether you want the PivotTable on a new worksheet, or somewhere on an existing worksheet within your Excel-file. Just click "Next" again. Now you get an empty PivotTable and a dialog with all the column labels in your data:

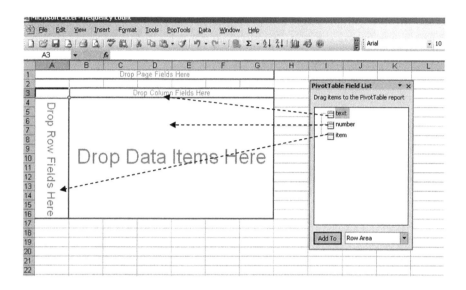

You may want to play with this a bit to familiarize yourself with how it works. Basically, you can drag each column label into each area of the PivotTable. For your purpose, we want to drag the "Number" label to where it says "Drop Data Items here", the "Text" label to where it says "Drop Column Fields Here" and the "Item" label to where it says "Drop Row Fields Here". When you have done that, your screen should look like this:

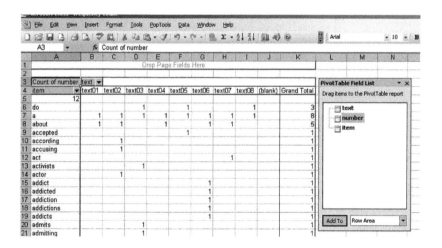

Note that virtually all cells contain only the number 1. This is because in its default format, the PivotTable just counts the number of occurrences of a certain type rather than tokens. For example, in row 7, the indefinite article *a* has one occurrence in each text. You can see that the table is of the type that only counts occurrences because that is what it says in the very top left cell: "Count of Number". However, what we want is for the table not to "count" the occurrences, but to add up the numbers in the cells "Number". So, we right-click again (put the cursor somewhere inside the table) to bring up the PivotTable menu, and click on "Field Settings".

	A	B	C	D	E	F	G	H	I	J
1					Drop Page Fields Here					
2										
3	Count of number	text ▼								
4	item ▼	text01	text02	text03	text04	text05	text06	text07	text08	(blank)
5		12								
6	do			1		1			1	
7	a	1							1	
8	about	1								
9	accepted									
10	according									
11	accusing									
12	act									
13	activists									
14	actor									
15	addicted									
16	addiction									
17	addictions									
18	addict									
19	addicts						1			
20	admits			1						
21	admitting			1						
22	after	1				1	1			
23	alive					1				

PivotTable Field [X]

Source field: number

Name: Sum of number

Summarize by:

Sum
Count
Average
Max
Min
Product
Count Nums

OK   Cancel   Hide   Number...   Options >>

'Count' was selected here before, but now click on "Sum". (This is a fantastically useful menu, as you see, you can have Excel calculate Averages, Standard Deviations (scroll down to get this option), and if you click on "Options>" to the right, you can have the results displayed as Percentages and all kinds of other neat things!).

Once you have clicked on "Sum", the table should be in the format you want. If you want to merge these results in one big table with other results, you can select the whole PivotTable and copy-paste it into a different sheet. Here you should choose "Paste Special" and then "Values".

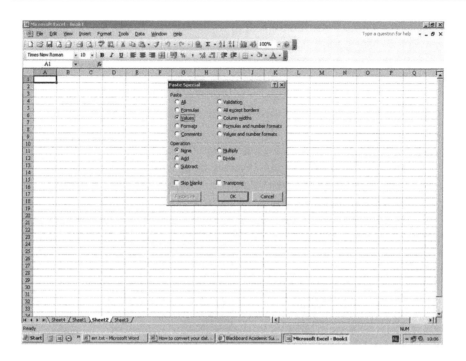

Now that you have all words, the number of times they have occurred in each text, and so on, you can sort your data by looking at which words are most frequent, least frequent and so on.

This analysis might be distorted, for example by the fact that some words appear in different forms – "is", "was" and "were" are all forms of "to be", "woman" and "women" are basically the same word, and so on. For some languages, CLAN offers the possibility of a morphological analysis, which allows the lemmatization of each word (that is, to bring each word back to its lexical stem). Otherwise you may have to change them by hand.

This was the last *How to* section for Chapter 3. We hope that these tools and techniques will give you a good start in coding your data efficiently and using excel pivot tables to their advantage.

2.5   Recalculating values to 0–1

In this *how to* we show how values can be recalculated to values from 0–1 so that originally different kinds of values and interactions of different constructs can be visualized and compared to each other more easily. For this *how to*, you can look at the Excel-file called "Recalculating values to 0–1" to see how the codes have been entered.

In Chapter 3 we compared three measures: D (lexical diversity) with a maximum value of 104 and a minimum of 44, the proportion of unique words, with a maximum of 41% and a minimum of 8%, and the average word length with a maximum of 8 and minimum of 4 letters. These three measures cannot be represented together in a single graph. In the chapter, though, these three measures were shown in one graph. To see how we did this, look at the Excel file called "Recalculating values". The procedure we followed is as follows:

1. At the bottom of the column with the original D values, determine the maximum value by typing: = max(C4:C27)
2. Below the maximum, determine the minimum value by typing: = min(C4:C27)
3. Next to the column with original D values, insert a new column.
4. Put your cursor next to the first value, in our case cell D4.
5. There you insert a formula that calculates the original value (C4) minus the minimum value (C29) divided (slash) by the maximum (C28) minus the minimum (C29). In the *fx* bar you see that the formula is written as follows: = (C4–C29)/(C28–C29)

			Microsoft Excel - Analysis for website chapter 3		
			File Edit View Insert Format Tools PopTools		
		D4		*fx* =(C4-C29)/(C28-C29)	
	A	B	C	D	E	F
2						
3			D			
4			67,52	0,40		
5			67,45			
6			93,52			
7			84,44			
8			51,90			
9			73,06			
10			75,25			
11			57,06			
12			43,60			
13			56,28			
14			58,29			
15			79,34			
16			63,17			
17			74,64			
18			90,92			
19			85,73			
20			103,78			
21			57,18			
22			66,43			
23			85,00			
24			80,92			
25			81,00			
26			43,60			
27			103,78			
28		MAX	103,78			
29		MIN	43,60			
30						
31						

6. Once you have inserted this formula and you have your newly calculated value in D4, you cannot just simply pull down this formula because Excel automatically moves down to the next cells for all the given values. So rather than referring to the cell C28 every time, it will go to cells C29, C30, and so on unless you make the reference "absolute" (i.e. make it refer back to the exact same cell every time). To make the reference absolute, you need to add dollar signs to the rows and columns in cells C28 and C29. In our case, we remain in column C, so we do not have to put a dollar sign in front of C, just in front of the row number. = (C4–C$29)/(C$28–C$29). (Note that C4 does not get a $ in it because we actually want this one to change to the following cell when we pull down our formula).

	D4	▼	fx =(C4-C$29)/(C$28-C$29)	
	C	D	E	F
2				
3	D	D-rec	Unique	U-rec
4	67,52	0,40	26,67	0,56

7. Now you can pull down the formula by putting your cursor on the little cross at the bottom right and as soon as you see a + sign, pull down the formula to the last data point.

After you have recalculated the D values, you can recalculate the other two values in the same manner. Once you have recalculated all the variables you want to compare as shown above, you can make a graph as will be explained in *how to* 3.1.

3. *How to* section – Chapter 4

3.1 Making graphs in Excel

In Chapter 4 we showed all kinds of graphs to visualize the data. This *how to* section illustrates how we created these graphs. For those who have very limited experience with Excel, it explains step by step how to create these graphs, how to format the graphs, and how to insert trend lines Finally, it shows how to make a min-max chart. From the web site you can download the folder called "Practice materials 3-1" which contains an Excel file, called "Making line graphs and min-max graphs". The screenshots that you see in this section were taken from that file, so if the screenshot is not clear enough, looking at our original files may be helpful.

3.1.1 Making a line graph

1. Select the part that you want in your chart, for example Alberto's, including the heading *No V* and *Don't V* by moving your cursor from the spot you want to start to where you want to end. (You do not have to select the column called *Tape*).

	A	B	C	D	E	F
1	Alberto					
2	Tape	No V	don't V	aux-neg	analyzed don't	
3	1	4	32			
4	2	57	20			
5	3	79	5			
6	4	62	23			
7	5	53	27			
8	6	48	32			
9	7	62	21			
10	8	52	20			
11	9	59	12			
12	10	88	1			
13	11	62	1			
14	12	69	21			
15	13	60	22			
16	14	56	23			
17	15	60	31			
18	16	43	17			
19	17	60	34			
20	18	53	15			
21	19	41	26			
22	20	40	38			
23						
24						

(Microsoft Excel - Cancino data for website; File Edit View Insert Format Tools PopTools Data Window; B2 — *fx* No V)

2. Once you have selected the part, click on the Chart icon or go to Insert and then Chart.

3. Choose Line graphs and then press Next > Next > Finish. You should now have a nice line graph in color.

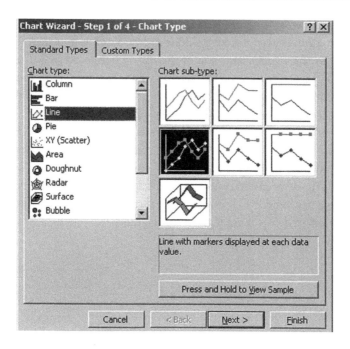

3.1.2   *Formatting headings, legends and lines and adding a trendline*

1.   Once you have a line graph, you can change the way the chart (larger square) and plot (smaller square) looks. If you put your cursor on the chart as a whole and click the right button, you can select Chart Options. In our case, we changed the color of the background and the color of the lines so they would be visible in black and white.

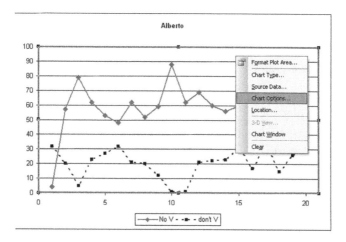

2.   In Chart Options you can also select titles and add whatever you need.

3. Put your cursor on a line and click the right mouse button. Select Format Data Series. You can change the color, width and type of line you want. You can also change the shape, color and size of the dots. Look to see which combination makes the variability most visible. Remember, the points are more important than the lines, so try to foreground the points by making them more visible and background the lines by choosing a thin line or a dotted line.

4. You can add a trend line by selecting Format Data Series again and clicking on Add Trend Line. You can choose different kinds of trend lines; to smooth the variability a little but still keep it visible, a polynomial to a high order (e.g. 6th) may be useful. To see the general trend a polynomial to the 2nd degree is useful. When formatting the trend line, remember that for our purposes the trend line is just background, so do not make it stand out too much.

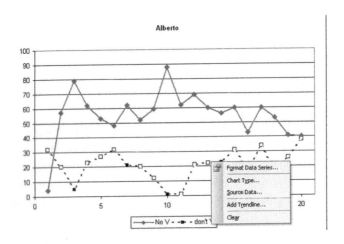

3.1.3   Making a min-max graph
For reference see the example Excel sheet of a min-max graph.

1. First select a column of data, copy it and paste it somewhere so you have an empty column next to it.

2. The size of the window depends on the number of data points you have. The smaller the dataset is, the smaller the window should be. For our data (20 data points), we chose a "window" of five data points. With your cursor first go to the empty cell next to the third data point (the middle of five) so that it is highlighted. That is the cell where the new numbers will appear.

3. In the cell (or move your cursor to the function bar fx right below the toolbar) type: = min(

4. Then with your cursor select the five data points you want to have the minimum value of. The cell numbers (here B57:B61) will appear.

54				
55	**Alberto's use of don't V**			
56	Tape	Alberto		
57	1	32		
58	2	20		
59	3	5	=min(B57:B61)	
60	4	23		
61	5	27		
62	6	32		
63	7	21		
64	8	20		
65	9	12		
66	10	1		
67	11	1		
68	12	21		
69	13	22		
70	14	23		
71	15	31		
72	16	17		
73	17	34		
74	18	15		
75	19	26		
76	20	38		
77				

5. Close off with a closing bracket and press Enter. If you did it right you will now have the minimum value of the five data points in the cell you had selected and there is a little green triangle in the top left corner of the cell, meaning it has a formula in there.

6. Once you have the formula, you can copy it by dragging the bottom right square down to the bottom of the column (stop at two points above the last one).

7. After you have made a column with minimum values, do the same for the maximum values. Go to the next column and repeat everything, except put in *max* instead of *min*.

8. Once you have the three columns (data, min values, and max values) you can make a min-max graph by selecting these columns. You can also reformat it so that the lines of the real data disappear and the min-max lines are not too obtrusive.

In the next *how to* section we will discuss how you can test for significance.

3.2 Resampling techniques

In Chapter 4 we compared the variability in Alberto's data with those of Jorge by using resampling techniques. In this *how to* section we will discuss the exact steps needed to resample our data. For ease of reference some figures and text are repeated here from the chapter. Our resampling analysis is performed in Microsoft Excel 2003 by means of the statistical add-in Poptools (Hood 2008), which can be downloaded at http://www.cse.csiro.au/poptools/. On the web site SLD_Methods (DOI:10.1075/lllt.29.website) there is also an Excel file called *Practice materials 3.2*, which you may want to download so that you can practice the steps and see the codes we used. In this file, one worksheet is called Hypothesis 1 and the other Hypothesis 2.

3.2.1   *Installing add-ins for Excel*
1.   Download Poptools (Hood 2009). To install the add-ins, first make sure you close Excel before you go through the installation!
2.   Go through the installation (Click Run > Yes > Next > I accept the agreement > Next > Next > Install). Excel will now open a Readme file, and you will see Poptools appear in the menu (You may need to go to Tools > Macro > Security and select medium). Click OK.

3.2.2   *Testing hypothesis 1: Jorge is generally more variable than Alberto*
Remember, the null-hypothesis is that the differences between values in succeeding data points stem from one single distribution (in other words, as if all these distances occurred in the values of one person rather than two, as our alternative hypothesis states).

For ease of reference, we show the same screenshot as in the chapter again. For the reasoning behind the steps, please read the chapter. Here we explain how to do the different operations.

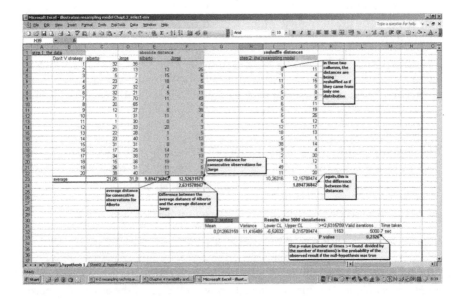

Column B has the number of the tape session, column C Alberto's percentage of *don't V* strategies and column D Jorge's percentage of *don't V* strategies.

3.2.3 Step 1: Calculating absolute differences

1. Give columns E and F headers (*absolute difference, Alberto, Jorge*).
2. Put the cursor in cell E4.
3. Type in: = abs(C4–C3), which means calculate the absolute difference between C4 and C3. Press Enter.
4. Pull this formula down until you get to Alberto's last data point.
5. Pull the formula first to the right and then down until you get to Jorge's last data point.

3.2.4 Calculating average differences and their difference

1. In cell E23, type the following formula: = average(E4:E22)
2. Pull the formula to the right (cell F24).
3. In cell F24, type: = F23–E23 (Note: this difference is our testing criterion).

We now proceed to step 2, which is to set up a resampling model. The resampling model takes the original data in columns E and F and reorders them randomly.

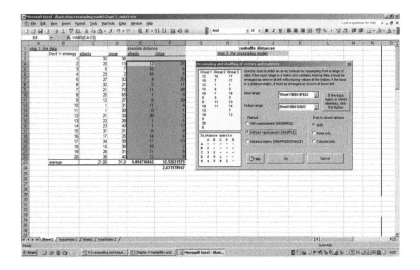

3.2.5 Step 2: Reshuffling distances

1. Create two new columns, one for Alberto and one for Jorge in columns I and J and put appropriate headings (so you will know later what is what).
2. Click on Poptools > Resample.

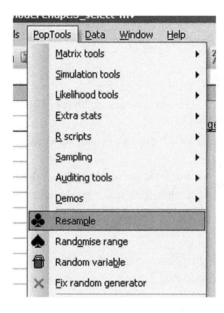

3. Put your cursor in the window for "input range", and highlight simultaneously the two columns you want to resample. For Alberto that would be E4:E21 and for Jorge F4:F21.
4. Put your cursor in the window for "output range", and highlight the two columns (I and J) where you want the numbers to appear.
5. Select Without replacement (Shuffle) (because you want the exact same numbers as in the original data).
6. Click on Go.
7. If everything goes well, you will have the exact same numbers as in the original two columns, but in a randomly different order across the two columns. Every time you press F9, the order will change.
8. Below the two columns, put the average distance and calculate the difference between these averages (In cell I23, type the following formula: = average(I4:I22). Pull the formula to the right (cell J23) and in cell J24, type in: = F23–E23 (Note: this difference is our dependent range).

The third step is to reshuffle the data 5000 times, i.e. simulate 5000 resampling simulations in a so-called Monte Carlo Analysis. This means that 5000 times we have a new number in cell J24. By comparing our testing criterion (which is the original distance in cell F24) with the newly calculated distance (cell J24), we can test our null-hypothesis.

3.2.6   Step 3: Running a Monte Carlo

1. In the Excel file go to Poptools > Simulation Tools > Monte Carlo analysis.

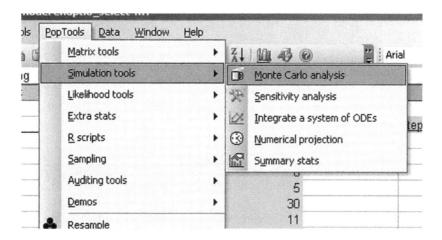

2. For the dependent range, select J24, which is the newly calculated difference between averages.

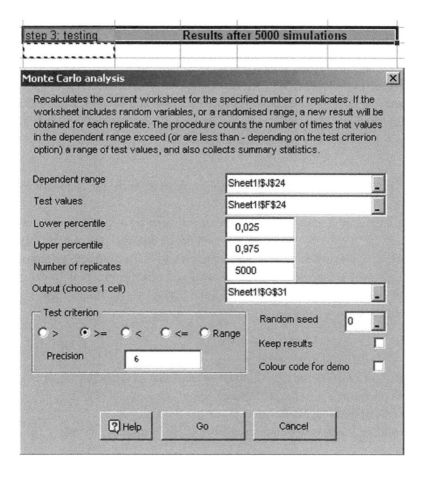

3. For the test values, select F24, which is the testing criterion based on our empirical data.
4. For Output, move your cursor to the cell where you want your results to appear, in our case G31.
5. Select as Test criterion equal or greater than (> =).
6. Press Go. You will see the number of iterations on your screen and after 9 seconds you will have the descriptives.

step 3: testing		Results after 5000 simulations				
Mean	Variance	Lower CL	Upper CL	>=2,6315789	Valid iterations	Time taken
-0,046042105	11,273312	-6,63158	6,315789474	1153	5000	9 sec

7. To interpret the results of the simulations, you have to calculate the p-value by dividing the number of times the same or greater value than our testing criterion occurred (here 1153) by the number of iterations (here 5000). Put your cursor in cell L33 and type: = K32/L32. Note that when you repeat this simulation, slightly different numbers will appear, but they will be in a similar range.

The p-value gives us the frequency with which the original difference between Jorge and Alberto (cell F24) was replicated in the 5000 randomized simulations. Only if this frequency is very low (below 5%, which corresponds to a p-value of 0.05), can we reject our null-hypothesis. In our illustration, the p-value is 0.2326, which means that roughly 23% of all simulations produced values that were similar to the original data. This means that we cannot reject the null-hypothesis and must conclude that on average, Jorge is not more variable than Alberto.

3.2.7 Testing Hypothesis 2: There are significant peaks in the use of don't V by Jorge and Alberto

In step 1 we started again by defining what we mean by a "peak". In this case, we stipulated that if there is a real peak, it should not be just one isolated jump. In order to be able to ignore isolated, one-time fluctuations, we started out with a simple moving average over 2 observations. Then we calculated what the maximum distance was between data points, e.g between 1 and 2, 1 and 3, 1 and 4, 1 and 5 and finally 1 and 6, then 2 and 3, 2 and 4, and so on.

3.2.8 Calculating moving averages

1. Move cursor to D7 and type the following formula: = average(B6:B7), press Enter.
2. Pull the formula down to the last data point.
3. In D6 put the same number as in D7.
4. Repeat for Jorge's data by pulling the formula to E7 and then down.

3.2.9 Calculating the maximum distance between data points

1. For the 2 step difference, move the cursor to H7 and type: = D7–D6, press Enter.
2. Pull this formula down to the last data point.
3. Repeat the same procedure for Jorge's data.
4. For the 3 step difference, move the cursor to J8 and type: = D8–D6, press Enter.
5. Pull this formula down to the last data point and repeat the procedure for Jorge's data.
6. For the 4–6 step difference repeat all the steps and increase the distance between the cells.
7. To determine the maximum difference between data points, type in cell H27: = max(H6:H25).
8. To determine the maximum values for Alberto, type in cell H29 all his maximum values: = max(H27;J27;L27;N27;P27).
9. Repeat for Jorge.
10. The values in H and I29 are our empirical criteria: the testing criterion. In our resampling we will see what the chance is that this same value will appear again.

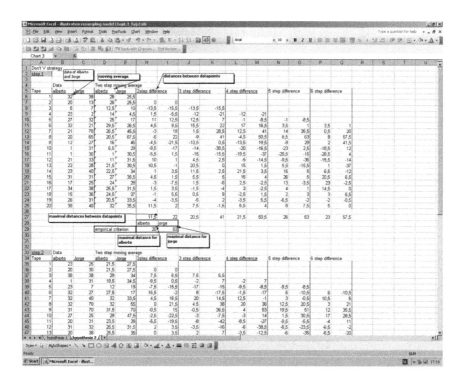

In step 2, we formulated our resampling model, i.e. we defined *what* has to be resampled. In this case, we took the null-hypothesis that by resampling the original data per person, we will get the same maximal distance as in the observed set. It is important to note that we resampled our data with replacement, which implies that in each simulation, a new set is randomly drawn from the original pool, and not all observations are necessarily selected in each simulation. Because we are looking at the individual trajectories, we compared the maximal simulated distance for Alberto with the maximal distance in the data. After that, we did the same for Jorge.

3.2.10   *Resampling*

1. Copy the original data and formulae from step 1 (Columns A–Q and Rows 1–29) and paste it after putting the cursor in cell A33.
2. In this new data set, delete Alberto's data. (You will see all the calculated values disappear and be replaced by #DIV/0!).
3. Click Poptools > Resample.
4. In the Input range select Alberto's original data (B6–B25).
5. In the Output range select the empty cells under the heading Alberto (B35–B54).
6. Under Method, choose With replacement (Resample).

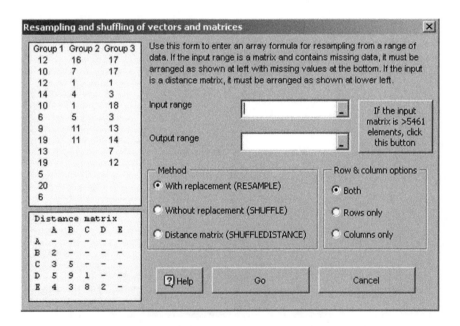

7. Press Go. You will now see the resampled figures and all the values have numbers again. Every time you press F9, all values will change again.
8. Repeat the exact same procedure for Jorge.

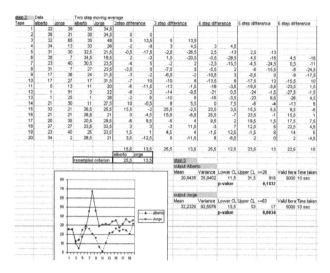

In step 3 we ran two separate Monte Carlo Analyses, one for Jorge and one for Alberto, with 5000 simulation steps.

1.   Go to Poptools > Simulation tools > Monte Carlo analysis.
2.   For the dependent range, select Alberto's resampled criterion (H58).
3.   For the Test values, select Alberto's original value (H29).
4.   Write down 5000 for the number of replicates.
5.   Choose a cell in which you want to put the results of the simulation.
6.   Select as Test criterion equal or greater than (> =).
7.   Press Go.

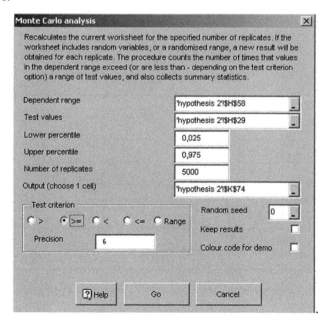

7. Calculate the p-value by dividing the number of times the same or greater value than our testing criterion occurred by the number of iterations.
8. Repeat these steps for Jorge.

The screenshot with all the data shows that for Alberto, the resulting p-value was 0.1832 (cell L73), which means that in almost 19% of all simulations, the random model was able to reproduce the peaks in the order of magnitude of those of Alberto. Therefore, we cannot reject the null-hypothesis for the data of Alberto. For Jorge, on the other hand, the result turns out to be highly significant (p = 0.0034) and we can safely conclude that the peaks are not likely to be the result of coincidental fluctuations (cell O73).

In this *how to* we have given two examples in which we operationalized the measurements in a hypothesis (Jorge is more variable than Alberto, or there are significant peaks in the data) and developed a reasonable testing criterion which we then resampled. These examples will hopefully give you ideas of how to resample your own variability data to test for significance.

3.3 Detrending

In Chapter 4 we briefly mentioned that it is sometimes necessary to detrend the data.

In *how to* 3.2, we showed how we can resample our data to test if a certain peak is meaningful or not by running a Monte Carlo simulation. In our example in the chapter and in the accompanying *how to*, it appeared that the peak in Jorge's use of *don't V* did not occur by chance, and can therefore be considered a developmental overuse of this construction. In the chapter we also mentioned that we did not have to detrend the data because, as the figure in the chapter showed (here repeated as Figure 1), there was not an overall increase in the use of *don't V*. The polynomial trend line actually goes down again at the end.

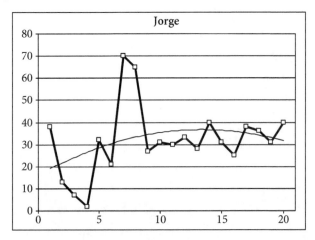

Figure 1. The use of Jorge's *don't V* strategy in the CRS study with a polynomial trend line (2nd degree).

In some cases though, it may be necessary to detrend the data, especially if you are interested in local variability rather than in a general trend. Our CRS data did not have any clear examples where this would be the case, so we decided to create a fictive example from the data to make clear why detrending may be useful and how to do it. Figure 2 shows Juan's actual use of *aux-neg*, and as the polynomial shows, the use of this strategy increases for a while and then goes down again, just as in Jorge's use of *don't V*, so there is no need to detrend the data here either if we want to test whether a local peak is meaningful or not.

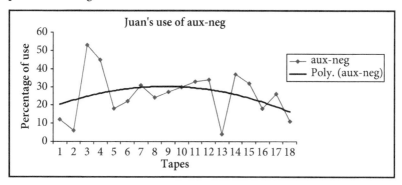

Figure 2. The use of Juan's *aux-neg* strategy in the CRS study with a polynomial trend line (2nd degree).

However, if we were to examine only the first 12 data points, a different picture emerges. (Note: There is no real reason to do so except to give an example of detrending!) As Figure 3 shows, there is now a general increase in the use of the *aux-neg* strategy. If we want to test if the peak at data point 3 is one by chance or not, we have to keep in mind that even though there seems to be a strong peak, part of this increase may be explained by the fact that there was a general increase anyway (as the linear trend line shows). So to make sure the peak is not just due to the general increase, we can deduct the degree of general increase from each data point by "detrending".

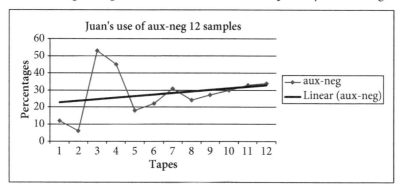

Figure 3. The use of Juan's *aux-neg* strategy in the CRS study with only 12 data points and a linear trend line.

Detrending basically means taking away the slope, which is the general increase over time. Once we take away the general increase, we can see how the "pure" residual values behave and test for significance as in *how to* 3.2. For this *how to*, you can download the Excel file called "3.3 detrending" to see how we entered the formulae.

3.3.1 *Detrending the raw data*

To detrend, we need to subtract the values created by a linear trend line. We do so by first creating a "model" of the trend line and then deducting it from the raw data.

In your Excel sheet, first create two rows and write down "intercept" and "slope", so you will know where you can find the figures you will need. Then be sure to have a column of data points in numerical order (rather than the date) and the actual values. In addition, get two new columns ready by putting headings for "model" and "residual".

	A	B	C	D	E	F
1	intercept					
2	slope					
3						
4	tape	aux-neg		model	residual	
5	1	12				
6	2	6				
7	3	53				
8	4	45				
9	5	18				
10	6	22				
11	7	31				
12	8	24				
13	9	27				
14	10	30				
15	11	33				
16	12	34				
17						

Once you have created your columns, proceed as follows:

1. Put your cursor in B1 and type: = intercept(
2. You should see the appropriate formula (known_y's; known_x's) pop up. The known y's are the actual values under "aux-neg" and the known x's are the tape numbers.

	A	B	C	D	E
	Microsoft Excel - 4-3 Detrending				
	File Edit View Insert Format Tools PopTools Dat				
	GEOMEAN ▾ X ✓ *fx* =intercept(				
1	intercept	=intercept(			
2	slope	INTERCEPT(**known_y's**; known_x's)			
3					
4	tape	aux-neg		model	residual
5	1	12			
6	2	6			
7	3	53			
8	4	45			
9	5	18			
10	6	22			
11	7	31			
12	8	24			
13	9	27			
14	10	30			
15	11	33			
16	12	34			

3. With your cursor, select the data values (in our case B5:B16), type a semi-colon and then select the tape numbers (A1:A16).
4. Close off with a closing bracket and press Enter.
5. Repeat these steps for slope. With your cursor in cell B2 type: = slope(B5:B16);(A5:A16) and press Enter
6. If you did this right, you should now have numbers in B1 and B2.

To calculate the model (which is basically the values of the linear trend line), add the intercept and slope, which is multiplied by the tape number.

7. Put the cursor in D5 (the cell under "model")
8. Type: = B1+B2*A5 (Note that you can also do this by selecting the appropriate cells with your cursor)
9. Because the cells with the intercept and slope values need to remain absolute references, you need to put dollar signs before the column and row numbers. The tape numbers are not absolute, so there should be no dollar signs before A or 5. In our case, the formula should look as follows: = $B$1+$B$2*A5.

D5	▼		f_x =$B$1+$B$2*A5	
	A	B	C	D
1	intercept	21,98485		
2	slope	0,912587		
3				
4	tape	aux-neg		model
5	1	12		22,89744
6	2	6		23,81002
7	3	53		24,72261
8	4	45		25,6352
9	5	18		26,54779
10	6	22		27,46037
11	7	31		28,37296
12	8	24		29,28555
13	9	27		30,19814
14	10	30		31,11072
15	11	33		32,02331
16	12	34		32,9359
17				

10. Pull the formula down in the columns.

If you did everything right, your model will show the linear trend line, which is the average "growth" in development. To calculate the detrended data (here called the residual data), you basically take the raw data and deduct the values of the linear trend line (the model data).

11. Put your cursor in E5 (under Residual) and type: = B5–D5
12. Pull the formula down and you will have your detrended data in column F.
13. If everything goes right, then you should be able to make a graphs as follows, with a trend line that is level.

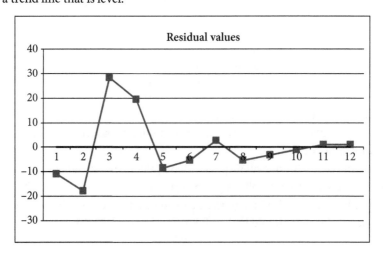

To conclude, detrended data are useful when you want to make sure the degree of variability and interaction between variables is not distorted by the incline of the slope. Detrended data can be used to examine the strength of local peaks or to look at the interaction of different variables as discussed in Chapters 5 and 6 if the variables show steep slopes or different growth patterns.

4.   *How to* section – Chapter 5

4.1   Correlations and moving correlations

In Chapter 5 we examined interactions between variables more closely to see how they develop over time. Are they connected or competing growers, or do their interactions change over time? As we pointed out in the chapter, it is important to first look at the raw data to determine if our expectations (based on theoretical insights) seem to be met. Then to be able to see the interactions more clearly we smooth the data (in our case with Loess functions, which we will not be able to show because the calculations are done with a program that needs to be bought; however, more information on this function can be found on the web, e.g. at http://research.stowers-institute.org/efg/R/ Statistics/loess.htm).

We can also normalize (recalculate figures from 0–1), which has been discussed in the *how to's* 2.5. Finally, we can run correlations over the numbers obtained during the whole time period, but because the interactions may change over time, it is also useful to create a moving window of correlations. In this *how to*, three rather simple Excel functions are explained: how to add variables, how to calculate a correlation in Excel and how to create a moving window of correlations. For this *how to* you can download the Excel-file called "Correlations and moving windows of correlation" from the web site SLD_Methods (DOI:10.1075/lllt.29.website).

4.1.1   *Adding variables*
In our original coding of the advanced learner's data we distinguished between simple, compound, complex and compound-complex sentences. Because we wanted to see the interactions between sentences with main clauses only on the one hand and sentences containing dependent clauses on the other hand, we added the simple and compound sentences together and complex and compound-complex sentences after we had normalized the data. (See the worksheet called Interactions sentence types).

1.   To add numbers, simply type: =
2.   Select the first cell, type + and select the second cell.

An alternative way is as follows

Type: = sum(

Select the cells to be added and close off with a closing bracket.

3. Pull the formula down by putting the cursor on the little square in the bottom right hand corner and then pulling it down to the last values.

Microsoft Excel - 5-1 correlations and moving windows

File   Edit   View   Insert   Format   Tools   PopTools

D31 — f_x =C31+B31

	B	C	D
29	**normalized data**		
30	simple	compound	Simple + compound
31	0,38	0,68	1,06
32	0,51	0,00	0,51
33	0,78	0,00	0,78
34	0,70	0,00	0,70
35	0,28	0,50	0,78
36	0,28	1,00	1,28
37	0,00	0,36	0,36
38	0,18	0,00	0,18
39	0,20	0,00	0,20
40	0,14	0,25	0,39
41	0,18	0,00	0,18
42	0,51	0,00	0,51
43	0,31	0,00	0,31
44	0,47	0,00	0,47
45	0,53	0,31	0,84
46	0,23	0,00	0,23
47	0,18	0,00	0,18
48	0,80	0,00	0,80
49	0,88	0,00	0,88
50	0,20	0,36	0,56
51	1,00	0,00	1,00
52	0,40	0,00	0,40

4.1.2   *Normalizing the data*

As we discussed in the *how to 's* 2.5, we can normalize any data (even smoothed data) as follows. Calculate the minimum and maximum values of an array (see B110 and B111 as examples). Then put your cursor in the appropriate cell (in our case H88) and calculate the present value (in our case B88) minus the minimum value (B110) divided by the maximum value (B111) minus the minimum value (B110). Be sure to put brackets around the pairs of cells on each side of the division mark and put dollar signs in front of row numbers that are absolute references (in our case 110 and 111). In the function bar you can then see the following formula: = (B88–B$110)/ (B$111–B$110)

4.1.3 Calculating correlations

In Excel we can calculate correlations. However, to see if it is significant, we need a statistical program such as SPSS. (Note that on our excel sheet, we have also shown the results that we obtained through an SPSS analysis.) Here we will just discuss how to do so with Excel.

1. Put your cursor in the cell where you want your result to occur (here J3).
2. Type = correl(
3. Select the first array from B4 to B25 and type a semicolon.
4. Select the second array from C4 to C25 and close off with a closing bracket.
5. Press Enter.
6. In our case the result will be 0,07637.

GEOMEAN ▾ ✗ ✓ ƒₓ =correl(B4:B25;C4:C25)

	Words/FV	Simple + c	Complex		correlation		
Smoothed and normalized data							
normalized							
	Words/FV	Simple + c	Complex		correlation Words/FV; simple compound	=correl(B4:B25;C4:C25)	
1	0	0,982386	0		correlation Words/FV; complex		
2	0,04673	0,916264	0,011042		correlation simple compound; complex		
3	0,080946	0,867849	0,029883				
4	0,116079	0,888456	0,013034				
5	0,083951	1	0,066889				
6	0,041525	0,832874	0,341151				
7	0,128315	0,539515	0,615445				
8	0,283892	0,177493	0,887522				
9	0,305577	0	1				
10	0,251536	0,035688	0,929498				
11	0,124374	0,129529	0,805509				
12	0,151602	0,171279	0,717207				
13	0,378931	0,314227	0,545021				
14	0,511808	0,419307	0,459572				
15	0,494015	0,361324	0,540696				
16	0,535461	0,335459	0,563978				
17	0,687717	0,391766	0,448471				
18	0,854065	0,546901	0,25945				
19	1	0,782226	0,018306				
20	0,89646	0,779847	0,011549				
21	0,72958	0,698003	0,106442				
22	0,570218	0,604002	0,206023				

4.1.4   Moving correlation

Just as we can make a moving min-max window as discussed in *how to* 4.1, we can create a moving window of correlations. In our case with a total of 22 data points, we used a window of five.

1. Put the cursor in the appropriate cell, preferably in the middle of the window to be created. Our window will be from 128–132, so we put the cursor in C130.
2. Type the formula for a correlation for the first 5 data points. Your function window should show the following formula: = correl(A128:A132;B128:B132).
3. Pull the formula down till 2 points away from your last data point.
4. Create a graph as usual.

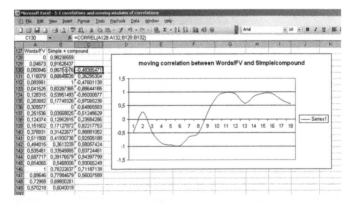

This *how to* has shown some Excel techniques to add data, to calculate a correlation and to create a moving window of correlations. The last two techniques are useful in discovering the relation between two variables. Remember, though, that correlations on their own do not tell us whether the results are significant or not, so there could be a correlation by chance; correlations only make sense when they test measures that are based on some theoretical insight; and finally, correlations do not say anything about causation.

5.   *How to* section – Chapter 6

5.1   Data fitting

In Chapter 6 we discussed data modeling. Before being able to model the data, it is necessary to "fit the data". In this *how to* we will show how you can apply a data fitting technique to create a simple one-dimensional model. For this *how to*, you will need the Excel sheet called "5.1 data fitting". The data in this sheet represent a child's lexical knowledge in weekly measurements, starting when the child was 45 weeks old. (We will not use all the original data from the chapter because they would be too complex to explain in simple steps.) The first column contains the number of weeks (age) and the second column contains the number of words.

As we discussed in Chapter 6, lexical knowledge growth can be defined as a combination of the knowledge one has at one moment in time (L), the new words learned a*L, and the words one does not yet know b*(1-K/L). In short, growth can be defined as r*L(1-L/K), which is derived from the Verhulst logistic growth equation (Verhulst 1838) (K stands for carrying capacity. In the formulas below, we will label it as carcap.) If we want to create a model of the data, each next step in time should be based on the previous step AND the two growth parameters.

First, the following three variables – initial condition, growth rate and carrying capacity – need to be defined and entered in Excel.

1.   In cell J4 (or any other empty cell), type: 1
2.   In the box left to the *fx* bar, type Ini_L (see figure below)
3.   In cell J5, type: 0.2
4.   In the box left to the *fx* bar, type: Rate_L
5.   In cell J6, type: 500
6.   In the box left to the *fx* bar, type: Carcap_L

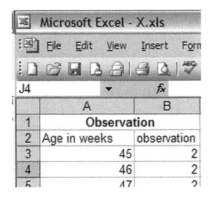
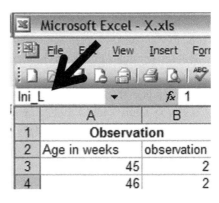

7. For extra clarity, you may want to add these terms in the cells immediately before the numbers:

H	I	J	K
	Ini-L	1	
	Rate_L	0.2	
	Carcap_L	500	

Note that if you did this right, you will see "Ini_L" in the box left to the *fx* bar when you select a cell with one of the values you have entered (for instance J4).

To the right of the columns called "Observation", create two "Model" columns: "Level Model" and "Increase". In the "Level Model" column we are going to simulate the observed data by manipulating the three variables we have just defined.

8. Put your cursor in the first cell of the Level model (C3), and refer to the initial level of vocabulary knowledge by typing the equal sign (=) and then selecting the cell with the initial value (J4). Press Enter.
   If you did everything right, you will see that value 1 appears in this cell. When you change the initial value in J4 (Ini_L) into 1.2, the first value in the Level Model column will also change to 1.2.
9. The increase is the result of the equation $r*L(1-L/K)$. To calculate this, leave the first cell of the Increase column (D3) empty and in the second one (D4) type: = Rate_L*C3*(1-C3/carcap_L). Press Enter.
10. In the second row of the Level Model column (C4) add up the previous value of the model plus the increase, so type: = C3 + D3 and press Enter.
11. Pull the formulas in the two new columns (Level Model and Increase) down to row 34.
12. Create a line graph that includes the observed values and the Level Model. The resulting figure should look something like the figure below if you have used the example values of 1 for initial value, 0.2 for growth rate and 500 for carrying capacity.

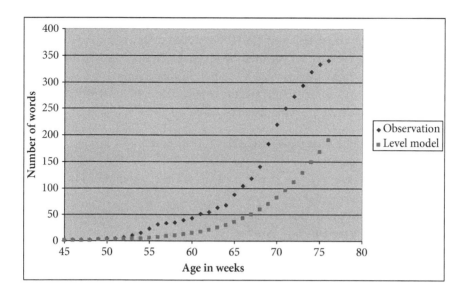

Although the trend of the model is a reasonable match to the observed values, it is far from perfect. Now adjust the values you set for the initial value, growth rate and carrying capacity slightly to try and create a better fit. The resulting figure should look something like the figure below.

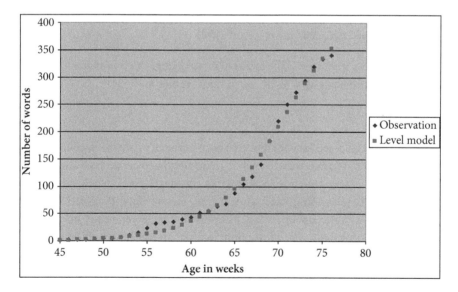

To evaluate the fit of the model to the data, we are first of all dependent on visual inspection, but we can also calculate which is the best fit. To make all this clear to you, we started a new sheet called "fitting the data". (Because Excel does not allow you to reuse the same formula we renamed "Ini_L" and called it "Ini_M". We did the same with the rate and carrying capacity names.) To set up the sheet, create a column SqDiff, immediately to the right of the Increase column. In this column, you calculate the squared difference between the model and the observed data. Immediately right to the SqDiff column, add a column called "Sumofsquares".

1.   Put cursor in cell E3 and type: = (B3-C3)^2. Press Enter.
2.   Pull down the formula.
3.   In cell F3, calculate the sum of all the squares. Type: = sum(E3:E34) and press Enter.
4.   The best fit is the model that has the smallest sum of squared differences between the data and the model.

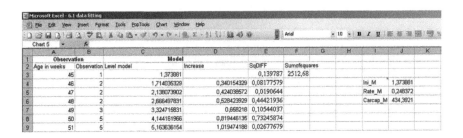

Source: Dromi 1986, 1987 in van Geert 1994b

The data fitting technique is the first step in modeling. Once you have fit the data, you can model the data as we will discuss in the next *how to* (5.2).

5.2   Modeling

In Chapter 6, we discussed how we modeled our vocabulary data using coupled equations. In this *how to* section, we will explain in detail how to create such a model. For this *how to* section, you need a special tool that was developed by Paul van Geert to create precursor models using Excel, so you need to download the Excel file called "5.2 Modeling". This file contains a Macro that will enable you to set up precursor simulations in a systematic way. Please note that the spreadsheet is Excel only, so it will not work with Open Office or other spreadsheet programs. After reviewing some relevant terms, we will describe how to use this tool in general. Then we will show how to model two of the L2 vocabulary levels as discussed in Chapter 6, and finally we will show a fictitious precursor model.

Note: Before you start, make sure the spreadsheet security settings allow Macros (set Macro security level to Medium in Excel). Activate the Macro that is included.

5.2.1 Terms used in the model

The modeling tool asks you to enter terms and values in separate steps. First, it asks how many "growers" will be modeled and then for each grower different values can be set. For ease of reference, we will quickly review the terms to be used here.

- A *grower* is a variable that changes quantitatively on the basis of a principle of increase (e.g. learning) or decrease (e.g. forgetting or suppressing). In our vocabulary example, the different growers were defined as recall, recognition, controlled production and free production.
- *Resources* help maintain and/or increase the level of the growers in the system. *Specific resources* are the actual growers that either support or compete with each other. In our vocabulary development data, recognition supports (i.e. stimulates) recall, which in turn supports controlled production. We have also seen that free production competes with (i.e. suppresses) controlled production. *Background resources* are resources that are not explicitly specified in our model (e.g. support from the environment, size of working memory, time spent on tasks, etc.). The *carrying capacity* is defined as the maximal stable level of a grower that the resources can maintain. And as we have seen in Chapter 6, it is the sum of the specific resources and the background resources of the system.
- There are four *property parameters*: The *growth rate* is the proportion of change of a grower for each time step. The *initial value* is the value of the grower at the beginning of the growth process. The *carrying capacity* is the maximal stable level of a grower that the resources can maintain and its *timing* is concerned with the onset of the growth process. The fourth property parameter specifies the level of *random variation* of the growers.
- The *relational* parameter, as we explained in Chapters 5 and 6, are the relationships of *support* and *competition* among growers. Another relational parameter is the *precursor* relation, which specifies that one grower needs to be at a certain level before another grower may develop.

5.2.2 Working with the model: general introduction

This is a general introduction on how to work with this Excel add-in. In 5.2.3 we will go through the same steps again, but then applied to the vocabulary data discussed in Chapter 6.

1. Open the Excel file called "5.2 Modeling". Open the sheet called "model setup". When you scroll down, you will see three sets of "boxes", blue, yellow and orange ones.
2. Click on the button "Click to set number of growers". (Do not start with the button add grower).

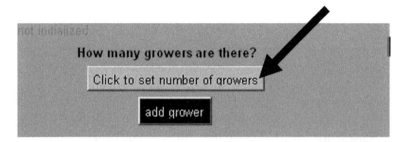

3. A window will appear that will ask you to specify the number of growers. Begin with 1 or 2. After clicking the OK button, windows will appear that will ask you to specify the names of your variables or "growers". By default, the names are Grower1, Grower2, etc., but you can replace them with your own names.

4. After having completed this, select the name of a grower by clicking on it. Specify the properties of the grower by clicking on the desired values in the list boxes extending downwards.

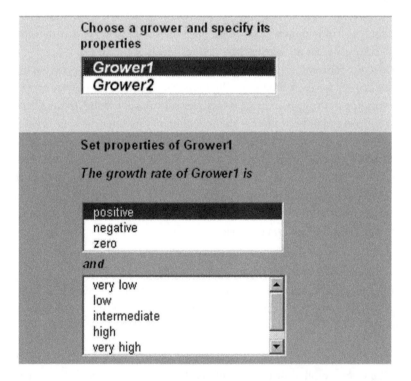

5. The texts and selected values in the list boxes will form sentences, e.g. "The growth rate of Grower1 is positive and low." To the right of the list boxes, texts will appear and specify the model you are making. In addition, while you are selecting the

words in the list boxes, the numerical values that correspond with the terms you have selected are shown in a separate worksheet, called "parameters". (As we will point out below, these numerical values can be changed later manually to obtain different model specifications).

The best way to proceed is to first specify all the property parameters (given in the blue boxes) for each grower.

6. After having specified the property values for each grower separately, specify the relationships between growers in the "Competition and Support" boxes (yellow). Select a variable from the list box at the top of the yellow block and work your way down to the button.
7. The choice between "by level" and "by change" can be explained as follows: When a certain level of one component is reached, the growth of the other component will be stimulated; the alternative, by change, would mean that a certain amount of change in one component will affect the growth of the other component.
8. Click to confirm choice. The procedure is similar for the precursor relationship.

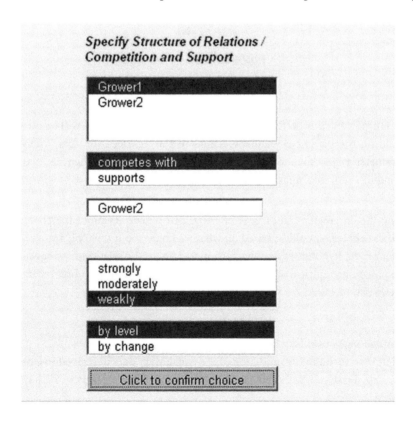

After confirming your choice, you can open the worksheet called "parameters". At the left you will see a range with the parameter values for each separate grower that corresponds with the options you have chosen in the list boxes. At the right you will see a matrix that contains the relational parameters you selected. For instance, in the matrix beginning with "by level", the cell specified by "from Grower1" and "to Grower2" might contain the value −0.1. This value means that Grower1 competes with Grower3; the value −0.1 specifies the strength of the competition.

9. Either in the growth model or in the parameters worksheet, select "Simulation" and then "Calculate model" from the toolbar. (In Excel 2007/2010, you will have to click on the "Add-ins" menu item and then select Simulation > Calculate model.). This command will calculate the values of your growth model and specify its results in the worksheet "growth model" (you will be automatically directed toward that worksheet).

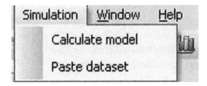

10. Each time you click on the calculate growth button, the model will be calculated based on the parameter values specified in the matrices. You may change the parameter values manually, e.g. by dividing or multiplying them by two or by changing them into small increments.

In setting the parameter values, it is important to remain aware of the choices you make. These choices should be based on what we know about the topic from previous studies or on the hypotheses we have formulated about the relationships between the growers based on empirical data. By fitting the parameter values to observed data, the hypotheses can be tested.

5.2.3   Modeling vocabulary growth
We will now go through the modeling of the vocabulary data described in Chapter 6 step by step. First, we included the data on which Figure 1 (also in Chapter 6) is based.

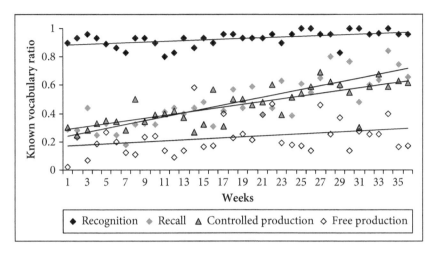

Figure 1. Development of academic English vocabulary knowledge levels over 36 weeks' immersion in the case study data

The smoothed data of the vocabulary learning levels is represented in Figure 2.

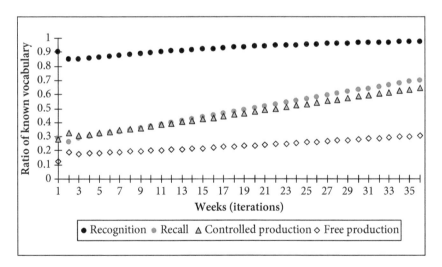

Figure 2. Smoothed data of the development of the four vocabulary levels

In Figure 2, you can see the four learning curves for the different levels of vocabulary knowledge. We will now simulate the development of these curves using a complex growth model. To simplify matters in our explanation here, we will limit the number of growers to 2: recall and controlled production. These are the most interesting two because their interaction is the strongest. Once you have gone through all the steps you may want to try and build the full model with four growers.

1. Open Excel file "5.2 Modeling". Save the file using a different name. (It may be a good idea to produce several files to try different settings of the model, each of which should get a different name, but be sure to keep the worksheets within the file intact.). Select the "model setup" worksheet from the tabs at the bottom of the screen. Set the number of growers to 2. Name the two growers *Recall* and *ConProd*.

2. We will begin by setting the values of Grower1, *Recall*. The settings will be based on our observations of the actual data and insights from previous research. At first we make educated guesses, and later we will fine-tune the parameters to fit the actual data. Put the settings as follows:

    –   Growth rate: *positive* and *intermediate*. (We expect the recall of vocabulary items relatively easy to acquire, more easily than production)
    –   Initial value: *intermediate* (This is a high intermediate learner, so the number of academic words known is well beyond zero)
    –   General support: *moderate* (The carrying capacity for word learning, depending on the resources, can be expected to be moderate, which is the default value for carrying capacity)
    –   Timing: *not delayed* (There is no reason to assume that the learning effect is delayed)
    –   Level of variation: *zero* (We will start off with a deterministic version of the model, which means that the random factor is zero).

3. Using the scrollbar, return to the top of the worksheet. We will now enter the settings of Grower2, *ConProd*. Put the settings as follows:

    –   Growth rate: *positive* and *low* (Production can be expected to grow relatively slowly compared to recall.)
    –   Initial value: *seed* (We expect the initial value of productive academic vocabulary to be lower than that of the recall parameter.)
    –   General support: *moderate* (The carrying capacity for production, depending on the available resources, can be expected to be moderate, which is the default carrying capacity.)
    –   Timing: *slightly delayed* (We expect the development of productive skills to start a bit later than that of receptive skills.)
    –   Level of variation: *zero* (We start off with a deterministic version of the model, which means that the random factor is zero).

4. We will now set the relations between the two growers we have defined. Scroll down in the worksheet until you reach the windows with the yellow shading. Select

    –   *ConProd* in the first field
    –   *Supports* in the second field
    –   *Recall* in the third field

- *Weakly* in the fourth field
(If there is any support between these growers, we can expect it to be from Recall to ConProd, but from the literature we know that this support will have to be really minimal.)
- *By level* in the fifth field
- Then click on "Click to confirm choice"

We have now defined how one variable affects another variable – an increase in the recall may slightly support the productive knowledge

5. Select the worksheet "growth model", and activate Simulation/Calculate model from the menu. Inspect the resulting graph. The overall pattern matches the data, but there are several deviations from the data on one of the parameters. First of all, the initial value in the data is almost identical for both growers. Second, the resulting graph of the model shows much stronger growth than we find in the data. We will roughly optimize the model based on these observations. Go back to the "model setup" worksheet and make the following changes:

- Change the growth rate of both growers into *very low*
- Change the initial value of ConProd into *intermediate*

Check the result again by selecting Simulation /Calculate from the menu. The resulting graph shows that we must have overestimated the amount of support from *Recall to ConProd*. Apparently, our assumption was wrong. This is in agreement with the general observation that there is a gap between the levels of vocabulary knowledge, and that growth in one level does not seem to promote the growth at another level. So we will change this by fine-tuning the model.

6. Fine-tuning the model can be done in the "parameters" worksheet. Open this worksheet. In this worksheet, you can see two areas (see screenshot).

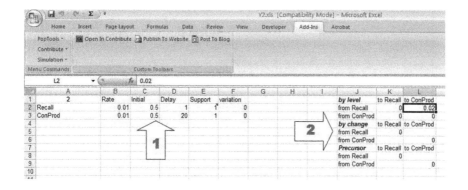

In area 1 you can see the basic parameter settings that you have set in the "model setup" worksheet. In area 2, you can see the definitions of the relationships between the growers in the model. Here you can see that there is a support from Recall to ConProd of 0.02, which is the default of the "weak" support. For fine-tuning, we can change these values. In this worksheet, you can also reset the values to 0. Try out different settings and each time simulate a model to see the effect of your change. Please note, once you have started changing parameters in the parameters worksheet, you cannot change the settings in the model setup worksheet anymore. So the sequence is always to first set up a rough model using the model setup worksheet and then fine tune the model in the parameters worksheet.

You can also use the model to test hypothetical assumptions, sometimes referred to as a "WhatIf" approach. For instance, when the growth rate of *ConProd* were faster than *Recall*, but if there were a small negative influence of *Recall* on *ConProd*, the graph would look like the one in Figure 3. The settings used for this graph are shown in the screenshot below. This is not in agreement with the data, so we can see that this setting is not appropriate. Try out different settings to test WhatIf situations.

Whatever you do in modelling, make sure that the parameter settings you enter are based on informed choices, based on either theoretical assumptions or empirical observations. Also note that you may not be able to simulate a pattern of interaction between Recall and Controlled Production that is identical to the pattern in Figures 1 (with variability) and 2 (without variability). The reason is that these graphs are based on four growers instead of two.

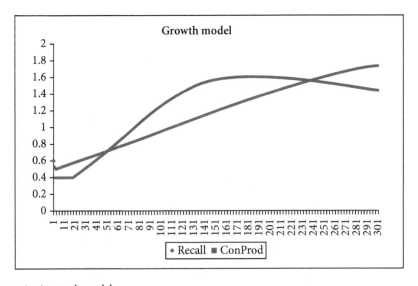

Figure 3. A growth model

	A	B	C	D	E	F	G	H	I	J	K	L
1	2	Rate	Initial	Delay	Support	variation				by level	to Recall	to ConProd
2	Recall	0.01	0.5	1	2	0				from Recall	0	-0.008
3	ConProd	0.03	0.4	20	2.5	0				from ConProd	0	0
4										by change	to Recall	to ConProd
5										from Recall	0	
6										from ConProd		0
7										Precursor	to Recall	to ConProd
8										from Recall	0	
9										from ConProd		0
10												

Here are some tips to organize the way you work with models:

- When you set a parameter value or an interaction, the program keeps track of your choices by adding text in the cells next to the menu windows (for instance, "the growth rate of Recall is positive and low"). You can copy this text and paste it in a new worksheet, which you can for instance call "model definitions". You can also copy the parameter values from your worksheet and paste them in a new worksheet (for instance below the verbal descriptions you have pasted earlier). In this way you can create a step-by-step report of the model you have created.
- It is generally advisable to explore the model systematically. So rather than wildly changing all parameters to see how that affects the model, do so in a planned and systematic way. Keep a log of the system you use, so that your argumentation can be included in a report and can be replicated by others.
- While experimenting with interactions (competition, support, precursor), you may want to change the type of interaction. To avoid old parameter values to affect your model, it is best to reset these values manually (so not in the model setup worksheet). To avoid confusion, it is also advisable to delete the verbal descriptions in the model setup worksheet once you have started working with parameters values, as the settings in the model setup worksheet will be overruled by the parameter settings.

5.2.4   Modeling precursor relations

In Chapter 6 we discussed precursor relations in our vocabulary data. Unfortunately, the relations were so subtle that they are difficult to simulate and therefore may be confusing to use as an example. Therefore, we will discuss precursor modeling based on Fischer's hierarchical development model, one that is very similar to the precursor relations shown in Figure 7 in Chapter 6.

Fischer distinguishes four stages of cognitive development. In each stage, several growers may occur and some growers only become active when a new stage is reached. Figure 4 shows three growers, A, B and C, in three developmental stages.

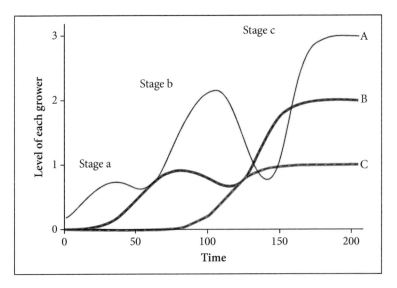

Figure 4. Development of individual Growers A, B, and C at Stages a, b and c. As a new grower begins to spurt it induces a spurt in the prior grower. Also, competition between growers produces a drop before each spurt in a grower.

For instance, Grower A is the capacity to make sums. Fisher calls this the stage of operations. Grower B would then be the capacity to comprehend relations between operations, like the relation between addition and subtraction. Grower C then is the capacity to understand relations between relations, like the whole of all operations like subtraction, addition, multiplication and division. This is the systems stage.

Each grower develops in a stepwise fashion. The hierarchically higher grower supports the grower that is hierarchically lower. For instance, B supports A, and C supports B. This predicts that as soon as children are able to understand relations between operations, the ability to carry out operations, such as doing sums, will also increase. Technically, this can be seen as an example of support by level, as the better the capacity to understand relations is, the easier it is to make progress in doing sums.

Simultaneously, there is a competition between the hierarchically higher grower and the hierarchically lower ones. So B competes with A and C competes with B. For instance, when children are absorbed in discovering relations (Grower B), they will temporarily have less attention for the operations themselves (such as adding up). Technically, this can be seen as competition by change, as doing sums will be inhibited more strongly when the *change* in developing the capacity to see relations increases.

The fact that these two relations both have an influence on the developmental process causes regression in the trajectory of the individual growers. This is a classical phenomenon in developmental psychology, in which regression is preceded by a growth spurt (u-shaped growth). In language development we will for instance see that children make more errors in formulating sentences when they are learning a new grammatical construction.

Based on this background information, we will now attempt to model Fischer's developmental growth.

1.   Open Excel sheet "Modeling". Save the file with a different name, like "Complex Growth Models Fischer". Select the model setup worksheet. Set the number of growers to 3. Change the name of Grower1 into *operations*; Grower2, *relations*; and Grower3, *systems*.
     For all growers set the parameters as follows::
     Growth rate: *positive*, and *low*
     Initial value: *seed*
     General support: *moderate*
     Timing: *not delayed*
     Level of variation: *zero*

2.   Now fill in the relations according to the description above. Since in this type of hierarchical developmental models, the lower level growers are conditional for the higher level growers, you will also have to set the Precursor fields. The growth of lower level growers will need to be nearly complete (so close to its carrying capacity), for the higher level grower to start growing. This means that you will have to set the precursor values as follows: a *high level* of *operations* is a precursor to *relations*, a *high level* of *relations* is a precursor of *systems*. Click on "confirm choices". Try out the model. These settings may not yet lead to a full similarity to Figure 2, so adjust the model to match the figure by changing the growth rates in the parameters worksheet.

This *how to* has shown you the very basics of modeling. In some cases, it will only be possible to create a good fit when the model is made more complex. Models can be made more complex by increasing the number of Support / Competition relations and by adding Precursor relations (see Chapter 6). We hope, however, that you have now reached the "threshold level" in modeling and can continue to be a creative modeler on your own!

References

Adolph, K.E. (1997). Learning in the development of infant locomotion. *Monographs of the Society for Research in Child Development, 62* [3, Serial No. 251].

Atkinson, D. (2002). Towards a sociocognitive approach to second language acquisition. *Modern Language Journal, 86,* 525–545.

Bassano D., & van Geert, P. (2007). Modeling continuity and discontinuity in utterance length: A quantitative approach to changes, transitions and intraindividual variability in early grammatical development. *Developmental Science 10*(5), 588–612.

Beckner, C., Blythe, R., Bybee, J., Christiansen, M., Croft, W., Ellis, N., Holland, J., Ke, J., Larsen-Freeman, D., & Schoenemann, T. (2009). Language is a complex adaptive system: Position paper. *Language Learning, 59* (suppl.1), 1–26.

Beer, R. (2000). Dynamical approaches to cognitive science. *Trends in Cognitive Sciences, 4,* 91–99.

Behrens, H. (2002). Learning multiple regularities: Evidence from overgeneralisation errors in the German plural. In A. Do, L. Dominguez, & A. Johansen (Eds.), *Proceedings of the 26th Annual Boston University Conference on Language Development* (pp. 72–83). Somerville, MA: Cascadilla Press.

Behrens, H. (2009). First language acquisition from a usage-based perspective. In K. de Bot & R. Schrauf (Eds.), *Language development over the lifespan* (pp. 40–59). London: Routledge.

Bertenthal, B. (1999). Variation and selection in the development of perception and action. In G. Savelsbergh, H. van der Maas, & P. van Geert (Eds.), *Non-linear developmental processes* (pp. 105–121). Amsterdam: Royal Netherlands Academy of Arts and Sciences.

Bybee, J. (2008). Usage-based grammar and second language acquisition. In P. Robinson & N. Ellis (Eds.), *Handbook of cognitive linguistics and second language acquisition* (pp. 216–236). London: Routledge.

Byrne, D. (2002). *Interpreting quantitative data.* London: Sage.

Cancino, H., Rosansky, E., & Schumann, J. (1978). The acquisition of English negatives and interrogatives by native Spanish speakers. In E.M. Hatch (Ed.), *Second language acquisition: A book of readings.* (pp. 207–230). Rowley, MA: Newbury House.

Caspi, T., & Lowie, W.M. (2010). A dynamic perspective on (Academic English) L2 lexical development. In R.Chácon-Beltrán, C. Abello-Contesse, M. Torreblanca-López, & M. López-Jiménez (Eds.), *Further insights into non-native vocabulary teaching and learning.* Bristol: Multilingual Matters.

Clark, A. (1997). *Being there.* Cambridge, MA: The MIT Press.

Clark, E. (2009). *First language acquisition.* (2nd Ed.) Cambridge: CUP.

Cowan, N. (2003). Comparisons of development modeling frameworks and levels of analysis in cognition: Connectionist and dynamic systems theories deserve attention, but don't yet explain attention. *Developmental Science, 6,* 440–447.

Coxhead, A. (2000). A new academic word list. *TESOL Quarterly, 34,* 213–238.

Coyle, T.R., & Bjorklund, D.F. (1997). Age differences in, and consequences of, multiple- and variable-strategy use on a multiple sort-recall task. *Developmental Psychology, 33,* 372–380.

de Bot, K. (2008). Introduction: Second language development as a dynamic process. *The Modern Language Journal, 92,* 166–178.

de Bot, K., Lowie, W., & Verspoor, M. (2005). *Second language acquisition: An advanced resource book.* London: Routledge.

de Bot, K., & Makoni, S. (2005). *Language and aging in multilingual societies: A dynamic approach.* Clevedon: Multilingual Matters.

de Bot, K., Verspoor, M., & Lowie, W. (2007). A dynamic systems theory approach to second language acquisition. *Bilingualism, Language and Cognition, 10,* 7–21.

Dowker, A., Flood, A., Griffiths, H., Harriss, L., & Hook, L. (1996). Estimation strategies of four groups. *Mathematical Cognitions, 2,* 113–135.

Dörnyei, Z. (2009). *The psychology of second language acquisition.* Oxford: OUP.

Dromi, E. (1986). The one-word period as a stage in language development: Quantitative and qualitative accounts. In I. Levin (Ed.), *Stage and structure: Reopening the debate* (pp. 220–245). Norwood, NJ: Ablex.

Efron, B., & Tibshirani, R. (1993). *An introduction to the bootstrap.* New York, NY: Chapman and Hall.

Ellis, N. (1998). Emergentism, connectionism, and language learning. *Language Learning, 48,* 631–664.

Ellis, N. (2002). Frequency effects in language processing: A review with implications for theories of implicit and explicit language acquisition. *Studies in Second Language Acquisition, 24,* 143–188.

Ellis, N. (2008). The dynamics of second language emergence: Cycles of language use, language change, and language acquisition. *Modern Language Journal, 92,* 232–249.

Ellis, N., & Larsen-Freeman, D. (2006). Language emergence: Implications for applied linguistics. *Applied Linguistics, 27,* 558–589.

Ellis, R. (1994). *The study of second language acquisition.* Oxford: OUP.

Elman, J. (1995). Language as a dynamical system. In R. Port & T. van Gelder (Eds.), *Mind as motion* (pp. 195–225). Cambridge, MA: The MIT Press.

Evans, N., & Levinson, S. (2009). The myth of language universals: Language diversity and its importance for cognitive science. *Behavioral and Brain Sciences, 32,* 429–492.

Eykhoff, P. (1974). *System identification: Parameter and state estimation.* New York, NY: Wiley & Sons.

Feldman, H.M., Dollaghan, C.A., Campbell, T.F., Kurs-Lasky, M., Janosky J.E., & Paradise, J.L. (2000). Measurement properties of the MacArthur communicative development inventories at ages one and two years. *Child Development, 71,* 310–322.

Fenson, L., Bates, E., Goodman, J., Reznick, J.S., & Thal, D.J. (2000). Measuring variability in early child language: Don't shoot the messenger. *Child Development, 71,* 323–328.

Furrow, D., Nelson, K., & Benedict, H. (1979). Mothers' speech to children and syntactic development: Some simple relationships. *Journal of Child Language, 6,* 423–442.

Gaddis, J.L. (2002). *The landscape of history.* Oxford: OUP.

Gass, S., & Selinker, L. (1994). *Second language acquisition: An introductory course.* Hillsdale, NJ: Lawrence Erlbaum Associates.

Goldberg, A. (2003). Constructions: A new theoretical approach to language. *Trends in Cognitive Sciences, 7,* 219–224.

Goldin-Meadow, S., & Alibali, M.W. (2002). Looking at the hands through time: A microgenetic perspective on learning and instruction. In N. Granott & J. Parziale (Eds.), *Microdevelopment: Transition processes in development and learning* (pp. 80–105). Cambridge: CUP.

Good, P.I. (1999). *Resampling methods: A practical guide to data analysis*. Boston, MA: Birkhauser.

Grant, L., & Ginther, A. (2000). Using computer-tagged linguistic features to describe L2 writing differences. *Journal of Second Language Writing, 9*, 123–145.

Hart, B., & Risley, T. (1995). *Meaningful differences in the everyday experience of young American children*. Baltimore, MD: Brookes.

Herdina, P., & Jessner, U. (2002). *A dynamic model of multilingualism: Perspectives of change in psycholinguistics*. Clevedon: Multilingual Matters.

Hernandez, A., Li, P., & MacWhinney, B. (2005). The emergence of competing modules in bilingualism. *Trends in Cognitive Sciences, 9*, 220–225.

Hood, G. (2009). Poptools [Computer software]. Canberra, Australia: Pest Animal Control Co-operative research Center (CSIRO).

Hopper, P. (1998). Emergent grammar. In M. Tomasello (Ed.), *The new psychology of language: Cognitive and functional approaches to language structure* (pp. 155–175). Mahwah, NJ: Lawrence Erlbaum Associates.

Jahn-Samilo, J., Goodman, J., Bates, E., Appelbaum, M., & Sweet, M. (2000). *Vocabulary learning in children from 8 to 30 months of age: A comparison of parental reports and laboratory measures*. San Diego, CA: University of California.

Jarvis, S. (2006). Examining the properties of lexical diversity through quantitative and qualitative means. Paper presented at the 16th Sociolinguistics Symposium, Limerick, Ireland.

Jessner, U. (2008). A DST model of multilingualism and the role of metalinguistic awareness. *Modern Language Journal, 92*, 270–283.

Jordan, G. (2004). *Theory construction in second language acquisition*. Amsterdam: John Benjamins.

Klima, E. & Bellugi, U. (1966). Syntactic regularities in the speech of children. In J. Lyons & R. J. Wales (Eds.), *Psycholinguistic Papers: The proceedings of the 1966 Edinburgh Conference* (pp. 183–207). Edinburgh: EUP.

Köpcke, K. (1998). The acquisition of plural marking in English and German revisited: Schemata vs. rules. *Journal of Child Language, 25*, 293–319.

Langacker, R.W. (2008). Cognitive grammar as a basis for language instruction. In P. Robinson & N. Ellis (Eds.), *Handbook of cognitive linguistics and second language acquisition* (pp. 66–88). London: Routledge.

Larsen-Freeman, D. (1976). An explanation for the morpheme acquisition order of second language learners. *Language Learning, 26*, 125–135.

Larsen-Freeman, D. (1997). Chaos/complexity science and second language acquisition. *Applied Linguistics, 18*, 141–165.

Larsen-Freeman, D. (2002). Language acquisition and language use from a chaos/complexity theory perspective. In C. Kramsch (Ed.), *Language acquisition and language socialization* (pp. 33–46). London: Continuum.

Larsen-Freeman, D. (2005). Second language acquisition and the issue of fossilization: There is no end and there is no state. In Z. Han & T. Odlin (Eds.), *Studies of fossilization in second language acquisition* (pp. 189–200). Clevedon: Multilingual Matters.

Larsen-Freeman, D. (2006). The emergence of complexity, fluency and accuracy in the oral and written production of five Chinese learners of English. *Applied Linguistics, 27*, 590–616.

Larsen-Freeman, D. (2007). On the complementarity of complexity theory and dynamic systems theory in understanding the second language acquisition process. *Bilingualism, Language and Cognition, 10*, 35–37.

Larsen-Freeman, D. (2010). The dynamic co-adaption of cognitive and social views: A complexity theory perspective. R. Batstone (Ed.), *Sociocognitive perspectives on language use and language learning.*

Larsen-Freeman, D., & Cameron, L. (2008a). *Complex systems and applied linguistics.* Oxford: OUP.

Larsen-Freeman, D., & Cameron, L. (2008b). Research methodology on language development from a complex systems perspective. *The Modern Language Journal, 92,* 200–213.

Larsen-Freeman, D., & Long, M. (1991). *An introduction to second language acquisition research.* London: Longman.

Laufer, B. (1998). The development of passive and active vocabulary in a second language: Same or different. *Applied Linguistics, 19,* 255–271.

Laufer, B., Elder, C., Hill, K., & Congdon, P. (2004). Size and strength: Do we need both to measure vocabulary knowledge? *Language Testing, 21,* 202–226.

Laufer, B., & Goldstein, Z. (2004). Testing vocabulary knowledge: Size, strength, and computer adaptiveness. *Language Learning, 54,* 399–436.

Laufer, B., & Nation, P. (1995). Vocabulary size and use: Lexical richness in L2 written production. *Applied Linguistics, 16,* 307–322.

Laufer, B., & Nation, P. (1999). A vocabulary-size test of controlled productive ability. *Language Testing, 16,* 33–51.

Laufer, B., & Paribakht, T.S. (1998). The relationship between passive and active vocabularies: Effects of language learning context. *Language Learning, 48,* 365–391.

Lee, K., & Karmiloff-Smith, A. (2002). Macro- and microdevelopmental research assumptions, research strategies, constraints and utilities. In N. Granott & J. Parziale (Eds.), *Microdevelopment: Transition processes in development and learning* (pp. 243–265). Cambridge: CUP.

Lieven, E., Behrens, H., Speares, J., & Tomasello, M. (2003). Early syntactic creativity: A usage-based approach. *Journal of Child Language, 30,* 341–371.

Lieven, E. & Tomasello, M. (2008). Children's first language learning from a usage-based perspective. In P. Robinson & N. Ellis (Eds.), *Handbook of cognitive linguistics and second language acquisition* (pp. 168–196). London: Routledge.

Long, M. (1993). Assessment strategies for second language acquisition theories. *Applied Linguistics, 14,* 225–249.

Lorenz, E.N. (1963). Deterministic nonperiodic flow. *Journal of the Atmospheric Sciences, 20,* 130–141.

MacWhinney, B. (2000). *The CHILDES project: Tools for analysing talk.* (3rd. Ed.). Mahwah, NJ: Lawrence Erlbaum Associates.

MacWhinney, B. (2008). A unified model. In P. Robinson & N. Ellis (Eds.), *Handbook of cognitive linguistics and second language acquisition* (pp. 341–371). London: Routledge.

May, R.M. (1976). Simple mathematical models with very complicated dynamics. *Nature, 261,* 459.

McKee, G., Malvern, D., & Richards, B.J. (2000). Measuring vocabulary diversity using dedicated software. *Literary and Linguistic Computing, 15,* 323–383.

Meara, P. (2004). Modeling vocabulary loss. *Applied Linguistics, 25,* 137–155.

Melka, F. (1997). Receptive versus productive aspects of vocabulary. In N. Schmitt & N. McCarthy (Eds.), *Vocabulary description, acquisition, and pedagogy* (pp. 84–102). Cambridge: CUP.

Mitchell, M. (2009). *Complexity: A Guided Tour.* Oxford: OUP.

Mitchell, R., & Myles, F. (1998[2004]). *Second language learning theories.* London: Arnold.

Nortega, L. (2009). *Understanding second language acquisition*. London: Hodder Arnold.

Paulson, E. (2005). Viewing eye movements during reading through the lens of chaos theory: How reading is like the weather. *Reading Research Quarterly, 40,* 338–358.

Peters, A. (2009). Cracking the language code: Processing strategies in first language acquisition. In S. Foster-Cohen (Ed.), *Advances in language acquisition. Quoting.* (pp. 40–61). London: Palgrave Macmillan.

Pierrehumbert, J. (2003). Probabilistic phonology: Discrimination and robustness. In R. Bod, J. Hay, & S. Jannedy (Eds.), *Probabilistic linguistics* (pp. 177–228). Cambridge, MA: The MIT Press.

Plaza Pust, C. (2008). Dynamic systems theory and universal grammar: Holding up a turbulent mirror to development in grammars. *Modern Language Journal, 92,* 250–269.

Port, R., & van Gelder, T. (1995). *Mind as motion: Explorations in the dynamics of cognition.* Cambridge, MA: The MIT Press.

Redington, M., Chater, N., & Finch, S. (1998). Distributional information: A powerful cue for acquiring syntactic categories. *Cognitive Science, 22,* 425–469.

Reinking, D., & Watkins, J. (2000). A formative experiment investigating the use of multimedia book reviews to increase elementary students' independent reading. *Reading Research Quarterly, 35,* 384–419.

Ringbom, H. (1987). *The role of first language in foreign language acquisition.* Clevedon: Multilingual Matters.

Robinson, P., & Ellis, N. (2008). *Handbook of cognitive linguistics and second language acquisition.* London: Routledge.

Robinson, P., & Mervis, C.B. (1998). Disentangling early language development: Modeling lexical and grammatical acquisition using an extension of case-study methodology. *Developmental Psychology, 34,* 363–375.

Rumelhart, D., & McClelland, J. (1987). Learning the past tense of English verbs: Implicit rules or parallel processing? In B. MacWhinney (Ed.), *Mechanisms of language acquisition* (pp. 195–248). Hillsdale, NJ: Lawrence Erlbaum Associates.

Saffran, J. (2003). Statistical language learning: Mechanisms and constraints. *Current Directions in Psychological Science, 12,* 110–114.

Schmitt, N., & Meara, P. (1997). Researching vocabulary through a word knowledge framework. *Studies in Second Language Acquisition, 19,* 17–36.

Shatz, M. (2009). On the development of the field of language development. In E. Hoff & M. Shatz (Eds.), *Blackwell handbook of language development* (pp. 1–15). Chichester: Wiley Blackwell.

Shrager, J., & Siegler, R. S. (1998). SCADS: A model of children's strategy choices and strategy discoveries. *Psychological Science, 9,* 405–410.

Siegler, R.S. (2006). Microgenetic analyses of learning. In W. Damon & R. M. Lerner (Series Eds.) & D. Kuhn & R. S. Siegler (Vol. Eds.), *Handbook of child psychology, volume 2: Cognition, perception, and language* (6th ed., pp. 464–510). Hoboken, NJ: Wiley & Sons.

Siegler, R.S. (2007). Cognitive variability. *Developmental Science, 10,* 104–109.

Siegler, R.S., & Svetina, M. (2002). A microgenetic/cross-sectional study of matrix completion: Comparing short-term and long-term change. *Child Development, 73,* 793–809.

Spivey, M. (2007). *The continuity of mind.* Oxford: OUP.

Spoelman, M., & Verspoor, M. (2010). Dynamic patterns in development of accuracy and complexity: A longitudinal case study in the acquisition of Finnish *Applied Linguistics, 31,* 532–553.

Steinkrauss, R. (2009). Frequency and function: A usage-based case study of German L1 acquisition. Groningen Dissertation in Linguistics 75.

Thelen, E., & Smith, L.B. (1994). *A dynamic systems approach to the development of cognition and action.* Cambridge, MA: The MIT Press.

Thelen, E., & Ulrich, B. D. (1991). Hidden skills. *Monographs of the Society for Research in Child Development, 56*(1, Serial No. 223).

Tomasello, M. (2000). Do young children have adult syntactic competence? *Cognition, 74,* 209–253.

Tomasello, M. (2003). *Constructing a language: A usage-based account of language acquisition.* Cambridge, MA: The MIT Press.

van der Slik, F., Driessen, G., & de Bot, K. (2006). Ethnic and socioeconomic class composition and language proficiency: A longitudinal multilevel examination in Dutch elementary schools. *European Sociological Review, 22,* 293–308.

van Dijk, M. (2003). *Child language cuts capers. Variability and ambiguity in early child development.* Groningen: University of Groningen.

van Dijk, M., & van Geert, P. (2002). Focus on variability: New tools to study intra-individual variability in developmental data. *Infant Behavior and Development, 25,* 340–375.

van Dijk, M., & van Geert, P. (2007). Wobbles, humps and sudden jumps: A case study of continuity, discontinuity and variability in early language development. *Infant and Child Development, 16,* 7–33. Published online in Wiley InterScience <www.interscience.wiley.com> DOI: 10.1002/icd.506.

van Geert, P. (1991). A dynamic systems theory model of cognitive and language growth. *Psychological Review, 98,* 3–53.

van Geert, P. (1993). A dynamic systems model of cognitive growth: Competition and support under limited resource conditions. In L.B. Smith & E. Thelen (Eds.), *A dynamic systems approach to development: Applications* (pp. 265–332). Cambridge, MA: The MIT Press.

van Geert, P. (1994a). Vygotskian dynamics of development. *Human Development, 37,* 346–365.

van Geert, P. (1994b). *Dynamic systems of development: Change between complexity and chaos.* New York, NY: Harvester.

van Geert, P. (1998). A dynamic systems model of basic developmental mechanisms: Piaget, Vygotsky and beyond. *Psychological Review, 5,* 634–677.

van Geert, P. (2003). Dynamic systems approaches and modeling of developmental processes. In J. Valsiner & K.J. Conolly (Eds.), *Handbook of developmental psychology* (pp. 640–672). London: Sage.

van Geert, P. (2008). The dynamic systems approach in the study of L1 and L2 acquisition: An introduction. *Modern Language Journal, 92,* 179–199.

van Geert, P. (2009). A comprehensive dynamic systems theory of language development. In K. de Bot & R. Schrauf (Eds.), *Language development over the lifespan* (pp. 60–104). London: Routledge.

van Geert, P., Savelsbergh, G., & van der Maas, H. (1997). Transitions and non-linear dynamics in developmental psychology. In G. Savelsbergh, H. van der Maas, & P. van Geert (Eds.), *Non-linear developmental processes* (pp. XI–XX). Amsterdam: Koninklijke Nederlandse Academie van Wetenschappen.

van Geert, P., & Steenbeek, H. (2005). Explaining 'after' by 'before': Basic aspects of a dynamic systems approach to the study of development. *Developmental Review, 25,* 408–442.

van Geert, P., & Steenbeek, R. (2008). A complexity and dynamic systems approach to development assessment, modeling and research. In A. Battro, K. Fischer, & P. Léna (Eds.), *The educated brain* (pp. 71–94). Cambridge: CUP.

van Geert, P., & van Dijk, M. (2002). Focus on variability: New tools to study intra-individual variability in developmental data. *Infant Behavior and Development, 25,* 340–375.

Verhulst, P.F. (1838). Notice sur la loi que la population suit dans sonaccroissement. *Correspondance Mathématique et Physique, publicée par A. Quetelet 10,* 113.

Vermeer, A. (2000). Coming to grips with lexical richness in spontaneous speech data. *Language Testing, 17,* 65–83.

Verspoor, M., de Bot, K., & Lowie, W. (2008). Input and second language development from a dynamic perspective. In T. Piske & M. Young-Scholten (Eds.), *Input matters* (pp. 62–81). Clevedon: Multilingual Matters.

Verspoor, M., Lowie, W., & van Dijk, M. (2008). Variability in second language development from a dynamic systems perspective. *Modern Language Journal, 92,* 214–231.

Verspoor, M. & Sauter K. (2000). *English sentence analysis: An introductory course.* Amsterdam: John Benjamins.

Wolfe-Quintero, K., Inagaki, S., & Kim, H.-Y. (1998). *Second language development in writing: Measures of fluency, accuracy, and complexity.* Honolulu, HI: University of Hawaií, Second Language Teaching and Curriculum Center.

Xue, G., & Nation, I.S.P. (1984). A university word list. *Language Learning and Communication, 3,* 215–229.

Young, R. (1988). Variation and the interlanguage hypothesis. *Studies in Second Language Acquisition, 10,* 281–302.

Index

In the series *Language Learning & Language Teaching* the following titles have been published thus far or are scheduled for publication:

30 **TROFIMOVICH, Pavel and Kim McDONOUGH (eds.):** Applying priming research to L2 teaching and learning. Insights from Psycholinguistics. *Expected June 2011*

29 **VERSPOOR, Marjolijn H., Kees de BOT and Wander LOWIE (eds.):** A Dynamic Approach to Second Language Development. Methods and techniques. 2011. ix, 211 pp.

28 **PORTE, Graeme Keith:** Appraising Research in Second Language Learning. A practical approach to critical analysis of quantitative research. **Second edition.** 2010. xxv, 307 pp.

27 **BLOM, Elma and Sharon UNSWORTH (eds.):** Experimental Methods in Language Acquisition Research. 2010. vii, 292 pp.

26 **MARTÍNEZ-FLOR, Alicia and Esther USÓ-JUAN (eds.):** Speech Act Performance. Theoretical, empirical and methodological issues. 2010. xiv, 277 pp.

25 **ABRAHAM, Lee B. and Lawrence WILLIAMS (eds.):** Electronic Discourse in Language Learning and Language Teaching. 2009. x, 346 pp.

24 **MEARA, Paul:** Connected Words. Word associations and second language vocabulary acquisition. 2009. xvii, 174 pp.

23 **PHILP, Jenefer, Rhonda OLIVER and Alison MACKEY (eds.):** Second Language Acquisition and the Younger Learner. Child's play? 2008. viii, 334 pp.

22 **EAST, Martin:** Dictionary Use in Foreign Language Writing Exams. Impact and implications. 2008. xiii, 228 pp.

21 **AYOUN, Dalila (ed.):** Studies in French Applied Linguistics. 2008. xiii, 400 pp.

20 **DALTON-PUFFER, Christiane:** Discourse in *Content and Language Integrated Learning* (CLIL) Classrooms. 2007. xii, 330 pp.

19 **RANDALL, Mick:** Memory, Psychology and Second Language Learning. 2007. x, 220 pp.

18 **LYSTER, Roy:** Learning and Teaching Languages Through Content. A counterbalanced approach. 2007. xii, 173 pp.

17 **BOHN, Ocke-Schwen and Murray J. MUNRO (eds.):** Language Experience in Second Language Speech Learning. In honor of James Emil Flege. 2007. xvii, 406 pp.

16 **AYOUN, Dalila (ed.):** French Applied Linguistics. 2007. xvi, 560 pp.

15 **CUMMING, Alister (ed.):** Goals for Academic Writing. ESL students and their instructors. 2006. xii, 204 pp.

14 **HUBBARD, Philip and Mike LEVY (eds.):** Teacher Education in CALL. 2006. xii, 354 pp.

13 **NORRIS, John M. and Lourdes ORTEGA (eds.):** Synthesizing Research on Language Learning and Teaching. 2006. xiv, 350 pp.

12 **CHALHOUB-DEVILLE, Micheline, Carol A. CHAPELLE and Patricia A. DUFF (eds.):** Inference and Generalizability in Applied Linguistics. Multiple perspectives. 2006. vi, 248 pp.

11 **ELLIS, Rod (ed.):** Planning and Task Performance in a Second Language. 2005. viii, 313 pp.

10 **BOGAARDS, Paul and Batia LAUFER (eds.):** Vocabulary in a Second Language. Selection, acquisition, and testing. 2004. xiv, 234 pp.

9 **SCHMITT, Norbert (ed.):** Formulaic Sequences. Acquisition, processing and use. 2004. x, 304 pp.

8 **JORDAN, Geoff:** Theory Construction in Second Language Acquisition. 2004. xviii, 295 pp.

7 **CHAPELLE, Carol A.:** English Language Learning and Technology. Lectures on applied linguistics in the age of information and communication technology. 2003. xvi, 213 pp.

6 **GRANGER, Sylviane, Joseph HUNG and Stephanie PETCH-TYSON (eds.):** Computer Learner Corpora, Second Language Acquisition and Foreign Language Teaching. 2002. x, 246 pp.

5 **GASS, Susan M., Kathleen BARDOVI-HARLIG, Sally Sieloff MAGNAN and Joel WALZ (eds.):** Pedagogical Norms for Second and Foreign Language Learning and Teaching. Studies in honour of Albert Valdman. 2002. vi, 305 pp.

4 **TRAPPES-LOMAX, Hugh and Gibson FERGUSON (eds.):** Language in Language Teacher Education. 2002. vi, 258 pp.

3 **PORTE, Graeme Keith:** Appraising Research in Second Language Learning. A practical approach to critical analysis of quantitative research. 2002. xx, 268 pp.

2 **ROBINSON, Peter (ed.):** Individual Differences and Instructed Language Learning. 2002. xii, 387 pp.

1 **CHUN, Dorothy M.:** Discourse Intonation in L2. From theory and research to practice. 2002. xviii, 285 pp. (incl. CD-rom).

-2 issues:
  - Different things contribute to fluency perspectives
  - Lang. is a complex system